THE REAL
SWEENEY

Dick Kirby

To Derek Durrant —

Sincere best wishes from

the author,

Dick Kirby 29¹¹/₁₀.

ROBINSON
London

Constable & Robinson Ltd
3 The Lanchesters
162 Fulham Palace Road
London W6 9ER
www.constablerobinson.com

First published in the UK by Robinson,
an imprint of Constable & Robinson Ltd 2005

A copy of the British Library Cataloguing in
Publication Data is available from the British Library.

Most of the names of people and locations
have been changed to protect their families and themselves.

ISBN 1-84119-911-7

Printed and bound in the EU

1 3 5 7 9 10 8 6 4 2

To Ann
who waited, wondered and worried

Contents

Contents

Acknowledgements

My thanks go to my chum of many years, Joe Wambaugh, who has been a guiding light; and also to Nicky Benwell QPM, Harry Cole BEM, John O'Connor, Nipper Read QPM and Michael Winner, for their kindness and assistance.

Next, to Karen McCall and her husband, Merlin Unwin, for their kindness, good advice and tolerance; to Pete Duncan and Claudia Dyer at Constable & Robinson for their courage and perspicacity in taking me on board; and to my son-in-law, Steve Cowper, for guiding me through the minefield of computer land.

And then, all of the correctly named police officers who appear in this book, without whom it really wouldn't be the same, and in alphabetical order: Geoffrey Arnold MBE, Bill Best QPM, Peri Chapman, Jan Cheal, Ian Chiverton, Dick Elsey, Anna Giacon, Robin Gilles, Terry and Ann Hack, Mike McAdam and George and Ellen Woolard, all of whom offered constructive criticism or were gracious enough to laugh in the right places.

Last, and by no means least, my dear wife Ann and our children Suzanne, Mark, Robert and Barbara, who, with our grandchildren, Emma, Jessica and Harry, have been an inspiration with their love and support.

Foreword

So often the memoirs of policemen are those of very senior officers who concentrate on their promotions and contributions to controlling the traffic by the introduction of major road improvements or assessment of yet another style of beat policing.

Not this. Dick Kirby was a real copper, a man who made it his goal to be a successful detective, a 'thief-taker' in the fullest sense of that old-fashioned word. He committed himself to the hardest place in the force – the Flying Squad – and searched out like-minded officers he could trust implicitly and who would be there when the going got tough.

Frequently his position required him to engage with the most difficult of men – police informants. Dealing with informants is a specialized talent, and one which Kirby proved to have in abundance. The trust in such cases must be reciprocal and Kirby came to be recognised as a man who could be relied upon to achieve the purest, most up-to-date information from his 'snouts'.

The stories he tells here, enlivened with his trademark racy humour, often have a dark side. He dealt with some of the most experienced and unpleasant criminals from the major leagues of the underworld. He suffered more than his fair share of injuries in arrests or dealing with enquiries into criminal activities, often requiring hospitalization. His name became feared throughout the underworld.

Dick Kirby joined the Metropolitan Police Force in 1967. After a short spell as a uniform Constable, he was selected for appointment to the CID, which he took to like a duck to water, encouraging a desire to be posted to the Flying Squad. Not for him the comfort of an office job where cases could be solved methodically and securely. He was happiest plunging into the fray on a daily basis and engaging with the enemy – the active and persistent armed robbers.

On the Flying Squad he found his niche, and experienced phenomenal success. He was commended for his ability, persistence, devotion to duty and courage on no less than forty occasions, by the Commissioner, other Senior Officers, Judges, the Director of Public Prosecutions and magistrates. It is a remarkable tally. A Judge at the Old Bailey described him as 'one of the best detectives at Scotland Yard', an indication of how he was regarded in that most senior of courts.

Kirby finally left the Squad in 1991 in the rank of Sergeant and served the rest of his time as a Divisional Officer, before leaving the Police Service on a medical discharge two years later as the result of injuries received in a serious car accident whilst on duty.

He would argue that he was fortunate to serve at a time when professional criminals began to concentrate their activities on what became known as 'across the pavement' crimes. That is, attacks upon banks and security vans; because 'That's where the money is', as Willy Sutton, the American bank robber, famously replied when asked by the FBI why he persistently robbed banks.

The book opens with the sobering tale of the hunt for a high-profile band of armed robbers responsible for a series of frightening offences in the North London area. Kirby frankly describes not only the success in bringing them to book but also the mistakes made during the painstaking operation necessary to identify them and mount close and persistent surveillance.

Yet it is through the details of relationships with magistrates, judges, barristers and fellow police officers, and the delightful thumbnail sketches he draws of the criminals he encountered, that these memoirs spring so vividly off the page. A comparison with the chronicler of the American low-life, Damon Runyon, comes to mind.

There is nothing formal about this book. It deals in a random and haphazard way with experiences as though they had just occurred. But each chapter is a separate little gem. I loved *The Real Sweeney*; the narrative runs at a cracking pace and is reminiscent in some ways of those thrilling escapades on 'The Sweeney' series on television. The difference being, of course, that Dick Kirby lived every moment he so vividly describes.

Leonard 'Nipper' Read QPM

Introduction

Motorway service stations are often the most unprepossessing of places, aren't they? Particularly when a cold wind from the Strait of Dover whistles in through the frequently opened door of the cafeteria. This was the glum scenario in which Detective Constable Mick Geraghty found himself, when he was minding a couple of supergrasses, Joe and John, who were in the process of being relocated. Mick and I had worked on the Flying Squad together: a fact not known to these two rascals, who were busily engaged in a little character assassination of police officers with whom they'd had dealings.

'I'll tell you who's a good Old Bill,' said Joe. 'Dick Kirby.'

At the mention of my name, Mick began to listen most carefully, but prudently said nothing.

John nodded his agreement. 'Yeah, he's a nice bloke,' he said. 'Mind you, he'd fit you up as soon as look at you.'

'Oh, sure,' Joe replied. 'But only in the line of duty!'

Mick was hugely amused as he recounted this untruthful and slanderous assertion to me. But I don't know why I joined in the laughter – probably to keep Mick company!

In writing down some of the things that have happened to me and my contemporaries it is often difficult to remember events with absolute clarity and the order in which they occurred. An example was the other night after I'd dined with Dick Miles, with whom I had been a police constable and an aid to CID, over thirty-five years ago. During the course of

1

our nostalgic conversation, Dick mentioned the name of a local tearaway. 'I know the name, of course,' I told Dick, 'but only because it's an unusual one. I can't remember if I had any dealings with him.' Dick choked on his drink.

'Had any dealings?' he echoed. 'You silly bugger, you had a fight with him, that's all.'

Well, perhaps Dick, that former Assistant Chief Constable who has a reputation for accuracy, was right; but I could remember nothing. I just hope I won.

There are, however, some things I don't forget. Being a member of the Metropolitan Police was like being part of a big family. Because being a police officer was a vocation, it was a delight to go to work. And, in those days, it seemed to me that we were all pulling in the same direction.

So, as you read this book, if you think that the justice that was dispensed then was sometimes a little rough, if you think that the language used was rather immodest, and if you feel that the interests of the people who suffered at the hands of the criminals were put way in front of the perpetrator of the crime, well . . . you're probably right.

The late Rayner Goddard, the Lord Chief Justice, once said, 'Remember the victims.' I did.

D.K.
2005

Remote Control

In 1985, four armed robberies and attempted armed robberies were committed. They were almost certainly committed by the same gang, as there were links. The North-East London office of the Flying Squad, at Rigg Approach, investigated three of them. Later that year, there was a fifth robbery, and the investigators thought that this might, or might not, be linked to the others. It was. There was also a sixth offence which was not linked, although members of the same gang carried it out. It was unassociated, first, because it bore no resemblance to the first four offences, and secondly because it was not investigated by Rigg Approach. The gang were, in fact, responsible for a further four offences, but we only learned of those later. In total, they netted over £1.6 million. Busy bunch, weren't they? Luckily, so were the Flying Squad, and what followed was a tremendous investigation, which pushed open the door of criminality and allowed us a peek inside.

You'd probably breathe a sigh of relief as you turn off the M25 at junction 25. Not for nothing is it known as Europe's biggest car park. But it's still busy on the Great Cambridge Road, and as you drive south, on the left-hand side is the cheerless sight of Enfield crematorium. It was here, on 24 April 1985, that the first of the four linked offences took place. Early that morning, the staff had been taken hostage by three armed men as they waited for a PPR security van to arrive. In

3

fact, the delivery times had been changed and the gang left empty-handed.

Nine days later, a few miles to the north, at the premises of Cross & Herbert, in Charlton Mead Lane, Hoddesdon, in Hertfordshire, two of the gang struck again, once again taking the staff hostage as they waited for a PPR security vehicle. This time the van did arrive but the crew had sensed something was wrong because the area was so unusually quiet. Prudently, they decided not to deliver their load and the gang left too. No doubt they were exasperated at being balked twice, but that was no excuse for them to leave behind a viable, remote controlled explosive device for the police to find.

Several weeks passed. Then, on 27 June, at a company named Amtico, on the Trafalgar Trading Estate at Brimsdown, in Enfield, three of the gang once again took the staff hostage while they waited for a Group 4 security van to arrive, and promptly left when it didn't.

Three weeks later, yet another attempt was made. (I shall deal with this a little later, since it was not immediately linked to the other offences. I mention it now, to show how persistent the gang were.)

Almost two months passed, and although no other offences were committed, the gang were not idle. They were meticulously planning other raids, some of which would never come to fruition. Others would become spectacular successes.

Portland Road is a cul-de-sac off Green Road, Tottenham; beyond it lies the local technical college and the town hall. The gang's target, this time, was the Imperial Cold Storage, and it was there that two of them, armed with a pistol and a sawn-off shotgun, burst in, to take the gateman hostage. As usual, they waited for their prize – in this instance, a Security Express van – and when it arrived, they overpowered the guard who had entered the premises and strapped an explosive device around his waist. He was told, in no uncertain terms, that unless he carried out their demands, the gang would detonate the explosives by remote control. The terrified guard had no option but to take a tray of tea out to the rest of the crew who, as they opened the van door, were attacked by the gang. An employee who had just arrived saw what was happening and struggled with one of the gunmen, who fired a shot; the noise inside the warehouse was deafening and terrifying, just as the robber intended. At that moment the company director also arrived. He was dragged from his car and another warning shot was fired. Then the gang unstrapped the explosive device from the guard, and used the company director's car to get away, taking with them £98,702.52p. They probably thought: 'About time, too!'

Detective Constable Kevin Shapland had been posted to the Flying Squad at the beginning of that September. He was slim, good-looking with a head of premature grey hair, and he brought with him a record of successful investigations that was second to none. A meticulous investigator, a shrewd interrogator and a handler of some high-quality informants, there was no aspect of criminal investigation in which he faltered. Not only was he best DC with whom I ever worked, he also, in my opinion, would have made a fine commander. (He retired on 16 November 2001. The fact that he never took promotion cheated the Metropolitan Police of an outstanding senior officer.)

Kevin set to work on the four offences and on 14 November 1985, reconstructions were televised on the BBC television programme, *Crimewatch UK*. The response was poor. No real leads emerged. But then something happened which I believe was guided by divine fate. A fourteen-year-old boy was watching television two nights later, but finding the programme

boring, he slipped a videotape of *Crimewatch* into the recorder
and began to play it. As he watched, he gasped. He was
looking at the explosive device which had been left behind
after the abortive raid at Cross & Herbert's, and realized that
this looked remarkably similar to something that he had
found in a sack outside a house in Broxbourne, Hertfordshire,
that summer. It wasn't all he'd found, either: also inside the
sack was a face mask of an old man, some glue and false hair,
and a radio receiver. He'd brought them home and, after he'd
frightened his mother for the umpteenth time by wearing the
mask, she threw the bits and pieces away, including the electronic device – but not before he'd taken it to pieces and
studied it meticulously. The boy telephoned his local police
station, and they in turn contacted Kevin. The boy drew a
picture of the device, which bore an astonishing resemblance
to the one found at Cross & Herbert's, full details of which had
not been disclosed. He also took Kevin to Broxbourne to show
him where he'd found the sack. It was an expensive-looking
bungalow named 'Emerald', in a cul-de-sac called Riverside
Avenue. What was even more interesting, Kevin thought, was
that the former occupier was the owner of an electrical
company . . .

'How much time did you spend looking at the previous owner
of "Emerald"?' I asked Kevin, much later. 'Too long!' he
grinned. The former owner of 'Emerald' would turn out to have
had nothing to do with the robberies. The present owners, a
couple named David and Rita Croke, were checked out. David,
it transpired, had a minor conviction for shoplifting, years
before; nothing had been added to his CRO (Criminal Records
Office) file since then. It would be nice to think that a dedicated
band of detectives were relentlessly pursuing every lead, every
strand of evidence in these cases, but, alas! it would not be true.

Had they been able to do so, they would have discovered sooner that David and Rita Croke had lived in a council flat in Edmonton for eight years, prior to buying 'Emerald' in February 1985, for £85,000 cash. The deeds were put in Rita's name. But a separate operation, code-named 'Operation Safari', was generating an enormous amount of work at Rigg Approach and tying up nearly all the Squad personnel. With at least one robbery being committed every day, operations being conducted and arrests made, Kevin not only had his work cut out dealing with day-to-day routine, but he was very much on his own. He was reduced to driving past 'Emerald' once or twice a day, and noting the registration numbers of vehicles parked in the driveway. And that's how the investigation progressed until 11 December – or rather, the night before . . .

Joe Symes was one of the custodians at a security company named Armaguard, based at The Pinnacles, in Harlow. That night, Joe returned home to his small terraced house in time for dinner with his wife and daughter. As he pushed open the lounge door, his cheerful greeting froze on his lips: his wife and daughter were handcuffed to the dining-room table, and two balaclava-ed men, one with a sawn-off shotgun, the other with an automatic pistol, stood facing him.

'You know what we want,' the leader said.

As Joe told me later, 'Of course I bloody well did!' He was terrified.

His appearance, though, didn't betray his fear. I was told later, by one of the robbers, that he went on pretending everything was normal, 'just casually looked round the room at us, nodded, picked up his dinner, and started to eat. All the time he was looking round, just to see if he could get the jump on us. He had a lot of guts.' That was very true: during the Second World War, Joe had escaped from the Nazis, who had overrun his native Poland; he had anglicized his name, joined

7

the British Army and later became a prisoner-of-war of the Japanese. Joe was told that the house was surrounded by the gang's associates, and to reinforce this, a steady stream of chatter was kept up by the two men inside the house with the rest of the gang, through a walkie-talkie. Joe thought there were at least five members of the gang, but, in fact, there was only one more, who later joined them.

The two women were later released from their handcuffs and were allowed to go to bed, but Joe was questioned all through the night. The gang obviously knew a great deal about him, the company and the strongroom, but they produced their 'bomb' from a holdall and told Joe that this would be strapped around his waist when they went to Armaguard the following morning. If Joe attempted to alert his fellow key-holder in any way prior to opening the door, they warned, the bomb would be detonated and his workmate shot. The following morning, when they set out for Armaguard, the bomb was placed underneath Joe's driving seat. A member of the gang pressed a switch and a red bulb started to glow. Joe was told that the bomb was now armed. As the fellow key-holder arrived and opened the gates, he was attacked, his keys taken from him. The premises were unlocked. Another employee arrived. He too, was overpowered, and he and Joe's fellow key-holder were bound with cable. In an astonishingly short space of time, the gang helped themselves to £480,000 cash. 'That's it, lads,' the ringleader shouted. He locked the three employees into the security cage, and the gang escaped. The victims were unable to see what had been used for the getaway. If anyone had asked them to guess the type of vehicle used (and of course, nobody did) they would have probably said a high-powered Jaguar, maybe a Mercedes, perhaps even a Land Rover, because that would have fitted in with the sophisticated, slick way one would have expected of this band of robbers. If so, they would have been wrong.

The missing half a million had been slung into the back of a repainted and rather shabby Honda van, registration number PBM 263W, such as any workman might use. Sunrise still had another hour to go, as the van set off at a steady 30 mph en route to 'Emerald'.

News of the raid filtered into the office at Rigg Approach a couple of hours later. The guards had managed to wriggle free from their bonds and raise the alarm, and Mrs Symes and her daughter had been found handcuffed and bound in a rear bedroom at the family home. This was the biggest robbery in the history of Essex police, and an incident room, under the command of a detective superintendent and a detective inspector, together with a team of miscellaneous detectives drawn from across the county, was set up at Harlow police station. So could this be the same gang? The explosive device which had been recovered from the aborted raid at Cross & Herbert's had been a viable one; the one left behind at Joe Symes' car was not. Could this have been a copycat raid, inspired by the *Crimewatch* programme? It was certainly possible. Could this be the work of the same robbers who were the subject of Operation Safari? Again, possible. Kevin Shapland was seconded to the Essex enquiry team for one week, and at the end of that time, he was not convinced that the Armaguard offence was linked with the others.

Christmas 1985 came and went, and those who were able to, took some annual leave whilst they could, because their workload was about to go into overload. January's biting winds and freezing temperatures were the worst I had ever known, the more so because I was getting up at 4 a.m. observing, from the back of a 7-cwt Escort van, the address of Operation Safari's ringleader. I have never been *so* cold – no matter how much I was wrapped up, I was still freezing. To keep my mind from freezing as well, I would recite from one to one thousand in German, and then backwards, to one again. Then, I'd do the same in Greek, followed by the Greek alphabet. This would go on until the main suspect left his house and I would be driven off, shivering and blue-faced, to Hornchurch police station to thaw out over a cup of coffee. Day after day, in these sub-zero temperatures I would sit down the road from the house until, eventually, the gang leader left home, met up with his colleagues, told them that he was being watched, and that he was going to return to the house and shoot the bastard. Seeing that he had already shot an off-duty Flying Squad driver, who had tried to intervene during the course of one of their robberies, this was no idle threat. Luckily, this information was passed on to the Squad, who stepped in 'a bit lively' and swiped up the lot, thus saving me from being pumped full of lead.

The mopping-up work for Safari took a long time, and all the while work was pouring into the Squad office. Once again, Kevin was relegated to having the odd peek at 'Emerald' whenever he could fit it in. And then, one day, he saw three cars parked on the driveway: one, an already familiar Audi GT, which Kevin knew belonged to Dave Croke; a Porsche for which no current keeper was shown, and, finally, a Nissan Sunny Estate, which was registered to the wife of a man regarded as a top London robber. Was this the breakthrough that Kevin was looking for? He now arranged surveillance from SO11, the Yard's intelligence department, but for several months, it seemed that little, or indeed nothing was happening. Croke seldom went out and the Nissan Sunny did not reappear. Then, in July 1986, a green Volkswagen Golf GTi appeared at 'Emerald'. The driver was photographed and the prints hurriedly delivered to Rigg Approach. The

Squadmen scrutinized them and Detective Sergeant Phil Burrows (who had served on the Flying Squad previously) immediately recognized the man to be none other than one Donald Walter Barrett.

Though uneducated, Barrett was highly intelligent, cunning and manipulative. He was, quite properly, regarded as a first-division armed robber. At the time, he was nearly fifty, tall, balding, muscular and extremely fit. He had been a thorn in the side of the authorities for well over thirty years. His criminal past was as violent as one could possibly imagine: he had even bitten the nose off a self-confessed grass in prison. Barrett had worked with some of the top robbers in London, including Derek Creighton 'Bertie' Smalls, with whom he had raided the diamond merchants, Ralli Brothers of Hatton Garden, relieving them of precious stones, cash and diamonds, valued at £296,451 in March 1969. Both made star appearances during the robbery at the Skefco Ballbearing Company in Luton, two months later, when £57,741 cash was stolen, as indeed they did when Barclays bank, Ilford, was robbed of £237,736 in February 1970. This was the biggest post-war bank robbery in England. Nine men had taken part in the raid and the late Detective Chief Superintendent Bert Wickstead ('The Old Grey Fox') had roped in and charged three suspects: none of whom was Barrett or Smalls. I remember seeing Bert at one of their remand appearances at Barking Magistrates' Court, when they applied for bail. 'Why do you imagine my client will abscond, if granted bail, Chief Superintendent?' an effete barrister asked. "Cos I know 'im!' growled Bert, which was quite enough for the magistrates. The prisoner was remanded in custody.

Seven months after the robbery at Ilford, Barrett and Smalls turned their attention to Lloyds bank in Bournemouth and snatched a measly £2,226 cash. Smalls made himself scarce, but acting on a tip-off, Barrett was arrested and sentenced to a total of twelve years' imprisonment for the robbery. It was sometime after that, that Smalls himself was arrested and became a 'Resident Informant' – or, more colloquially, a 'Supergrass'. Smalls admitted every offence he could remember doing and implicated everyone he could think of. On 27 September 1974, following three separate trials of a large number of his associates, their sentences totalled 308 years' imprisonment. For his part in the Ralli Brothers robbery, Barrett was sentenced to seventeen years' imprisonment. Smalls was given complete amnesty. Six months later at the Court of Appeal (Criminal Division), Lord Justice Lawton, sitting with Lord Justice James and Mr Justice Milmo, allowed one of the appeals, and reduced the sentences in others (including Barrett's, whose sentence was reduced to twelve years). But Lawton said that what had happened when the DPP (director of public prosecutions) had given an amnesty to Smalls, should never be allowed to happen again. Later, in the House of Lords, Lord Dilhorne criticized Lawton for his remarks about the DPP – 'He must not be told what he has to do in the future' – but the fact remains that Smalls' case was the only one where the Director ever authorized the dropping of charges against a supergrass.

After his release, it didn't take Barrett long before he was going across the pavement once again, and once more, he was arrested. Supergrass fever was gripping the underworld and this time, Barrett wanted some of the action. He, too admitted every crime he had committed (the list was considerable) and implicated everybody with whom he had worked, but instead of receiving the almost mandatory five years (which was then the norm for supergrasses) he was sentenced to fourteen years' imprisonment. This was reduced on appeal to seven, and the parole board released him after serving three years and four months. Barrett was provided with a new identity and a job; but after living the high life for so many years, life as a £200-a-week scaffolder came hard. Just over a year later, Barrett succumbed, and after being introduced to Croke by another top armed robber ('He's got no form,' the robber said, 'but he's bloody good!') Barrett once again set his sights on the good life.

The whole investigation was taken over by Detective Superintendent Duncan MacRae. MacRae was a Squadman through and through – he had served in practically every rank on the Flying Squad and he ordered full-time surveillance to be set up on 'Emerald'. About a week later, things started to happen. Barrett drove his Golf GTi into 'Emerald's' driveway and Croke got into the passenger seat. With the surveillance team following, they drove to Battersea and then into an industrial estate at Nine Elms. They drove round the block and left, but not before the surveillance team had noted that there was a security depot in the estate. The name of the company was Shield Transit Ltd.

The surveillance team split, and now Shield was watched as well. A few days later, Detective Constable Ron Cuthbertson was strolling by the depot when he noticed a black Volkswagen Golf parked on the forecourt. Noting the registration number, he realized that he had seen the same vehicle parked on the driveway at 'Emerald', a few days before. The registered keeper of the car was a man named Al Turner, who lived in Clacton-on-Sea. What the connection was between him and Croke, nobody knew – certainly, Turner had no criminal record – but here was his car again, parked right outside the premises which Barrett and Croke had visited.

Croke and Barrett were seen together on several more occasions, and then on Friday 8 August 1986, Barrett, together with his family, flew out to Portugal, on holiday; and, of course, to establish an alibi. What better than to book a family holiday and then to return alone in the middle of it, commit a crime, return to Portugal and finally return home, complete with family? It might have worked, had not Barrett been spotted arriving back at London Heathrow on Sunday 10 August. From there, the surveillance team followed him all the way to 'Emerald' . . .

In the meantime, MacRae had made himself busy with what was to become known as 'Operation Standard'. First, it seemed that the target was Shield. If they had been the gang who had attacked Armaguard (and now it looked as if that were the case) it appeared that hostages would be taken. Could they go to the management, explain what was happening and replace the staff with Squad officers? No, they couldn't. If Turner was an inside man, word would filter through to him. If there was another inside man, he could warn the gang, the police would never find out who he was, and the gang could simply target other premises. No. If the premises were the target – and they must be – then the Squad would have to set up observation posts (OPs) in and around the industrial estate. Once Croke and Barrett were inside the complex, they would then be contained. How would they get in to the company? Would Turner let them in? How many key-holders were there? The robbers had used scanners to monitor the police radio frequencies during the Armaguard raid. How, then, to communicate? It was all ifs, ands and buts.

Meanwhile, after arriving at 'Emerald', Barrett and Croke drove off to Clacton-on-Sea and spent several hours in Al Turner's company before returning to Broxbourne. It was obvious that something was very imminent, and the SO11 surveillance team stayed out all night. In the most atrocious weather conditions imaginable, the rain poured down and two of the SO11 watchers lay in the grass, overlooking 'Emerald', their clothes sodden, not moving a muscle. There they stayed until 4.30 the following morning, when the lights went on in the bungalow. Shortly afterwards, Croke and Barrett emerged and went to a lock-up a short distance away, where a blue Ford Escort van, purchased for cash and not registered to anybody, had been stashed. As the van drove off, so the surveillance team started to shadow them, all the way to Battersea.

At the last moment, Duncan MacRae had been unavailable to supervise the operation and Detective Superintendent Peter Gwynne stepped into the breach. Again, Gwynne was a committed Flying Squad officer who had previously worked on the Squad, and who possessed a keen analytical brain. Furthermore he was completely unflappable. The team had been fully briefed at Lambeth police station and Gwynne had set up three OPs – Tom, Dick and Harry – and the police fire-arms team – the elite PT17 – formed part of the 80-officer team who now lay in readiness.

At exactly 5.45 a.m., Al Turner drove his black VW Golf into the estate and, seventeen minutes later, Croke and Barrett drove the blue Escort in after him. Then something odd happened: two minutes later, the Escort re-emerged from the estate, drove a little way down the road and parked up. Ron Cuthbertson and I were in the back of a lorry filled with the firearms unit – it was to be our job to assist with the arrests once the unit had contained them – and we looked at each other and raised our eyebrows. Minutes passed. Turner was nervously walking up and down, as though waiting for someone. A guard arrived and unlocked the premises. A few moments later, Turner entered the premises and re-emerged, carrying what looked like a shoe-box – one that was quite obviously heavy – and this he put into a white van. Three minutes later, both men got into the van and drove off, and as they left the industrial estate, they were followed by the blue Escort which, in turn, was followed by the surveillance team. Well – this was a how d'you do. 'Right', said Peter Gwynne. 'They may be going to pick something up and return to the depot, and Barrett and Croke will attack them then, and clear out the whole firm. On the other hand, they may be intending to attack the van in the near future. Therefore', said Gwynne, 'half the team will stay at the estate, the other half will join in the follow.' This, everyone agreed, was an eminently sensible course of action – even Ron and I, who were left behind. Detective Inspector Ken Grange was put in charge of the team to follow the convoy. He was a supremely capable officer and was no stranger to large inquiries. He had led 'Operation Safari' to a successful conclusion.

On, through central London and on to the M1 motorway, went the convoy: the white van followed, like a pilot fish, by the blue Escort, and then by the Squad officers. The police helicopter at Battersea had been scrambled and was now overlooking the whole scene, forwarding messages to the police chiefs of the areas for permission for officers from another force to enter their area, carrying firearms. Eventually, the white van signalled that it was pulling off the motorway and into the service station at Newport Pagnall, still followed by the blue van. Some of the surveillance team followed – the rest hung back on the hard shoulder, just before the slip road. Turner got out of the van; at 7.45 a.m. the watchers registered a meeting between him, Croke and Barrett, who was now wearing a wig and glasses. Turner entered the cafeteria and emerged carrying two cups of coffee and headed towards the white van, with Croke and Barrett walking purposefully in pursuit.

The white van left the service area, heading for the slip road to the M1, and it could be seen that Croke was driving; the blue Escort in close pursuit was being driven by Barrett. As they reached the motorway, there came the order, 'Attack! Attack! Attack!' and the Squad cars raced down the motorway, overtook the two vehicles and forced the white van to a halt on the hard shoulder. Croke was dragged from the van and reached towards his jacket pocket but before he could complete this manoeuvre, he was handcuffed. It appeared to be not a moment too soon. The .32 revolver in his jacket was fully loaded.

Barrett, meanwhile, had tried to make a break for it, but he too, was stopped and as Kevin Shapland ran towards him, Barrett, seeing there was no way out, surrendered both his loaded 7.65 mm automatic and his liberty.

Both men were in possession of radio scanners, CS gas cannisters and Croke, a flick knife. There was also, the gold bullion which they'd just stolen, valued at £283,500. In the back of the van, tied up, were Al Turner and the guard. Everybody was taken to Milton Keynes police station where the greatest possible assistance was given by the locals – everybody wanted to help. Croke, his cunning working overtime, engineered a move to hospital in order to get a little breathing space. Barrett and Turner admitted their involvement in the affair and the other guard was not, of course, involved in any way, save as a victim. Speed was now of the essence: the prisoners were held incommunicado and teams of detectives were sent to their homes. As Detective Constable Mark Bryant arrived at 'Emerald', so Rita Croke was getting into her car. She was stopped and the car searched. 'What's this?' asked Bryant, pointing to two sacks.

'Rubbish!' Rita snapped and, although it was unclear if she was referring to the contents of the sacks or the absurdity of Bryant's question, the sacks were seized and searched. They

contained a Reck .65 self-loading gas pistol and 28 gas cartridges, bullets, shotgun cartridges, spectacles, a holster, hats,
clothing and adhesive; also a quantity of correspondence. Rita,
too, was brought back to Milton Keynes police station. I had
been despatched to East London to pick up the professional
robber, whose wife's car had once graced the driveway of
'Emerald'. He wasn't at home, so I sat up on the address, until
a little later, he turned up and parked the Nissan Sunny Estate
round the corner. As he headed for the house, I ran across the
road after him and, with a couple of yards to go, I launched
myself at him, fully expecting him to go down flat on the
pavement. He didn't – he just stood there, as solid as an oak
tree with my arms wrapped round him and my little legs flail-
ing up and down. And d'you know what he said? 'Leave off.
You know I've got a bad leg!' So I climbed down to the ground
and arrested him. It was all a bit of an anti-climax – I did feel
silly. Soon he joined the others at Milton Keynes police
station, and that, chums, was that – end of round one.

I think I had a pretty good idea of what was running
through Barrett's mind as he sat in his cell: going into over-
drive. What could he do to minimize his predicament? He'd
been caught, bang to rights, for this offence and there was no
way out of that. He had committed a number of offences since
his release, three years before. Could we link him to them?
What did we know? Even if we knew nothing – not very
likely! – conviction for this offence alone, even with a guilty
plea, could still end in a substantial lump of porridge. Being
in possession of a loaded automatic didn't help, either. So
what could he be looking at? Well, with his form, practically
all for robbery, a twenty, certainly; in front of the wrong
judge, life imprisonment which would just about see him
out. And how could he do any normal bird, with all the chaps
he'd grassed up? He'd be dead in a week or two, a month top

whack. The alternative would be to go behind the door with all the sex cases: the nonces. What a thought. And what would happen if Dave Croke rolls over? He's got enough on me to hang me once those cunning Squad bastards get to work on Dave. Then Barrett would remember what a top London robber had said to him: 'I'm working with you, Don, because you're the best. Also, because you've been a supergrass, you can never be one again. Mind you,' he added, 'if you ever grass me, I'll find you and kill you.' He'd meant it, too. Because I can never be a supergrass again. Who says not? Because it's never happened, it doesn't mean to say it can't be done. And why isn't Crokey answering me? I've been calling out to him for bloody ages. Where is he? Upstairs? Spilling his guts? Time for me to make my play!

With that, Barrett had got to his feet, taken two quick paces across his cell, stuck his thumb on the bell-push and kept it there.

'A supergrass, twice?' Kevin said. 'Never heard of that before, Don. Don't think it's ever been done.' The three of us were seated round a table in the interview room.

'Doesn't mean it can't though, does it?' Barrett asked casually enough, but I noticed that the pulse in his neck was beating strongly.

'The thing is, Don,' I said, 'do we really need you? We can link you to Armaguard, Cross and Herbert's, Enfield crematorium and the rest.'

'You don't know how many I've done,' Barrett said. 'And you need someone like me to bring in the rest and point the finger at them and convict 'em. But if you reckon you can get me down for things that I'm not even admitting, fine. I'll just wipe my mouth and walk away.'

'So what are we talking about then, Don?' Kevin asked.

'Right,' said Barrett. 'Including today's job, I can tell you

19

about eleven robberies, attempted robberies and conspiracies. I can give you about the same number of top-class robbers. I can tell you where the guns are, I can tell you what happened to the money which comes to a couple of million and how to get it back and I can tell you where to look for corroboration.' He sat back, having laid down an impressive hand of cards and watched us intently. There was a bit of a silence. Of course, Barrett had left the best bit to last. He knew full well that independent corroboration was essential in any super-grass trial. 'First of all,' I said, 'if we're going to do anything, the Director of Public Prosecutions has got to agree.' Barrett nodded. This was nothing new to him. 'So what I'll need,' I continued, 'is something in writing, to show him.' Barrett threw back his head and guffawed. 'Leave off!' he laughed, although there was very little humour in his laughter. 'What I want to do,' I continued, 'is take a "without prejudice" state-ment. We'll put something like, "I, Donald Walter Barrett, make the following statement on the understanding that if I am not accepted by the Director of Public Prosecutions as a resident informant, nothing in this statement can be used in evidence against me." Then, what we'll do is just put down what you've said to us, as briefly as that.'

Barrett smoked and thought. Eventually, he said, 'All right, we'll do it.'

And we did.

As he signed the statement, he grinned wryly. 'Well, that's it,' he said. 'I'm bollocksed now, aren't I?'

I picked up the statement and put it in my briefcase. 'Whatever way it goes, Don,' I said, 'we're playing this one straight down the line.'

'You simply can't take a statement like this!' screamed the pimply representative from the Crown Prosecution Service. This worthless organization had just got underway and this little twerp was flexing his muscles. I gave him a look and said, 'Shut up! It's done.' He flounced away and I settled down for a long wait. To tell the truth, I didn't know if I had done the right thing, never having done anything like this before, but it seemed to me to be the fairest thing that I could do, for everybody concerned, in the circumstances.

The following day, Peter Gwynne emerged from the Director's office. 'Right, we've got the go-ahead,' he said. 'Mind you,' he added with a grin, 'the Director did wince when he saw your statement!'

Barrett, the two Crokes and Turner were all charged and, with the exception of Barrett, were remanded in custody. Barrett was moved into a suite of cells at an East London police station which had been especially adapted for resident informants. Entry to the suite was gained through a series of electronically controlled doors, each having to be closed before the next could be opened. This, the feeding facilities and the searching of permitted visitors were administered by armed uniformed officers, who worked a three-shift system in the claustrophobic atmosphere of what Kevin christened 'The Bunker'. It was here that the first six months of this intensive inquiry began, with Kevin and myself as Barrett's handlers. Ken Grange had the overall charge of this small squad of twelve, which included a typist, a woman police constable for indexing and filing, and Tony Freeman, to drive the Squad car in any further investigations.

One person who was to be an invaluable member of the team was Paul Millen, a civilian Scenes of Crime officer (SOCO). I have never had a particularly high regard for SOCOs in general. Apart from the fact that I thought they were a pretty useless bunch at solving anything, I didn't believe they had the commitment for the job. But with Paul Millen, I changed my opinion. It was an inauspicious beginning. I had been instrumental in getting rid of the previous nightmare SOCO attached to the Squad. And then along came Paul – short, balding, his eyes blinking owlishly behind his spectacles. I glared at him. 'You the new SOCO?', I asked. Paul nodded. 'Hope you're better than the last one,' I said. 'Because if you're not, out you fucking-well go!' Paul said nothing, just blinked at me once or twice, turned and got on with his job. I learned very quickly that Paul was the absolute Billy Bollocks. He was a keen and tireless worker and if Paul said something couldn't be done, it was because he had exhausted every other possibility of finding a solution. So Paul was with us on the case from the word go and had acquired samples from the suspects and had been at the houses for searches. Corroboration was the watchword and, with Paul, that's what we got. We badly needed it: not one incriminating fingerprint had been found at the scene of any of the robberies.

I took a separate statement for each offence, rather than one long, rambling one that tried to encompass everything. It was a lot easier that way and, if further evidence came to light, or if Barrett wanted to add something that had previously slipped his memory, it was simple to take a further, short statement and attach it to the first.

Barrett proved to have a phenomenal memory for detail. He recounted meticulously what cars were used, what guns, and also what clothing and disguises he and the team were wearing.

He admitted that the first offence occurred on 3 August 1984, at a warehouse, Brook Bond Oxo, in Suez Road, Enfield. Barrett, with two others, had taken the staff hostage and awaited the arrival of a Securicor van. The guards were seized and firearms were discharged, for the necessary 'frighteners'. When this failed to take immediate effect, one of the guards was doused in petrol and the others were told that unless the cash was forthcoming, their colleague would be ignited. The guards were left in no doubt as to the serious-ness of the threat, and the gang escaped with £78,431.37p.

Just over three months later, the gang struck again, this time in Jeffries Road, Brimsdown, Enfield. A Ford Sierra Estate travelling from Hatton Garden to Johnson Matthey plc was forced to a halt. One of the gang smashed the rear window, and the driver was threatened by another member of the gang who was armed with a gun. Gold and silver bullion, valued at a quarter of a million pounds, was hauled from the boot, the team leapt into the getaway car and drove it the few hundred yards to a railway bridge. There it was abandoned. They raced across the bridge and into a car waiting on the other side, then drove sedately away.

Three weeks later – a week before Christmas 1984 – Barrett and Croke hijacked a Vauxhall van en route from Bristol to Sheffield. The driver was threatened with a .32 revolver and an automatic pistol, was bound and gagged, and taken to Heston services on the M4 motorway where he and his van were dumped, minus his consignment of gold and silver, again valued at a quarter of a million pounds. A dust-coat, belonging to Croke, was later found and was tested for firearms residue: none was discovered. Particles of gold were.

I can remember when the teleprinter message concerning this robbery was sent from the Avon and Somerset Con-stabulary. I thought it odd at the time because, initially, the sum stolen was described as being a quarter of a million pounds; the next day, it was amended to £97,000. Eventually, matters became a little clearer. The company was Scadlynns Ltd, of Bishopsworth, Bristol. Six weeks after the robbery, Detective Constable John Fordham was stabbed to death, ten times in the head, back and chest. Kenneth Noye claimed it was in self-defence, but I feel that I can call him a murderer now, because of his life sentence for stabbling to death another young man. John had been observing Noye because of his links with £26 million worth of gold, stolen during the Brink's-Mat robbery on 26 November 1983. Part of the consignment had been smelted at Scadlynn's, who were raided shortly afterwards. Garth Chappell, the director of Scadlynn's, was later sentenced to ten years' imprisonment, fined and ordered to pay costs totalling £275,000 for his part in the conspiracy to handle dishonestly the gold from Brink's-Mat. For his part in the conspiracy, Noye was sentenced to thirteen years' imprisonment, fined a total of half a million pounds or one year's imprisonment consecutive, and ordered to pay costs of £200,000. I was in court at the Old Bailey when they were weighed off. A nice result – but it didn't bring John back.

On 24 February 1985, Barrett and another man, armed with a revolver, went into Select-a-Property, in Penn Road, Beaconsfield and attacked, bound and gagged two members of staff, a man and a woman, and stole two rings, which the woman later insisted were worth half a million pounds. 'Bollocks!' was Barrett's surprised and indignant response when I tasked him with that amount. 'I fucking wish they had of been!'

Then came the offences at Enfield crematorium, Cross and Herbert and Amtico. And what about the explosive device which had been so thoughtlessly left behind at the Cross and Herbert raid? Inside the bomb device we had found a shotgun cartridge stuffed with a piece of cloth. At the time it had been packed and sealed. Fifteen months later, Paul searched Croke's address and discovered an identical piece of fabric, with identical stitching.

Now, as I mentioned, between the unsuccessful raid at Amtico's and the far more successful raid at Imperial Cold

Storage, there was another, that previously had not been linked to the other offences. With so much going on, it's doubtful if anybody at the Rigg Approach office was aware of it, because this case was being investigated by the Tower Bridge office of the Flying Squad.

On 18 July 1985, as a Security Express van was waiting to enter premises on Mauritius Road, Greenwich, the vehicle was attacked by Barrett and three of the gang. Shots were fired and a Hilti gun was fired into the van window in an attempt to fracture it and gain entry. The police were alerted, and with the sound of their sirens drawing near, the robbers had abandoned the raid and fled. Barrett disclosed the whereabouts of the Hilti gun; forensic tests revealed that glass, inside the mechanism of the gun, exactly matched the laminated glass from the security van. Then a piece of cloth found inside one of the getaway cars matched cloth found at one of the suspects' addresses. Barrett told us that one of the gang had been experimenting with armour-piercing bullets on this raid. A search at 'Emerald' revealed a steel-headed, home-made bullet, together with home-made silencers.

Then came the Imperial Cold Storage robbery, and that was followed by Armaguard.

Experienced robbers do not simply commit one robbery and, when they've done it, think to themselves, 'Well – better look round for another one.' They have several on the go, all the time. If one fails, they've got another – probably several – to fall back on. So having just helped themselves to a quarter of a million pounds' worth of gold bullion from Scadlynn's in December 1984, Croke and Barrett immediately started planning the Armaguard offence, which took place a year later. During that time, they committed five more offences and the successful ones netted £590,000.

In fact, Armaguard was initially Croke's idea. He had seen

the company's vans and started following them back to their base – quite a small depot with just a few vehicles. Croke mentioned what he had seen to Barrett and, shortly afterwards, Barrett drove down to the premises in an Austin Princess saloon, parked the car and left. Croke was in the boot and from there he observed the firm, the comings and goings of its employees, through unobtrusive holes, bored in the bodywork. Weeks went by. He noted Joe Symes, and his friend Bill. They now formed a plan to take out the entire security company.

Bill was the original target. First, he was followed home and the tailing was carried out to MI5 standards. As Bill left the depot in his private car, so he would be followed until he reached a junction and turned left or right. The vehicle following him went straight on. This continued until such time as the gang were satisfied that this was Bill's normal route home. Then, they would park up near the junction until he appeared and follow him to the next junction. This might be for 100 yards along the road or for two miles. Then, as before, they would abort the follow. This went on for weeks until they successfully discovered his address. The next step was to follow Bill on his day off, when he went shopping with his family. As Bill, his wife and two children wandered through the crowds in Marks & Spencer's or Tesco's Supermarket, so Barrett and Croke would be alongside them, in front of them, trailing just behind them; hearing scraps of conversation, the names of the children, what they'd done at school, the name of the family pet, where they'd been on holiday. All this information was stored away, so that they could later casually mention it in conversation to them. And this technique works: it strips people naked and makes them think that their adversaries know everything and that they're defenceless. I knew exactly what Barrett meant: I'd been looking for a robber and couldn't immediately find him, so I read up everything that he'd ever done as well as details of his private life. When I eventually found him, I sat him down and just started casually chatting about him: his mouth fell open, more and more. 'Stop!' he finally shouted. 'You know everything!' He promptly made a full confession. Just as well, because the evidence against him, until then, had been pretty ropy.

So that was Bill all ready for the taking – until the obvious thing stopped them. 'You simply can't wrap up kids,' said Barrett to me and, of course, he was absolutely right and not from any moral or ethical grounds either. Try tying up young children in front of their parents and it's possible that they – particularly mum – will go berserk, and what could have been a sweet little job suddenly goes awry. So all those plans were scrapped and they started on Joe Symes, right from scratch – just as they'd done with Bill.

The third member of the gang was Glen Armsby. He had already taken part in the Imperial Cold Storage robbery some three months earlier, had conducted himself well on that occasion and since another gang member was necessary, Armsby was recruited. You know what happened next.

Following the robbery, the share-out came to £140,000 each. Barrett had told me that Croke had an account in the Bank of Ireland, Seven Sisters Road, Holloway in the name of T. & R. Moore. Shortly after the robbery, £140,000 was deposited in the account. During the robbery, a chain-link fence was cut. Wire cutters were found at 'Emerald' which revealed that they had been used. Adhesive, which had been used to make the explosive device found in Joe Symes' car, was also found at 'Emerald'. Several items were left behind: a battery cover plate was found at the scene – the radio device, minus the cover plate was also found there. A balaclava, too, was left and fibres were discovered inside it. They matched fibres found on the wig worn by Barrett at the time of his arrest. Croke was later picked out by Joe Symes and his daughter in an identity parade.

Remember the shabby Honda that was used to transport the money? A point was raised that needed clearing up. Barrett had told us that the van had been repainted yellow. Checking through the enormous bundle of witness statements taken by Essex police at the time of the robbery, a couple of witnesses had said that they had seen the Honda leave the vicinity of Armaguard at the relevant time. However, both said categorically that the van was white.

Could Barrett have made a mistake? No, he couldn't, he replied irritably and then, when he was pushed on the subject, he finally lost his temper. He knew what was yellow and what was white and that van had been painted yellow. He didn't care what the witnesses had seen. If they said the van was white, either they were wrong or they'd seen a different van – one that was white, right? Not fucking yellow! In fact, nobody had got it wrong; everybody was right.

Paul Millen solved the conundrum. The van had originally been supplied, painted white. It had been resprayed in accordance with the fleet colours. Paul demonstrated that under the street lighting in the area of Armaguard, this shade of yellow looked white; and at the time when the witnesses had seen the Honda van, the street lighting was still on, because dawn was still an hour away. This was carefully explained to a very sulky Barrett, still annoyed that his word had been doubted. 'Told you so!' was his only response. So the van had indeed been repainted yellow and Barrett mentioned that it had met with a slight accident when it struck the garage door in the lock-up. Yellow paint was found on the door of the lock-up: this matched yellow paint fragments found on a roof rack, which had been set to the exact dimensions for a Honda van of that model. But where was the van? Barrett knew. Following the raid, it had been driven by Croke, together with Rita and Glen Armsby, across France to a town named Chalon-sur-Saône, fairly close to the Swiss border. There, it had conked out and Croke had purchased another cheap vehicle, a Daf. From there, they had made their way to Malta where David and Rita had a flat, and while they relaxed in the sun, Croke purchased a boat. Now, there are two things that are considered bad luck by sailors: first, killing an albatross, and, next, renaming a boat. I can only assume that Croke had never heard of the second; it seemed the height of stupidity to paint the name 'ARMAG' on it to commemorate his latest piece of work. Perhaps he later realized his recklessness, because he painted over it, but that didn't really help. I went to Chalon-sur-Saône and discovered the Honda's fate; it had been scrapped, sawn up and the top part used as a chicken coop. Kevin and Ken Grange went to Malta, found the boat and, under ultra-violet light, discovered the incriminating word, which was photographed. Kevin, ever the perfectionist, obtained a statement from a suitably competent person to say that 'ARMAG' was not a word in the Maltese vocabulary.

Barrett never stopped blaming Croke for his current situation. 'It's all his fault,' he'd say. 'If he hadn't left that stuff in the sack outside his house for the kid to find, we wouldn't be in the mess we're in today. Well, fuck 'im!'

Thirteen others were pulled in. John Kenneth Johnson admitted to being one of the gang who had attacked the Ford Sierra in Brimsdown, Enfield. He also admitted to attacking the staff at Select-a-Property. Glen Armsby, too, came in and admitted his part in the Tottenham raid (which was later left on the file at court) and the Armaguard robbery. Two other men were charged with receiving the gold, stolen from the Brimsdown robbery.

Months passed in the bunker. The case correspondence in each offence was drawn, scrutinized and re-investigated. I was seconded to work on the details of the Armaguard case with the Essex detectives. What a good bunch they were. There was absolutely no resentment at our presence and they worked just as hard as we did to clear the matter up. Barrett came out in the Squad car to point out the robbery sites, where vehicles were parked, and where lock-ups were situated. He was given keep-fit equipment in his cell: a heavy punch bag and weights and, although they were seldom used at first, later they were, in order to sharpen his mind for the trials. His moods went up and down. Sometimes, thinking about his predicament and the possible outcome, he would be morose, because that was the question on his lips all the time: what sort of sentence was he going to get? It was a question to which nobody could supply the answer, and Kevin and I would pull his leg to cheer him up. Barrett's leg was seriously pulled one day, when he was in a pensive mood.

'You know,' he said. 'It's a pity you couldn't have got Croke to have rolled over. He knows a lot,' he added. 'More than me, I reckon.'

I think Barrett wanted Kevin and myself to rush to his defence, crying, 'Oh, no Don – there's no one like you!' If so, he was sorely disappointed.

'Be a change from listening to a boring fucker like you,' said Kevin, winking at me.

'That's right,' I replied, joining in. 'And what's more, Croke's got no form, either; he's got more cred than you! Come on, Don, get your kit together – we're fucking you off to Brixton this afternoon!' In the end, Don had to laugh with us – but it took a bit of time.

On another occasion, Barrett and I were talking about a very high-ranking armed robber, whom he knew very well.

'He really screwed his loaf, Don,' I said. 'He got nicked for a half-million pound VAT scam, involving Krugerrands, and copped just twelve months. All that dough and nothing like the same amount of bird you'd get for a blagging – didn't you ever fancy something like that?'

Barrett smiled and his eyes were far away, reminding me of Lawrence's quotation about 'men who dream with their eyes open'. The answer he gave provided another insight into the committed armed robber's psyche. 'You can't understand it, Dick,' he said, 'because you've never been across the pavement.' He shook his head. 'There's no other feeling like it,' he added, quietly.

But Barrett would often be in an amusing mood and we'd all have a laugh over things that had happened. On one occasion, Barrett mentioned the name of someone who was a prolific robber.

'Yes,' I laughed. 'Big fat fucker!'

Barrett frowned. 'Why'd you say that?' he asked.

'Well,' I replied, 'anybody who's 5 foot 8 inches tall and weighs over 20 stone has earned the right to be called a big fat fucker!'

Barrett shook his head.

'The bloke I'm talking about is 5 foot 8 inches all right,' he replied. 'But the last time I saw him was in Albany and he weighed about 11 stone and he was as hard as a lump of concrete. I wouldn't have gone up against him!' he added.

We *were* talking about the same man; inside, he'd work out as though there was no tomorrow and actually built himself an assault course in one prison; outside prison, he simply ballooned. In fact, he'd recently been arrested by the Squad during an ambush, and when I interviewed one of the small-fry, he'd been told that the flabby robber had been a member of the SAS, to keep him in line. I don't know if he was; I do

31

know that he'd been in Africa, because when he was chatting to the Squad officers, he proudly told them, 'I can speak Swahili.' This statement was met with derision by the Squad officers, with the robber insisting it was true.

'Go on, then,' said one of the officers. 'Say something in Swahili.'

'*Mimi nataka pesa!*' the robber snapped.

'Blimey!' replied one of the round-eyed Squadmen, impressed at the fluency and authority in his voice. 'What's that mean?' The robber grinned. 'It means, "Give me the money"!' he replied.

It did, too – he'd had two years' hard labour in Nairobi to prove it.

Barrett confronted the people he was accusing, giving them the opportunity to confirm or deny his accusations. Croke just sat in a corner, his body hunched, saying nothing, his eyes never leaving Barrett's face. With his perpetually downcast expression, his droopy moustache and his spectacles, he gave the appearance of one of life's losers. But he didn't fool us for one moment, nor Barrett, either. 'It's when he looks like that,' Barrett told me once, 'that he's at his most dangerous.' Not only did Croke have nothing to say on that occasion, he had little to say on any other occasion, either. It was only when my questioning got a little too persistent that he uttered his only words of the interview: 'I want my solicitor to be here.'

He needed one. The evidence against him continued to mount. Every time Croke had carried out a successful robbery, his share would appear the following day in the T. & R. Moore bank account in Seven Sisters Road.

Barrett pleaded guilty at the Old Bailey to a total of 23 offences. He was remanded, pending sentence, and his statements under caution were transcribed into witness statements and served on the defendants. Where independent corroboration could be found, the defendants were charged; where there was not, they were released. Tough, I know, especially when I and the rest of the team were utterly convinced of their culpability, but as Humphrey Bogart was prone to say, 'That's the way the piss-pot cracks'. After a series of trials at the Bailey, just one man was acquitted on a technicality; the rest pleaded or were found guilty.

Barrett was told that he was receiving a 25 per cent discount in recognition of his record as a police informant. 'What credit can I give you for the enormous assistance you have given police? In my judgement, rather less than last time,' said His Honour, Judge Michael Coombe QC. 'Nobody could be permitted for a second time the leniency you were given.' Barrett was then sentenced to sixteen years' imprisonment and was made criminally bankrupt in the sum of £840,519. Barrett, clasping a wide-brimmed Fedora against the front of his immaculate Savile Row suit, bowed slightly to the judge. Irony? Maybe. The Fedora wasn't the only thing that could be placed on Barrett's head; with it went a bounty of £250,000 put up by the underworld for his instant demise.

Faced with a mountain of overpowering evidence, Croke pleaded guilty to the robberies involving the gold bullion at Scadlynn's, the raid at Imperial Cold Storage, Armaguard and the bullion robbery for which he'd been arrested. In addition, he also pleaded guilty to kidnapping the Symes family, and associated firearms offences. Further offences were left on the file. Describing Croke as, 'a ruthless criminal with no feelings for the suffering and terror of others', and adding that the bomb device, used to encourage compliance from the victims, was 'a diabolical feature', Judge Coombe sentenced him to a total of 23 years' imprisonment and made him criminally bankrupt in the sum of £528,352.

Rita Croke pleaded guilty to possessing a prohibited

weapon, was sentenced to three months' imprisonment, suspended for one year and fined £5,000.

Glen Ronald Armsby had stepped from the ranks of being an unsuccessful criminal straight into the first division. Perhaps living with Rita Croke's daughter helped. For his part in the Armaguard robbery, the kidnapping of the Symes family and possession of firearms, he was sentenced to 15 years' imprisonment.

Al Turner was sentenced to seven years' imprisonment, after being found guilty of robbing his partner of the gold bullion at Newport Pagnell. He had been christened Al Capon, but tired of being teased about how similar it was to Al Capone, he had changed it to Turner. In fact, he could have changed it to Croke; after all, he was Rita's son.

John Kenneth Johnson, who had taken part in two of the robberies, was sentenced to two years' imprisonment. Two men who received the gold from Johnson Matthey were sentenced respectively to three and four years' imprisonment, and the senior of them was made criminally bankrupt in the sum of £219,000.

With the exception of Rita, the prisoners made their way to the cells, for onward transmission to various prisons.

So what happened next? Barrett appealed against his sentence and the Court of Appeal reduced it to 12 years. He was later released, given a new identity, but, oh dear! soon he was back to his old tricks, robbing a supermarket. Nobody wanted a triple supergrass and he wound up with a lengthy term of imprisonment.

Croke, too, appealed and his sentence was also cut, albeit less dramatically than Barrett's, and he was stuck with 21 years' imprisonment. Several times he attempted to escape and was finally released. Somehow I didn't think we'd heard the last of Mr Croke, and we hadn't. On 22 July 2002, Croke and

his associate, Robert Knapp, were sentenced to life imprisonment for the contract murder of a businessman. On 2 October
2002, the millionaire property tycoon, Nicholas van
Hoogstraten, who was found guilty of manslaughter in the
same case, was sentenced to ten years' imprisonment. Van
Hoogstraten's conviction was overturned on 9 December 2003
and he left the court a free man, vowing to 'sue everybody'.

Armsby wrote a mawkish letter to Joe Symes, apologizing
for his behaviour. Personally, I've no doubt that it was done
to curry favour with the parole board, and for no other reason.
Joe handed it to me. 'Look at zat,' he said scornfully, in his
thick Polish accent. 'Vat a load of bollix!' Mrs Symes went to
her grave, never having uttered a single word about her
ordeal. Joe, too, died shortly afterwards. His daughter told
me that she had no doubt that the strain of that night had has-
tened his demise. I am sure she was right. What a man he was.
And yet despite all the misery they cause to innocent people,
in prison armed robbers are highest in the pecking order.

The top London robber with whom I'd unsuccessfully wres-
tled, was charged and locked up for several weeks; but
eventually, he was released due to a lack of corroborative
evidence.

Peter Gwynne, Duncan MacRae, Ken Grange, Kevin
Shapland and myself all retired; Tony Freeman died. One day,
I was walking around an art exhibition when a small object
caught my eye and I decided to buy it, as a memento. It was
a golden frog, to commemorate all the bullion that was stolen
in this case. It sits on my windowsill now, as I type; I'm
almost sure that I can hear it 'croke'.

So that was the story of Operation Standard. Ken Grange,
Kevin Shapland and I were commended by the commissioner,
the trial judge, the Director of Public Prosecutions and the
chief constable of Essex. But out of all the commendations

given, if only one could have been awarded, the recipient would have to have been Kevin Shapland: it was always his case, no one else's.

For one who had so much to say, the last word must be Barrett's. He had been arrested, disarmed and handcuffed. He stood on the M1 motorway, the wind of the passing vehicles tearing at him, and he knew his life was in ruins. It was, as he told me later, 'the first time I've ever been caught on a ready-eye' – in other words, bang to rights. Surrounded by police and a wealth of incriminating evidence, he knew that his next step was into a prison cell, perhaps for the rest of his life. And yet, as he turned and calmly surveyed the scene on the motorway, he spotted Detective Sergeant Phil Burrows, his one-time handler. 'Hello, Phil,' he said, casually. 'Nice little tickle you've had here!'

A Cry For Help

Informants are a funny breed. For some, it's a full-time occupation and their work-rate can be so prolific that they can take over your working life. There were some who delivered an incredible, out-of-this-world job, right out of the blue, copped their reward, and were never seen again. A case I have in mind was of a snout who gave me the thief who had stolen a painting by Rembrandt, valued at £2.5 million, from the Dulwich Art Gallery. The thief pleaded guilty and received three years' imprisonment; the snout was paid out . . . well, quite a lot of money! And that was that – I tried all sorts of ways to find the little rascal afterwards, without success. The word was that he'd gone to Hamburg with a team of whizzers and that he'd been nicked – no, he'd been murdered – no, not murdered in Hamburg, somewhere else – Antwerp? Dunno, Guv. The enquiries that I made had to be extremely circumspect because whoever I was asking, whether it was my chums in West Germany's *Bundeskriminalamt* or the likes of Sammy the Snout, the inevitable question asked would be – 'Why d'you want to know?'

And then there were the part-timers. Snouts with whom you didn't really lose contact, and who would pop out of the woodwork maybe once a year. One such was Terry Chapman who was a bizarre informant: nervous, thin, with an odd line in rambling chat. We met during the investigation of the murder of a French prostitute in Soho. She had been

37

despatched by the Maltese Syndicate. Terry had seen and heard a little too much and he was badly frightened that he might well be next in line. I thought he had a point, so he was given a new identity and whisked off to the seaside town of Ramsgate. I had an excellent relationship with the Kent constabularies' Special Branch and we agreed that if swarthy strangers started making enquiries in the area, we should soon get to know about it.

From time to time, I would visit Ramsgate, but Terry was difficult to find. He was fascinated by the underworld and, instead of his brush with the Syndicate scaring him off, he was eager to pick up tips to pass on. So I'd book into my hotel, visit his local haunts and leave word for him to call me. Then I would return and unpack a large and varied selection of books. If I'd known how long he'd sometimes take to get in contact, I reckon I could have passed the Inspector's exam in about two weeks flat.

One day, I was in the London office, when I received a telephone call from Terry. His moods were mercurial; today, he was on a high. He tried to inject an air of mysterious authority into his voice but failed miserably because he was brimming over with excitement.

'Mr Kirby, you'll never guess what,' he gasped. 'I've been asked to take part in a robbery at Barclays bank, here in Ramsgate – it's going off tomorrow, at closing time!' Now, this *was* interesting.

'Go on, Terry,' I said. 'Who else is involved? What do they want you to do? How'd you get involved?'

There was a pause. 'Actually, I don't know his name, Mr Kirby.'

'Don't know his name?' I echoed. 'So how'd you get approached?'

'Well, I was walking down the High Street yesterday, on

my way to the library,' he said. 'And this bloke came up to me and said, "How'd you like to take part in an armed robbery on Thursday?"'

'Just like that?' I asked. 'Someone, who you've never met before comes up to you, right out of the blue and asks you to take part in an armed hold-up?'

'Put like that, it does sound a bit funny, Mr Kirby,' Terry said.

'So what was the plan then, Terry?' I asked. 'You do the bank and then run off down the road?'

'We didn't get that far with the fine detail,' he muttered.

'I only hope he didn't ask you to be the getaway driver,' I said, now rapidly running out of patience. 'I mean, bearing in mind you can't drive. If he'd asked you to do that, I hope you'd have been up front with him, so there wasn't any embarrassment later,' I added sarcastically.

'It would have been a bit worrying if he'd asked me to do that,' Terry agreed.

'This isn't a wind-up, is it Terry?' I demanded. 'You're not giving me the run-around, are you?'

Terry was mortally wounded. 'Certainly not, Mr Kirby!' he cried. 'You know I'd never do that! I'd never let you down – I look up to you, Mr Kirby, I –'

'Yes, yes,' I hastily interrupted, since Terry was beginning to sound like a first-year boarder, who's suddenly become enamoured of the sports master. 'But the whole thing does sound, well . . . a bit improbable, doesn't it – be honest?'

'I suppose so,' replied a very down-in-the-mouth informant.

'Look, what's the chap look like?' I asked. Terry provided a detailed description of a strange-sounding creature, clad in dungarees and sandals who wore pebble glasses. Not unreasonably, I commented that he sounded a bit of a nutter. 'He seemed all right to me,' Terry said indignantly, which I thought was no kind of recommendation at all, but promising Terry that I'd look into it, with the proviso that he stay away from the High Street on the following day, I put the phone down.

'Look, I know it sounds bollocks,' I said to the highly incredulous detective inspector at Ramsgate police station, and feeling every kind of fool, I ploughed on desperately, 'but he's been a good'un in the past. Do me a favour – can you just stick a couple of aids outside the bank tomorrow, just until closing time? I mean, we both know it's not going to happen but you know . . . just in case . . . next time I come down, we'll have a laugh about it, over a drink,' I trailed off, miserably. The Ramsgate DI gave his grudging agreement and having successfully passed the Queen of Spades, I put the phone down and got on with some proper police work.

The following night at five o'clock, I was about to book out to Gerrard Street, that thriving area of the Chinese community which is situated just off London's Shaftesbury Avenue, where I had a particular interest in a certain frequenter of a notorious gambling club, when the telephone rang.

'I don't know where you found your informant,' said the puzzled Ramsgate DI, 'but you'd better hang on to him, because he's solid gold!'

As my mouth fell more and more open, the DI explained that, that afternoon, two of his aids who had ostensibly been forming part of a bus queue opposite Barclays bank, had suddenly spotted a strange figure shambling along the High Street, towards the bank. His description exactly fitted that given by Terry, the time was precisely 3.24 p.m., he was looking up and down the street, as if for an accomplice, and he was carrying a bulging supermarket bag. The aids detached themselves from the bus queue and with a complete absence of ceremony, grabbed hold of the suspect and relieved him of his plastic bag. Inside, were eight yellow candles, taped together with a collection of wires which had been pushed into what proved to be Plasticine. 'All right, you've got me,' immediately admitted the strange young man, whose name was Dennis Collins. 'I was just about to go into the bank, tell them I'd got a bomb and unless they gave me the money, I'd detonate it. I was going to give them this.' With that, he pulled a grubby note from his pocket and handed it to the astonished young aids. The note outlined his demands, as he'd just described to the officers. It was also signed, 'Yours sincerely, Dennis Collins.'

'Did you really think you'd get away with it?' one of the aids asked incredulously. 'I've already done so,' Collins calmly replied. 'I did exactly the same thing at Barclays in Hastings, two months ago.' He had, too.

I suddenly shut my mouth, because I realized that an onlooker would think that I was giving an impersonation of a guppy. 'Yes, well, he is a pretty reliable snout of mine,' I said, trying to draw back a little credibility. 'You lying bastard,' the DI chuckled. 'That's not what you said yesterday!'

The judge at the Crown Court took a pretty dim view of Collins' activities and notwithstanding that he had no previous convictions, weighed him off with four years' imprisonment. The two aids were commended and I knocked out an informant's report for Terry. The late Ernie Bond OBE, QPM, probably the finest deputy assistant commissioner to serve at the Yard, minuted the report, saying, 'It was, in no small part, due to the sensitivity and tact on DC Kirby's part in handling this informant that the matter was brought to a highly satisfactory conclusion.' I basked in this richly undeserved praise for weeks afterwards.

Terry was pleased as well: he received a decent ex-gratia payment from the Yard's Informants Fund and the more

A Cry For Help

modest contributions from both the Kent and Sussex constabularies were more than balanced by the generous payment from Barclays bank. Whether he carefully husbanded the money for a rainy day or capriciously blew the lot, I've no idea. The last I heard from him was six or seven years later when I received a disjointed telephone call from him in the Flying Squad office. He excitedly demanded a meet with me in Shaftesbury Avenue – coincidentally, close to the spot that I was about to go to previously when I had received the astonishing phone call from Ramsgate police.

''E looked a weird one,' commented the Flying Squad driver, after I returned to the car, and he wasn't far wrong. Terry didn't have any information for me. By now he'd lost it and was becoming steadily unravelled and he merely wanted someone to unburden his soul to. During our conversation he was becoming more and more agitated and his wildly gesticulating arms were beginning to alarm passers-by. I tried to calm him and tactfully added that this wasn't a particularly good area in which to draw attention to himself because remnants of the Maltese Syndicate who had unnerved him several years before were still in evidence. Terry replied that he couldn't care less and, with that, he cut a pathetic, shambling figure as he stumbled off through the drizzle.

His body was found a few weeks later. The Syndicate hadn't caught up with him. The autopsy revealed that when Terry had imbibed an unwise cocktail of anti-depressants and alcohol, the Grim Reaper had finally crooked his skeletal finger at him and that was that. But in his hand was found a screwed-up page which had been torn from a diary with my name and telephone number on it. In the years that have passed, I wondered, as I do now, whether Terry was going to supply me with a piece of splendid, albeit implausible information – or was it another cry for help?

The Loneliest Place on Earth

'The witness box is the loneliest place on Earth,' a colleague said to me recently, and he was right. While everybody else in court may not be against you, there are precious few who will actually help you. It's rather like being in the stocks – some people have a better aim than others.

For a police officer to be able to give evidence at court in a clear, compelling manner and to disregard the sneering attempts by blustering barristers to get their clients acquitted (clients who, they know full well, are as guilty as sin) is not an exact science, but it is an art. To some police officers this ability comes as naturally as a duck takes to water, and, to others, it is a wretched, impossible business. They stammer, they stutter, they blush and, in the end, their credibility completely shot, they will agree with practically anything the defence barrister says, just so that they can get out of the witness box. I must tell you that as a new police constable, I belonged to the latter category.

As a probationary police constable, I was quite hopeless at just about any task that presented itself. My first crime arrest was a 'percher' – so called because the arrestee was 'on the perch': she had been detained by another person and passed over to a police officer to be officially arrested. The 'other person' in this case was a store detective, who had stopped a middle-aged civil servant after she had left the shop without paying for a dress. The tearful civil servant protested that absent-mindedness rather than larcenous intent had brought about her predicament, to no avail. She was charged and bailed to appear the following day at Barking Magistrates' Court. There, a remand was sought so that she might obtain legal representation since she was denying the charge. In addition, the store detective had contacted head office so that the prosecution might also be represented in court. A date was set several weeks hence for a full hearing and I was informed that a certain Mr Birtwhistle would be appearing for the defence. I mentioned this fact in the police station's canteen.

'Fucking Hell! Not Birtwhistle!' gasped one officer.

'He'll eat you alive, son!'

'Better get your story straight,' added another, shaking his head, sorrowfully. 'Otherwise, the next time you make an appearance at court, it'll be at the Bailey, with you gripping the rail!'

There was much more of the same, all of which got my Adam's apple bobbing like a yo-yo. I tottered out of the canteen, the unwitting victim of a classic wind-up; in retrospect I don't suppose that half of them had even met Birtwhistle, but their comments had been sufficient to put me into a muck sweat at the mere mention of his name. Mind you, I suppose there was a whisper of truth in what they'd said, because when I arrived at court on the morning of the hearing and saw Birtwhistle, all of my fears were confirmed. He was a Napoleonic figure and had much of that diminutive Emperor's aggression; he was also rude, arrogant and spiteful. Just how spiteful, I was about to discover. When I had first gone to Peel House, the police training establishment, I had been issued with a *Metropolitan Police Instruction Book* (or IB), which is now defunct. I believe that modern-day recruits are issued with a sort of a comic, containing cartoons, such as a police officer planting a suspect with cannabis, and this drawing has a big red cross through it and a stern 'NO!' just to reinforce matters. In my IB there was a passage which said that when police officers had their characters attacked in court by malevolent solicitors and barristers for the defence, they were to remain unfazed, since magistrates would always intercede at this unfriendly behaviour. Unfortunately, this edict had obviously not been passed to the bench of muppets at Barking Magistrates' Court, because far from squashing that obnoxious little squirt, Birtwhistle, they positively encouraged him.

'Can I ask you to stop mumbling?' Birtwhistle snapped. 'I'm so sorry, Your Worship,' he added, smarmily, 'but I can hardly understand a word the officer says. Could I ask you to implore the officer to speak up?'

'Certainly, Mr Birtwhistle,' simpered the utter drip of a chairman. Turning to me, he said sharply, 'Speak up at once! And stop mumbling!'

'Sorry, Your Worship,' I muttered. I dragged on with my minuscule amount of evidence – after all, it wasn't as if I'd seen the wretched woman take anything – to the accompaniment of Birtwhistle sneering, interrupting and doing his best to belittle me – doing rather well, too. At last, the whole sorry business came to an end and the case was chucked out. As the civil servant stumbled past me, sobbing her gratitude to Birtwhistle, I sought a modicum of solace from the store detective, who having given her evidence, had sat through my discomfort.

'That was nothing!' she scoffed. 'You should have heard what he had to say to me!' I crept back to the nick.

'Got off!' cried one of the canteen cowboys. 'How can a shoplifter get off? What did she do – bung you?'

I crept away, not having a clue as to what a 'bung' was and

45

therefore ignorant of whether or not the defendent had 'bunged me', although there was one thing I was sure of: this was the culmination of a dreary series of cock-ups that I had made, and was probably the lowest point in my short career. If I hadn't been married, with two young children and living in married quarters, I should have resigned on the spot. With the esteem in which I was held by my senior officers, I should think that the chief inspector would have accepted my resignation so quickly, that greased lightning would have looked positively sluggish by comparison.

And then something happened which made me change my mind. As a probationary police officer, I was expected to provide a respectable return of work every month to my reporting sergeant: arrests, 'stops' and process. Process was the reporting of motorists for their transgression of the Road Traffic and associated Acts. So I reported motorists – in police parlance, 'stuck them on' – because it was expected of me, and also because if I had not, my probationary reports would have been even bleaker. I was called to give evidence one afternoon at a Traffic Court, which again was held at Barking Magistrates' Court. I was amazed to see most of my relief, who worked the same shift as me, there, because so many of them worked assiduously at dodging the column, I could not imagine any of them leaping out into the roadway to stop a recalcitrant motorist. In fact, I was quite right – most were there because they had been unlucky enough to have been called to the front office by the station sergeant to report a motorist who had produced an out-of-date insurance certificate or test certificate. Now, my case was the very last one to be called, so I spent the best part of two hours listening to my peers giving the most straightforward of evidence and making utter arses of themselves in the process. All of them were older and more experienced than I – and certainly experienced at taking the piss out of newcomers like me – and yet here they were, giving me cause to believe that there was hope for me yet.

I went home, sat down and, nursing a mug of coffee, I evaluated my position. I now knew that I was no worse than my colleagues at giving evidence, but that was no criterion because none of us were any good. So how was I to improve? The obvious answer was more practice. Now, at that time, when an officer made an arrest for drunkenness, he filled in a pro-forma. There was no need for the officer to attend court, because the form was handed to the court inspector, who, following a plea of guilty, would read out the brief facts. Only in the case of a plea of 'Not guilty' would the officer be required to attend court. So, if I went out on patrol on Friday night-duty and arrested a couple of drunks, they would be charged, bailed to attend court on the following Monday morning and I would fill in my pro-formae. If, however, the following night I went out and arrested someone for, say, threatening behaviour, he too would be bailed to court on Monday but, for this offence, I would be required to attend. So on Mondays, I would go to court and ask the court inspector if I could give evidence of arrest of the drunks, as well as the other arrest. You may think it was a small point, but over a few months, it worked wonders in giving me the self-confidence to get into the witness box and speak. I would also sit in court while I waited for my case to be called, and listen to the other police officers giving evidence. Some, like me, were tragic. Others were solid, if unimaginative. And still others were brilliant. In this latter category were the CID officers. They were totally different from the majority of uniformed officers whose idea of giving evidence was to stand up and chant, 'On day, date, time and place, I saw the defendant and as a result of what I was told, I arrested him for the offence

47

charged, cautioned him and he made no reply. I took him to the police station where he was charged, the charge read over and cautioned and he made no reply.' It was like listening to a bloody mantra. And quite apart from being boring, it told the magistrates precisely nothing. They would call for probation reports, advise the defendant (if he was in danger of getting a bit of porridge) to be legally aided. Then the whole case would be moved to another day, thereby not only wasting everybody's time but creating a lot of unnecessary work for the probation department and the police, as well as making the local solicitors richer. The CID officers, on the other hand, had gathered a wealth of experience by giving evidence at the Courts of Assize and Quarter-Sessions and when they got into the witness box, they dominated the whole court room. The words flowed from them and the magistrates were entranced. They made a fascinating story of the whole case and were able to give motivation for the crime and also plead extenuating circumstances; in short, they acted both as prosecutor and defence. The magistrates were now in a position to dispose of the case immediately and, as the detective stepped from the witness box, the congratulations of the bench ringing in his ears, he had saved himself a lot of work and, indeed, had procured a possible snout. It is something, alas, denied to the young police officers of today.

So, as the years passed, I was gathering a lot of experience of courts. I was appointed to the CID and, as a detective constable, it was normal for me to attend the Magistrates' Court at least three times a week. Newham (West) Magistrates' Court was ruled with a rod of iron by its clerk, Frank Knight, who had a terrifying reputation for rudeness, barracking and belittling police officers, particularly young ones. But he met his match in Tony Diamond, who was a detective constable with a reputation for eccentricity and sarcasm. On this occasion, Tony stepped into the witness box to make an application to the bench. There was a short pause as he put his papers down and cleared his throat. Exasperated by this unacceptable delay, Frank Knight blew his short fuse.

'Well?' he bellowed.

'Not bad,' Tony answered laconically. 'You?'

Having heard of Frank's fearsome reputation, I sought advice from one of my many mentors, Detective Sergeant (2nd Class) Paul Maddy. 'It's easy,' Paul said. 'All you do is ask to see him in his office before court commences. Then you say to him, 'Mr Knight, I'm a bit concerned about a case I've got this morning. I wonder if I could ask your advice?' You then mention anything about the case – it doesn't matter if it's bollocks – he'll be flattered that you asked him in the first place, and then, when you get into court, if he ever thinks about bollocking you, he'll suddenly realize that you would then be in a position to say, 'Oh, but Mr Knight, when we discussed this case in your office this morning, you told me . . .' and he'll be too embarrassed to say anything. Simple, see?' And yes, it was simple, and yes, it did work – every single time. And yet, off-duty, Frank Knight could be the nicest of men. He was a fishing companion of the late Detective Superintendent Randall Jones, and during one of their trips, Randall said, 'Frank, it's great having you along, you're terrific company – but why do you act like such a shit in court?' Frank paused, deep in thought for a moment, and then suddenly shrugged his shoulders. 'I just can't help it!' he said.

Over fifteen years passed since that first bruising encounter with that little swine Birtwhistle and I never saw him again. But along the way I met plenty like him (and many far worse) and with hundreds of appearances at Magistrates' and Crown Courts throughout the capital I felt reasonably confident about any court appearance. On this particular occasion,

I had arrested a troublesome young screwsman, Danny Perkins, for a fairly unpleasant burglary. There was a mass of evidence against him and his immediate future looked fairly grim. With his previous, I felt tolerably certain that following an appearance at the Magistrates' Court, he could expect a carpet or quite possibly half-a-stretch for his endeavours. Keeping this gloomy forecast to myself, I strove to explain to him the advantages of a quick plea at the lower court, whereas the alternative would be a trip to the Crown Court where, under the gentle ministrations of the likes of Judge Argyle, he could confidently expect about three years' imprisonment. If it was necessary to prove strictly every aspect of the case, I could certainly do it, but it would be an immensely time-consuming matter, and with my enormous work load, it was something I could well do without – hence the need for young Perkins to admit his undeniable guilt at the earliest possible opportunity. My arguments fell on deaf ears, since Danny Perkins was having none of it.

'Please yourself,' I said. 'You must be some sort of a mug, though – just think, you could get it all out of the way tomorrow. Instead, you'll be on remand in Brixton, having your arse punched by some big nonce.'

'I won't be on remand at all,' sneered the overly optimistic Mr Perkins, "cos my brief'll get me out on bail, no sweat.'

I gave a scoffing laugh as I led him off to the cells, telling him that we'd see about *that*.

The following morning, I arrived at the local Magistrates' Court, where I had another case, in addition to Perkins'. Looking at the lists, I saw to my trepidation that my cases were in separate courts and that Perkins was appearing in front of a stipendiary magistrate whom I shall rename Oliver Sharpe. Mr Sharpe was a true eccentric – nice as pie one moment, a raving lunatic the next. He had a loathing of inefficiency and unprofessionalism which was matched with a strange longing to redeem the ways of the prostitutes who regularly appeared before him. He would give fantastic lectures to them, about how they should change their worthless lifestyle, before fining them the most paltry amounts. I should like to report that the Toms were grateful for being so leniently dealt with, but they would stand in the dock, sighing, impatiently tapping their feet and looking at the ceiling, waiting for Sharpe's homily to finish, so that they could pay their fines and get back on the street for an indolent pimp. So that was Mr Sharpe – a beak to be handled as dexterously as weeping gelignite. I tried to get both cases transferred to the same court without success, so working on the assumption that my case in Court No. 1 would be dealt with quite quickly, I informed the usher in Court No. 2 – Sharpe's court – of my predicament and he agreed to put back Perkins' case.

But in No. 1 court, one delay followed another and it took a considerable time for my case to be dealt with. As I walked towards No. 2 court, the usher rushed towards me, his eyes wild with anxiety. 'Quick!' he gasped. 'Sharpe's gone berserk – he's talking about chucking your case out – run!' Now, running into court was something I'd done once at the Bailey and after that gasping, wheezing performance, I vowed I'd never repeat it. So taking slow, deep calming breaths, I strolled into Court No. 2. Sharpe was absolutely furious and as I walked towards the witness box he yelled, 'Where the devil have you been, sir? How dare you behave in this disgraceful manner?' Out of the corner of my eye, I saw that Perkins, who was sitting in the dock, had a look of glee. Stepping into the witness box, I replied, 'I'm extremely sorry, Your Worship. I was detained in another court.'

'And that was more important than appearing in my court,

was it?' Sharpe roared. 'We'll see what your chief superintendent has to say about this!'

I meekly bowed my head and answered, 'Very well, sir.'

'Right, get on with it then,' Sharpe snapped.

'This is an application for a remand in custody,' I said, carefully arranging my papers. 'Before I outline my objections to bail, Your Worship,' I continued, 'would it be of assistance if I were to explain the facts of the case to you?'

'No it would not, sir!' Sharpe snapped back. 'Just get on with your objections to bail!'

This proved too much for Perkins, who guffawed with laughter from the dock.

'*Silence!*' shrieked Sharpe. 'One more sound from you and we'll deal with this application in your absence!' Having well and truly vented his spleen, Sharpe turned to me, now somewhat calmer. 'Perhaps it would be helpful to hear the circumstances of the case before you put your objections, Sergeant Kirby,' he said courteously. 'Please proceed.'

Having done so and then outlined my objections to bail, it took very little time for Sharpe to remand the now crestfallen Mr Perkins in custody and as he was led off to a possibly bruising encounter in HM Prison Brixton, Sharpe prepared to rise. Before he could do so, I leant forward in the witness box.

'Excuse me, Your Worship,' I said, 'but before you rise, I should just like to apologize unreservedly for my tardiness in appearing before you this morning.'

Sharpe frowned. 'That was hardly your fault, Sergeant Kirby,' he replied. 'You were, as I understand it, giving evidence in another court.'

'So I was, sir,' I replied, 'but I feel with a little forethought on my part, I do think that I could have handled the situation better by keeping you fully informed about the situation.

Because I failed to do so, you were thoroughly inconvenienced which, I think, was inexcusable.'

Sharpe beamed. 'My dear fellow!' he cried. 'Not another word, I won't hear of it! It's always a delight to hear your applications!'

Not a bad morning's work, I thought as I left court: my cred. restored intact and Perkins shafted.

Not so fortunate with Sharpe was a young and keen-as-mustard police constable who fell foul of him – not, as you'll already have realized, that this took much to do so. He stammered and stuttered his way through his evidence until, Sharpe, growing more and more furious, suddenly shouted, '*Stop!*' The poor PC was frozen to the spot. 'I've never heard such incompetence! Get out of my court and don't come back until you've learnt how to give evidence! *Get out!* Next case!'

The next case was, in fact, mine and, as I got to my feet, Sharpe spotted me and addressing the red-faced PC who had almost reached the sanctuary of the exit, he again shouted, '*Stop!*' The wilting officer turned and pointing dramatically towards me, Sharpe snapped, 'If you don't know who this is – and I don't suppose you do, because you don't seem to know anything at all – this is Sergeant Kirby, who really knows how to give evidence. Sit down, listen, and perhaps you'll learn something!'

I gave my evidence and, at the conclusion, I was cordially thanked by Sharpe who then turned to the unfortunate young probationer and said contemptuously, 'That's how you give evidence! See if you can do anything near as well the next time you appear before me!'

I walked outside with the young fellow, who was close to tears. I laid a comforting hand on his shoulder. 'Son,' I said quietly. 'If a beak had spoken to me like that when I had your service, I would have put my papers in, become a monk, taken

53

a vow of silence and never said another fucking word to anyone!'

'I just can't get the hang of going to court, Sarge,' he replied miserably, 'and as for that bloody Sharpe . . . !'

'I know,' I said. 'I've been down that road myself and I assure you that when I had your amount of service, I was far worse than you. Come and have a cuppa and I'll give you a few tips.'

We sat and talked and later we talked again. I gave him some hints to make his life a little easier in the witness box, told him of the blunders that I'd made and how to avoid these pitfalls. He listened eagerly to every word, asked questions and made intelligent suggestions of his own. If only I could tell you that I later saw him in the witness box, clear, fluent, amusing and compelling, to have the bench rise to their feet and commend him for the skilful way he had solved a tricky case and the way that he presented it. It was not to be.

In 1984, brave, resolute Police Constable Stephen Jones attempted to stop a group of drunken drivers racing each other along the Seven Sisters Road, Holloway and was knocked down and killed. What a fine young man he was. I sometimes wonder if, upon receipt of that news, a tear ran down the cheek of Oliver Sharpe? One did, down mine.

An Afternoon Stroll

Whenever possible, I avoided the CID office at Holloway police station: it had an overpowering aura of defeat and decay. But on this occasion, my attendance was really necessary – I had a report on the activities of Sammy the Snout and rather than entrust it to the vagaries of the internal despatch system, I drove over from the Crime Squad office at Highbury Vale police station to place it personally on the detective superintendent's desk.

Mission accomplished, I was beating a hasty retreat, when I was called back by Detective Sergeant Dave Crompton, a conscientious and hard worker with whom I got on well. Dave sought my assistance with a robbery which he was investigating. Securicor had made a delivery to a local company. No sooner had they left, when two youths rushed in, attacked the staff and grabbed a sackful of money and ran off. 'They were both black,' Dave said, 'and they ran round the corner and completely vanished.' The descriptions were sketchy: both were masked, there was no CCTV, and no forensics. 'I know you've got a snout in that area, Dick,' Dave said. 'Any chance you could put a few feelers out?'

'Sure,' I said. 'When did you say this happened?'

'Last Friday afternoon at 3 o'clock,' he said.

He was right: I did have an informant in that area, and what Gerry didn't know wasn't worth knowing. I set up a meet with him and told him what had happened. Gerry had heard nothing but agreed to get to work. 'Leave it with me,' he said.

A couple of days later, Gerry telephoned to say he'd got something for me and, later that day, we met in one of our agreed locations.

'You say it happened last Friday?' he queried.

I agreed that this was so.

'Well,' said Gerry, scratching his chin, 'this pair had it off on Friday,' and he named them. 'I couldn't make out what it was they'd had off,' he continued, 'because they were giggling about it so much. But I do know, that on the same day they stuck the dough that they'd nicked into their Building Society accounts. They've both got accounts at the same branch,' he added.

'You wouldn't know where, by any chance?' I murmured.

'Course!' Gerry replied, irritated that I could even question his expertise. Gerry, I should mention (if you haven't already guessed it), was one of my better informants. 'There's just one thing,' he added. 'You did say that the blokes who did the blag were black?'

'Yes, why?' I asked.

'Well, one of these two's black but the other's white.'

I thought for a moment. 'The two guys who did the blag were black, no doubt about that,' I said. 'But when they ran round the corner, they vanished. I suppose they could have jumped into a car, with a white guy driving.'

Gerry nodded. 'I suppose so,' he said, unwillingly, 'but I got the impression that those two had done the job themselves and that nobody else was involved.' He shrugged his shoulders. 'Just a hunch,' he added. 'I could be wrong.'

Early the following morning, I turned up at the black youth's address, together with a couple of aids from the Crime Squad. Detective Constable Clive Jamieson was in charge of the

team to arrest the white suspect. Both of these young miscreants had got form, and normally, for a serious violent offence
like robbery, I would make my entrance by kicking the door in
and using the crash-bang-gotcha technique both to disorien-
tate the suspect and prevent him from harming me or my officers. But I looked round at this council house and noticed that
there were quite a lot of potted plants in the tidy garden, giving
a cheerful look to an otherwise glum area and I paused mid-
kick. I must have had a flash of intuition – or something. So I
tapped on the front door and, within seconds, a large and pleas-
ant-looking woman, named Doreen Griffiths, answered my
knock. I quietly introduced myself and she rolled her eyes.

'I s'pose you've come for Junior,' she sighed.

I nodded. 'I'm afraid so, Madam,' I replied.

She glanced up the stairs. 'He's in bed,' said Mrs Griffiths.
'At least you can get him up; it's more than I can,' she added.
'That boy is so worthless – just like his father!'

Hello, I thought, as I trotted up the stairs. I could have an
ally, here.

Junior Griffiths was lying indolently in his bed, reading a
book entitled, *101 Famous Trials*. 'Right, get up, you're
nicked,' I said. 'And bring that book with you. You might
need some inspiration!'

'You got nuffin' on me,' Junior replied scornfully, swing-
ing his legs out of bed, 'less you goin' to fit me, that is.'

'Less of your lip, Sonny,' I said, 'and get dressed. You two,'
I said to the aids, 'turn his room over – you know what you're
looking for.'

The aids did – and soon found the pass book for his building society. I had a quick look: a very impressive amount had
been deposited on the Friday in question – good old Gerry!
The aids continued searching. Then they found some krugerrands. And then some expensive-looking jewellery. This was

a bonus. 'You've got a lot of explaining to do, Junior,' I said, pointing to his spoils. 'This little lot could mean a lot of porridge for you.'

'Rass, man,' sneered Junior. 'Me say nuffin'!'

I raised my eyebrows, shocked at such insolence. 'Have a word, will you?' I said to the aids. 'I'm going to have a chat with my new friend.'

The sound of raised voices drifted away as I walked into the lounge. 'Sorry about all the upset,' I apologized to Mrs Griffiths. She shrugged, philosophically. 'That Junior,' she sighed. 'I've tried, but what can you do?'

I nodded sympathetically and looked around the room. Potted plants were everywhere. 'I like that,' I said, pointing towards a magnificent specimen of a Snakeskin Plant, which was impressively tumbling over the rim of a very pretty pot. 'You mean me *Fittonia argyroneura nana*,' she replied, with the self-assurance of an expert.

'My daughter's got one of them,' I said, 'but it's nothing like yours – the leaves keep on shrivelling.'

'Ah. You tell her it got to be kept moist and she got to mist it, regular,' said Mrs Griffiths, authoritatively, 'And it got to be kept out of direct sunlight. Did she repot it in the spring?'

'I don't think so,' I replied.

'She got to,' said Mrs Griffiths, firmly.

I smiled. 'I'll tell her,' I said, 'but when have kids started doing as they're told?'

'Ha!' she retorted and her eyes flashed. 'That's a fact!'

'Anyway,' I added, 'I don't think hers would be as good as this one; I bet you got the Obeah woman to get it like that!'

Mrs Griffiths roared with laughter and slapped me on the chest with a hand the size of a dinner plate. 'You bad man!' she shrieked. 'Where'd you hear about the Obeah woman? Anyway,' she chuckled, 'it ain't true!'

Just then, Junior appeared at the top of the stairs, hand-cuffed and escorted by the aids who were carrying a plastic bag, filled with exhibits. 'Mum,' called Junior, loudly. 'Get me probation officer!'

Mrs Griffiths raised an eyebrow. 'I'm not gettin' nobody, Junior,' she replied, decisively.

Junior registered consternation. 'Mum,' he repeated, urgently. 'Jus' get me probation officer, I said. This lot, they goin' to fit me for sumfin' I ain't done. Just do it, Mum!'

Mrs Griffiths raised her head and gave her offspring a look that was so piercing, that it would have felled an experienced CIB2 officer in his tracks at 20 paces. 'Junior,' she said, calmly, folding her massive arms across her broad bosom, 'I hope they do. Fit you up and beat you up. That's what you need to bring you to your senses. Nothin' I ever done, never done no good. Well, I'm goin' to work – I'm late already.'

A wild-eyed, abandoned Junior was dragged down the stairs and out to the waiting police car. Pausing at the door, I turned and gave a brief bow. 'Goodbye, dear lady,' I said. 'It was a great pleasure!'

It was enough to cause Mrs Griffiths to rock with laughter again. 'Bye, Sarge!' she chuckled. 'You sure got a lot of style!'

Arriving at Holloway police station, Clive Jamieson and his team had already turned up with their prisoner. I took Clive to one side. 'How'd you get on?' I said quietly. 'Not bad,' replied Clive. 'He's not having the robbery, but we got his building society pass book – has he got a load of dough in there!'

'Deposited on the Friday?' I queried. Clive nodded. 'We got some tom, as well,' he said.

I strolled over to the prisoners. 'Right, you mugs, now listen up,' I said, sternly. 'Both of you have been captured bang to rights and both of you are bang in trouble. You can

59

have a sit down in the cells and think about what you're going to tell us.'

Both of them looked very downcast and stared at their trainers. 'Right,' I said to the aids. 'Stick these two down the flowery and we'll have some breakfast.'

We'd just finished our meal in the canteen when Dave Crompton walked in. 'What's this I hear about you nicking that team for my robbery?' he grinned.

'Nothing to it,' I said.

'Are they having it?' Dave asked.

'Expect an early confession,' I replied.

Dave laughed. 'Nora!' he shouted to the canteen manageress. 'Teas all round for the heroes, over here – put it on my bill!'

'Be sure you pay it!' Nora grunted.

Now, in those days, if a police officer wanted to inspect a prisoner's bank account, he had to obtain a warrant from a magistrate under the provisions of the Bankers' Books Evidence Act, 1879. This warrant had to be served on the bank and then the officer had to wait three clear days before obtaining a statement; then the statement, unsigned, had to be forwarded to the bank's legal department for perusal; oh, what a performance.

So it was a good thing that our prisoners had lodged their ill-gotten gains in a building society where these strictures didn't apply. All that was required to obtain the desired information was a nice smile and good manners. Clive and I left the aids to have a chat with the prisoners and we strolled off along the Holloway Road towards the suspects' building society.

'Yes, that's right,' the assistant said. 'It was me who checked the money into their accounts. I remember them, not only because it was quite a large sum of money but because they were both giggling, fit to bust.' Funny – that's what

Gerry had said – it was as though they'd played a huge joke on somebody, rather than just carried out a blagging.

'Now, I know this may be difficult,' I said, 'but can you tell me when it was on the Friday afternoon that they deposited the money?'

'Certainly,' nodded the assistant. 'I've got an exact note of the time. Here it is,' and she showed me. My jaw dropped open. Both sets of money had been deposited at 2.30 p.m. – half an hour *before* the robbery.

Shaking our heads in bewilderment, Clive and I returned to the nick. We were so stunned that I don't think we even attempted conversation. The assistant was quite adamant; wherever the money had come from, it wasn't from Dave Crompton's robbery.

So all would have been lost, had it not been for the persuasive charms of the aids, who had neatly unravelled the mystery for us. On the Friday, this worthless pair had got up late, met and with the prospect of another aimless day in front of them, decided to enliven things by indulging in a little petty thieving. Except that it didn't turn out to be little, or petty, either.

Lunchtime found them in Southampton Row, WC1, and as they strolled by a solicitor's office, they glanced in through the window. Not only was everybody at lunch, they could see right through a series of open doors, straight into a back room. There, in the middle of the room was a safe. The safe's door was open.

They pushed at the door of the premises; it swung noiselessly open. The pair could hardly believe their luck. They quickly made their way to the safe and helped themselves to several thousand pounds' worth of cash, some krugerrands and a selection of antique jewellery: about £15,000's worth, in all.

No wonder they were giggling when they deposited the money! I made two quick phone calls, first to the Building Society to freeze the accounts and then to Holborn police station to come and collect a couple of prisoners, adding that there was no work to do at all, because we'd done it all for them. It was misery all round, as far as the police were concerned. The valuables were returned intact to the negligent solicitors, who received them without a word of thanks. The CID at Holborn couldn't be bothered to put the aids up for a commendation, which they richly deserved. Dave Crompton was distraught. 'What about my fucking robbery?' he kept exclaiming.

But Gerry did well out of it. He got a very nice drink out of the Informants Fund and I ensured that his contribution to the investigation was properly recognized by requesting that the deputy assistant commissioner also write to the insurance company for the dopey solicitors, who coughed up 10 per cent of the recovered property for Gerry.

Gerry wasn't the only one who was pleased. No wonder Junior Griffiths kept banging on about his probation officer: she must have had some clout. She managed to persuade the bench of Muppets at the Magistrates' Court that imprisonment was not the only option for an offence as serious as this. The magistrates agreed and sent both of them on an adventure training course.

It was set just off the coast of Trinidad.

On board a fucking yacht.

Not Everything's What It Seems

Jessie Harris sighed with relief as the very capable crew helped her into the ambulance. Her health hadn't been good for some time; at 78 years of age, she was suffering from asthma, Parkinson's disease and an obstruction to the airways to her lungs – probably chronic bronchitis. Now, to cap it all, she'd had a fall in her home in Marlborough Road, Dagenham. Its blue light flashing, the ambulance set off to Oldchurch hospital, Romford. The date was 6 October 1991.

The casualty doctor smiled reassuringly. 'Not too much to worry about, Mrs Harris,' he said. 'You're suffering from hypothermia and there's a bit of a chest infection, as well. I think we'll send you to St George's hospital for a few days. Some antibiotics should soon have you up and about again.' Blood samples had been taken from Mrs Harris; the result of the tests would accompany her to the new hospital.

And now, Mrs Harris was in the ward at St George's in Hornchurch. She was bright and cheerful; all the staff were very kind. The kindest of them all was the young American, Dr Brafman; he had such a nice bedside manner. He had just taken a finger-prick test from her. 'Hey!' he exclaimed. 'Did you know you're diabetic?' A fellow patient overheard the question and also the answer. 'Nonsense,' chuckled Mrs Harris. 'I'm not diabetic.' Brafman shook his head. 'Think you are,' he muttered.

What Mrs Harris would never know was that Brafman had not checked the results of her blood tests from Oldchurch hospital, nor did he make his own tests. He did not administer the antibiotics that her condition required. And when Mrs Harris' condition started to deteriorate, he did not seek the help or advice of any of the other doctors. The nursing staff telephoned Brafman to inform him of her condition and he told them to administer insulin.

When Jessie Harris died, she had been Brafman's patient for just twelve hours.

Brafman was shocked. 'She was the last person I expected to die,' he told the staff.

Brafman was employed as a senior house officer at St George's hospital at a salary of £18,000 from 1 September 1991 until 31 October 1991. During his two months' service, he treated 210 patients in the hospital's day centre. Forty of them had died. This was not thought to be particularly unusual at the time; after all, St George's was a hospital for the elderly, and elderly people who are ill do tend to die.

At about the time that Jessie Harris was admitted to St George's, vacancies existed for posts in obstetrics & gynaecology, geriatrics and Accident and Emergency (A & E) within the Havering Hospital Group. Brafman applied for A & E; a senior consultant at St George's gave him a glowing reference.

But that was in the future for Brafman. Right now, he had to sit down and write out the death certificate for Jessie Harris. Like the subjects of twelve other death certificates he had written, Jessie Harris was cremated. Whatever was written on the death certificate was accepted as being correct, because no post-mortem examinations had been carried out on any of his former patients. And now, no trace of them existed. Out of this unfortunate state of affairs, two matters of the utmost importance arose.

The first was that insulin should not have been administered to Jessie Harris, because she was not diabetic.

And the second was that Brafman was not a doctor.

Matthew Levi Brafman was born in 1959 in Monticello, north-west of New York City. His school record was appalling – he had great difficulty with grammar and spelling – and inevitably, he finished bottom of the class and left without graduating.

He dreamt of becoming a doctor, but with his complete lack of academic qualifications, this dream could never be realized. At the age of seventeen, he joined the town's volunteer ambulance service and became a traffic policeman. The following year, he joined the US Army. Again, he failed to distinguish himself and, after a fruitless three years spent on low-grade medical and administrative duties, he left.

During a holiday in England, Brafman met a girl named Allison at a Jewish summer camp and, in 1982, they married. In July of that year, Brafman rejoined the army, and his wife (and later, their son) followed him as he worked in a succession of US Army hospitals in Germany and America. But Allison was growing weary of army life and was homesick for England. It was probably sometime in 1990, when Brafman was stationed at Fort McClellan Army Base, Alabama, that they began to hatch the plot that would cause so much unhappiness to so many innocent people.

Because of Brafman's appalling spelling and grammar, Allison prepared a letter and a Curriculum Vitae, which, on 1 May 1990, was sent to the Joint Committee on Postgraduate Training for General Practice in England, stating that Brafman was a Doctor of Medicine, and requesting a licence for him to practise medicine, unsupervised. The Brafmans entered into correspondence with that body and also with the General Medical Council (GMC). To substantiate these claims, Brafman forwarded photocopies of certificates of his achievements issued by the Anniston College of Medicine and the Oxford Medical Centre, stating that he had graduated as an MD from Anniston Medical College in July 1987 and had passed his post-graduate training with distinction at the Oxford Medical Centre. The certificates were forged by Brafman and the colleges did not exist. The addresses of these bogus establishments were given as post office box numbers in Anniston, Alabama. Brafman had taken the precaution of renting both these post office boxes, nine days before sending the first letter; in this way, he would be able to intercept and reply to any queries that might arise.

And arise they did. Having been told that Brafman had graduated as an MD from Anniston Medical College in July 1987, the GMC wrote to him regarding the photocopy of the diploma which he had sent them. This showed the date of his appointment as MD as being 22 May 1986. This certificate did, in fact, belong to a genuine doctor. Brafman had got hold of the certificate, superimposed his name over the genuine doctor's name and photocopied it. They had also discovered that the Anniston Medical College did not exist, and in a letter to Brafman, dated 22 June 1990, they actually requested that he ask the college's registrar to confirm its details to the GMC.

Brafman duly forged a letter from the Anniston Medical Centre, giving details of its history and explaining that one year after Brafman was issued his diploma, the college closed. The GMC wanted to hear from the doctors who had been appointed referees. Brafman provided glowing testimonials about himself. Had the GMC looked closely, they would have seen that these doctors shared the same post office box numbers as Anniston Medical College. Had they checked the fictitious telephone number that Brafman had provided for the college, they would have found that it did not exist; but then they knew that. Didn't they? They could have checked to see if Brafman was listed on the US medical register. They didn't. And then the GMC contravened their own guidelines by accepting photocopies of diplomas instead of originals.

In the face of such a bureaucratic cock-up, you will not be unduly surprised to discover that Dr Brafman was granted a certificate to practise medicine by the GMC. Your life in their hands. Makes you shudder, doesn't it?

Following his honourable discharge from the US Army on 9 July 1991 and his successful interview at Oldchurch Hospital, Dr and Mrs Brafman settled into their flat in the hospital grounds and Brafman began work at St George's. He was pleasant and had a good bedside manner. The staff were amused when he strolled through the wards, wearing green operating clothing, even though the hospital had no operating theatre. But they put this down to American eccentricity – after all, he *was* a doctor, for heaven's sake.

So the two months at St George's passed quickly enough, with his patients dropping dead all around him, at the rate of five per week, and on 1 November 1991, Brafman began work as a senior house officer in the A & E department at Oldchurch hospital. It's rather interesting to note that at his selection board for his permanent appointment to A & E, not one single question of a medical nature was asked of him. Had it been, his deficiencies would have been exposed and the following shambles would never have occurred.

Right from the word go, Brafman's inadequacies became apparent. The ludicrous aspect of prescribing a diet of Kentucky fried chicken to a patient suffering from gastro-enteritis initially caused amusement amongst the staff, followed by an embarrassed laugh. Well, he was a Yank, wasn't he? And of course, he *was* a doctor!

The next case was far more serious. A six-year-old boy was left with his face permanently scarred, because of Brafman's inability to stitch the wound. Blunder followed blunder. A man was admitted, suffering from supra ventricular tachycardiac (racing heart beat) and the electrocardiogram showed the seriousness of his condition. Brafman, unable to understand the electrocardiogram print-out, tried to discharge the patient, who could have died. Fortunately, other experienced hospital staff intervened and the patient was given proper treatment. A child was admitted, suffering from a severe asthma attack. Brafman, not having a clue as to the appropriate treatment for asthma, attempted to discharge the child. Luckily, experienced staff again intervened. Had they not done, there was a very high risk that the child could have died.

The staff were running out of excuses for Brafman ('He's a Yank, isn't he?' was running a bit low, by this time) and when a doctor – a real one – said, 'There are good doctors, there are bad doctors, and there are no doctors – and Brafman is no doctor,' the hospital administration staff stepped in and contacted the GMC. Amazingly, he was still allowed to continue working for another two-and-a-half weeks because the GMC told Oldchurch that Brafman's registration had been sanctioned by a senior official. The hospital tried telephoning the non-existent Anniston Medical Centre and when they discovered from international enquiries that no such number was listed and that no trace of the college could be found, they informed the GMC that, with that information, along with Brafman's incredible behaviour in A & E, they believed that he was a fraud. The GMC, who by now had been stirred into an advanced state of panic, shrilly demanded that the police be informed.

It had just gone 5 o'clock on that Friday afternoon and few

of the staff were left in the CID office at Romford police station; either they'd gone for their refreshment break if they were late-turn or they'd gone home for the weekend. This was what I had in mind, as I tidied up my desk – the sooner I could get away from the wretched place, the better. I was off-duty for the next three days and I was not due to resume until 2 p.m. the following Tuesday.

The senior uniform personnel at Romford were a pretty decent bunch, but as the superintendent marched purpose-fully into the CID office, there was no one I wanted to see less. From the concerned look in his eye, I could tell that a lumber of catastrophic proportions was about to descend on me, unless of course, I could just reach the sanctuary of the fire escape which led to the car park . . .

'Dick!' he called – too late! 'I need to have a word,' he said quietly and, since my escape had been foiled, I swiftly resorted to Plan 'B' which involved sighing and letting my shoulders sag, just to convey my sense of apathy at being asked to do *any-thing*. 'What is it, sir?' I asked dully, but as I did so, I noticed that he looked very concerned, a marked change from his normal cheery countenance. 'I've had a phone call from the registrar at Oldchurch hospital,' he replied. 'It looks very much as if they've got a doctor on their staff who's bogus.'

'Can you get somebody else, sir?' I asked. 'I've weekend leave and I don't get back until Tuesday afternoon.'

'That's not a problem,' the superintendent replied, 'because he's gone on leave; he won't be returning until 9 December.'

I had more than enough on my plate. 'Yes, but even so –' I said, vainly attempting to wriggle out of it.

'I want the best man on the case, Dick, and that's you,' the superintendent said firmly. Now, although I'd had one or two modest successes during my short time at Romford, this was no more than a bit of man-management buttering-up, and I was having none of it. But this shrewd man realized this and added casually, 'Oh, did I mention that he's American?'

My ears pricked up. 'American?' I mused.

'Yes, I expect whoever deals with this would have to go to the States to make follow-up enquiries,' he said, diffidently, 'but of course, if you're too busy . . .'

'Ah!' I exclaimed. 'I might just be able to fit this one in!' We looked at each other and burst out laughing: me at his guile, him at my indolence.

The superintendent explained what had happened and added, 'The hospital trust is terrified that news of this will leak out and that there'll be widespread panic.'

This was something I could understand. Also, if the man was bogus and using a false identity and he heard about the investigation, he simply wouldn't come back. 'We'll have to keep this under wraps,' I said. 'I'll inform the DCI and nobody else; you do the same with the chief superintendent and warn your contact at the hospital to keep it tight, there. There's nothing that won't keep until Tuesday – in the meantime, I'll put in a dodgy crime report to cover my commitment to the investigation. I'll show an allegation of theft of bedsheets or something from the hospital, mark it "not for press" and allocate it to myself.'

'Right,' the superintendent said, 'I'll see you on Tuesday then Dick – oh, and thanks again for your – er – commitment – to this one!' We both laughed again and I busied myself, writing out the mendacious crime sheet.

After my return from weekend leave, I began making enquiries at Oldchurch hospital. It took days. I checked and re-checked documents and letters and noted details of Brafman's scandalous behaviour and who could strictly prove them, when the time came. I took a long statement from the hospital registrar, followed by one from one of the doctors. I hadn't wanted to do this because it meant admitting somebody else into the confidentiality of the inquiry but it was essential. I had to have a blueprint upon which to base the prosecution of Brafman. Finally it was done. I was ready to arrest Brafman, and if he exercised his right to remain silent when he was arrested, I would have a strong case for keeping him locked up whilst I conducted further enquiries.

At 8 o'clock on the morning of 9 December 1991, I was in the secretary's office at Oldchurch hospital. I had a couple of useful aids with me. One of the rumours that Brafman had circulated was that he had been a member of the US Special Forces in the Gulf War and I had discussed contingency plans with the aids about what action they should take in the event that I was rendered *hors de combat*.

'Phone him up,' I said to the secretary, 'and tell him there's a query with his salary that's got to be sorted out before he goes on duty – that'll bring him running.' She nodded and, with trembling fingers, dialled his number.

Brafman, plump, fair-haired with a wispy moustache and wearing glasses, strolled into the administration building and I pulled him into a side office and fired six prepared, cogent questions at him. Any thoughts I had about him being a member of Special Forces quickly evaporated, because Brafman collapsed like a pricked balloon. He sagged. The man who, seconds before, had held the fate of seriously ill people in the palm of his incapable hands, was a broken reed.

In his flat, we found certificates, thirty-three forged references, 62 partly forged documents – and piles of medical reference books. Taken to Romford police station, he was detained, and later, in the cells, he was formally sacked by a member of the hospital trust, who told me that the GMC had been very relieved to discover that I had recovered his certificate to practise; about the only genuine medical document in his possession.

Even though he was admitting the offences – 'I was amazed when I was accepted and then I lost control of things' – he still could not stop lying. He told me that all the names of the doctors who had allegedly provided references for him, were fictitious. At the time, it made no difference to me because it only corroborated the fraud case against him. Later, I was to discover the truth.

Allison Brafman was also questioned. She stated that she had no idea that his qualifications were false and there was no evidence to connect her with any of the offences – at the time.

But now that Brafman was in custody, there was no further need for secrecy, and when word filtered through about his time spent at St George's Hospital, the deaths were regarded as suspicious and the Area Major Investigation Pool or AMIP was called in.

Each of the four Metropolitan Police areas had an AMIP with a dedicated staff of detective superintendents with detective sergeants as their bag carriers. They were called upon to deal with the most serious crimes – murder, rape etc. – and following the telephone call going into the area's AMIP headquarters at Arbour Square police station, the officer appointed to head this enquiry was Detective Superintendent Russ Allen.

I'd known Russ Allen when he was DCI at Holloway. He was quiet, avuncular and a committed Fraud Squad officer. He had prepared an Annual Qualification Report on me and, as I read it, I noticed that under the section headed 'Temperament, self-control, stability & reactions', he had marked me down as 'a good standard' and added, 'Can be temperamental.' 'Can be temperamental!' I roared. 'What do you fucking mean, "temperamental"?'

72

Russ raised his hands in mock surrender. 'Nobody's perfect!' he said mildly. So Russ was in charge; he brought along Colin Johnson as his bag carrier, plus an exhibits officer and a card indexer. I was co-opted on to the squad, as was Trainee Investigator (the names they give them!) Cliff Lyons. Cliff was one of the aids with me when Brafman was arrested and he was one of those young officers who soak up work like a sponge. I thought he was outstanding and had the makings of a very fine CID officer.

What a highly complex inquiry this was. All of us on the team were entering an area of investigation which we had never encountered before. I interviewed doctors, specialists and administrators. Cliff interviewed the nursing staff and, because he proved so successful in this aspect of the investigation, Russ directed him next to obtain the most detailed statements from biochemists and pharmacists. And all the time we were learning – grasping the intricate and complicated medical issues in order to try to appreciate the enormous difficulties there are when dealing with expert witnesses. My head was spinning as I tried to assimilate the interaction of administering a specific type of insulin to an elderly patient who was suffering from other independent ailments. Sometimes, I swam strongly in these muddied waters; on other occasions, I floundered and often sank.

If only it had been a simple case of seeing a witness and saying (as I would in many other straightforward cases), 'You were there – what did you see?' First was the staggering cock-up when Brafman had been granted a licence to practise. This was exacerbated when he was given two appointments and recommended and selected for a third. Then there were the times when Brafman had bumbled his way through the wards and the A & E Department, acting in the most overtly ludicrous manner whilst the staff simply looked on in amazement.

Many of them thought that they could be held accountable for Brafman's actions. They had a point.

Let's look at it this way. Supposing someone, purporting to be a New York cop, came over here and, on his first day out, he started shooting shoplifters. It's no use saying, 'Well, he's a Yank, isn't he? – that's probably the way they do things over there,' and just sort of hoping for the best, when the streets are littered with the corpses of absent-minded old ladies. You've got to take decisive action about behaviour like that.

I had to say (and keep on saying to the staff), 'Look – don't try to protect him – keep on saying to yourself, "He's not a doctor".' Mind you, it was debatable whether they were in some way trying to shield Brafman or minimize their own inadequacies.

Some of the doctors and consultants genuinely wanted to help; others were pompous to defence barrister standards. I had to bite my tongue to be civil to some of them; I did so, because their evidence could be crucial. Others, who had misguidedly championed Brafman, were terrified and went to extraordinary lengths to avoid meeting me.

There was one doctor whom I thought was as bonkers as conkers. I had obtained the notes for the patients whom Brafman had treated. Because of his appalling writing and spelling, they were almost incomprehensible to me, so I asked her to study the notes, to try to decipher the writing and then tell me what was wrong with the action he had taken. I later saw her, in order to take a statement from her, recording her findings. To my horror, I discovered that she had scrawled all over these notes in red ink – and remember, these were important court exhibits – with comments on Brafman's actions, such as, 'You must be kidding!' and 'Is this man serious?' 'Really!'

But, eventually, we managed to cobble together sufficient

evidence to charge Brafman with the manslaughter of Jessie
Harris. This was due, in no small part, to Cliff Lyons who proposed that there could be a multiple cause of death, rather
than a single one. Lengthy consideration was given to prefer-
ring manslaughter charges in respect of the 39 other people
who had died whilst under Brafman's care, especially those for
whom he had signed the death certificates, but it was not
thought that there would be a realistic prospect of obtaining
a conviction.

1991 passed into 1992 and still we pushed on, against a
tide of arrogance, apathy and fear – as well as some good,
genuine assistance.

One thing that is helpful in an investigation is now and
again to stop, and go back, and check what's been done. I've
often done this successfully myself. In this way, by checking
statements, actions and exhibits you can see not only what
might have been overlooked but also new lines of enquiry
which might bear fruit for the investigation. That's just what
Detective Sergeant Colin Johnson did. Colin was sifting
through the enormous amount of documentation when he
noticed the original letter sent to the GMC. So what?
Brafman had acknowledged that he had sent it and that the
contents were false. Colin was about to continue his perusal
of the documents, when he paused. He had realized that the
handwriting in this letter bore no resemblance to Brafman's
handwriting on the patients' notes. And what was more,
Colin knew he had seen similar handwriting before – but
where? It took several more hours of patient searching
through the 1,600 pages of documentation before he found
it. It was Brafman's CV. Now, if Brafman had not written
these two documents, who had? The obvious suspect was
Brafman's wife, Allison, who had previously stated that she
knew nothing about her husband's deception. What was

needed now was a handwriting sample from her. All of us feverishly searched the miscellaneous correspondence from the flat; nothing could be found which suggested her handwriting. A handwriting sample was essential – if she were to be arrested, she could legitimately refuse both to answer questions or to give a handwriting sample. In fact, when she was arrested, she did exercise both of these options.

I discovered that she was applying for housing benefits. I had a quiet word with the local council and got them to request a written statement from her in furtherance of these claims. I duly obtained this statement and to the layman's eye, her handwriting on the statement and the handwriting on the letter to the GMC and the CV appeared identical. It was not enough; other samples would be required in order to obtain a conclusive comparison. But how to acquire them? I had no idea. Within a month, they would be dropped into my lap.

In March 1992, Colin Johnson and I travelled to the United States – Colin to New York and Washington and I to Georgia and Alabama. To help us carry out our enquiries, we had the most enormous assistance from the Federal Government. The Naval Investigative Service had offices all across the country and no facet of the investigation was too small or mundane for them. They eased our way into places that would otherwise have been barred to us and I cannot speak too highly of their commitment, nor the friendship they showed us.

I like America and the Americans – I always got on well with the ladies.

In 1976, I was seated in a Lufthansa aircraft at Tempelhof Airport, Berlin, awaiting clearance for take-off to London Heathrow. I'd blotted my copybook by carrying out a sensational (and rather illegal) arrest at the city's prestigious

Hotel Kempinski, so the authorities had been rather glad to get shot of me. I'd been staying in a hotel where the staff were so hostile that I quickly formed the impression that they were on day-release from serving a sentence for war crimes. I'd taken to slipping wedges under my door at night, so I was quite happy to be heading for London. Not so the plump lady from New York in the window-seat next to me. As the engines revved up for take-off, she grew more and more agitated. Her tubby fingers squeezed her prayer beads so hard, they were beginning to resemble Smarties and as the brakes were released and we hurtled down the runway, her repeated babbling of 'Hail Mary, full of grace' rose to a crescendo. I patted her chubby, be-ringed fingers reassuringly. 'Courage, dear lady,' I murmured. 'Oh, my Gahd,' she sighed. 'You sound just like Ronald Colman!' As the famous film-star heart-throb had actually served in the First World War, I was somewhat alarmed at the disparity in our ages!

The Colman charm re-emerged some sixteen years later, after that initial encounter. I'd gone into a florists in Mississippi to purchase a bouquet for the wife of one of the Federal Agents and on my way out of the shop, I was spotted by two elderly matrons, both sporting blue rinses.

'Mah Lawd, Angie,' said one. 'Will yew look at those flowers?'

'If mah man bought me flowers like that,' rejoined the other, 'Ah'd fergive him *anythin'*!'

'Madam,' I replied, 'if I were your man, you would never have cause to forgive me anything at all!'

Both the blue rinses shrieked with laughter. 'Go on, honey!' squealed the first lady. 'Say anythin' you like – Ah jus' *lurve* that accent!'

But leaving aside the elderly waitress who leant over the table and murmured, 'I'm off in half-an-hour, honey – wanna take in a movie?' I think I'll leave the most productive encounter with a lady until a little later on. I wouldn't want you to run away with the idea that my time in the States was one long round of hedonistic pleasure – I got a bit of work done, as well.

Remember the photocopy of the medical licensure which Brafman had submitted to the GMC? I checked the number on the certificate and discovered the real identity of the doctor to whom it had been issued, who incidentally knew Brafman. I was also able to do a 'belt and braces' job on proving the falsity of the document by tracing the calligrapher who had prepared the certificate. I made myself busy round the printing companies in Anniston and discovered the one who had printed up the certificates for the fictitious two colleges. I gave the proprietor's memory a prod: he recalled crucial aspects of the transaction.

I made enquiries at the Alabama Board of Medical Examiners to prove that Brafman had never been licensed as a doctor in that state. You might think that I was verifying the blinding bleeding obvious but, with a sociopathic liar like Brafman, you could leave nothing to chance. Remember the doctors who had provided such glowing references for Brafman, who, he stated, were fictitious because he had written the letters himself? They weren't. Two of them actually practised in the state of Alabama and others practised in Ohio and Florida. All of them were found and interviewed.

I spoke to Brafman's commanding officer at Fort McClellan. The whole sorry story of Brafman's army career was exposed. Special Forces? No, not really. His CO described him as being 'a chronic liar'.

One evening, I was invited to the house of a special agent who had spent quite a lump of his career in Japan; he loved the country and spoke the language. His house was now filled with the most beautiful selection of that country's collectables that I'd ever seen. As we were sipping our drinks, the lounge door opened and in walked my host's coltish, bored fifteen-year-old daughter. 'Hi,' she sighed.

My host perked up. 'Honey,' he said importantly, 'I wanna introduce you to Dick Kirby. He's from Scotland Yard,' he added, impressively.

A frown creased the lovely forehead. 'Ain't we got kin in Scotland, Daddy?' she asked.

'Not Scotland, Scotland, stoopid!' roared her Father. 'Scotland Goddam Yard – the home of the British bobby!'

'Oh,' replied his daughter, mightily unimpressed with the whole thing. As she made her exit, she was kind enough to tell me that meeting me had been 'real neat'. I came to the irrevocable conclusion that whatever charms I possessed for the opposite sex in America were aimed largely at the more mature model.

I thought I'd have a wander around the housing estate where the Brafmans had lived. 'Sure, I remember them,' said the manageress, sourly. 'He weren't too bad but she was a snotty bitch with that crummy English accent – present company excepted,' she added ungraciously.

'Did they have any friends round here?' I asked.

'She had one,' admitted the manageress. 'She's still here. Wanna meet her?'

Well, why not? The young woman had indeed been friends with Allison Brafman – still was, in fact. 'She's written me some swell letters since she went back to England,' she enthused.

And all of a sudden, Bingo! 'Have you –' I asked, hesitantly, 'by any chance – kept any of them?' She had. All of them.

The forensic science laboratory later compared them with the original letter and CV sent to the GMC and came to the

79

conclusion that Allison Brafman had written the suspect documents, to the exclusion of anybody else. This evidence was so decisive that without answering a single question at her interview, Allison pleaded guilty to the charge levelled against her.

So the Brafmans came to trial at the Old Bailey and Matthew pleaded not guilty to the manslaughter of Jessie Harris. He was ably defended by Ann Curnow QC, a lady for whom I've got a lot of respect.

Remember the eccentric doctor who scribbled all over the court exhibits? Having fixed the date of the trial months in advance, so that nobody was inconvenienced by having their holidays disturbed, this doctor simply cleared off on holiday, just before the trial began. She failed to tell anybody in advance, and although failure to appear at court in these circumstances was punishable with three months' imprisonment, not one word of criticism was levelled against her. Until now, that is.

A geriatric expert told the court that by Brafman ordering Jessie Harris' insulin injection, it was, 'as certain a cause of death as if a knife had been stuck into her'.

Brafman's superior disagreed; then again, he had recommended him for the A & E job at Oldchurch hospital. A third doctor thought that the use of insulin was inappropriate but was irrelevant to the cause of death. A fourth thought that she might have died of septicaemia. After legal submissions from the defence, the Recorder of London, Sir Lawrence Verney, ordered the jury to return a verdict of not guilty to the charge of manslaughter. 'If the doctors are not certain of the cause of death,' said the recorder, 'how can the jury be?' In these particular circumstances, it was the only course of action that could have been taken.

Brafman pleaded guilty to posing as a doctor, forging certificates and committing perjury by unlawfully signing thirteen death certificates, and was sentenced to three-and-a-half years' imprisonment. For her part in the offences, Allison Brafman was placed on probation for two years.

In my opinion, the arrogance of the GMC throughout the inquiry was breathtaking. In an attempt to regain some semblance of credibility, a ludicrous, blustering letter was sent to the *Daily Telegraph*. The arguments did not impress a lay member of the GMC who was appalled by the case. 'I find it difficult with honour to remain on the GMC,' she said, adding, 'the GMC doesn't protect the public.'

Retiring at more or less the same time as me, Detective Superintendent Russ Allen told the press that, 'Brafman was an egotist, living a lie.'

Brafman? I thought he was a twerp who became a dangerously egotistical twerp, simply because he was allowed to become one. And never forget, it was Allison Brafman who had penned the letter and the CV to the GMC which started the whole sorry ball rolling. Whenever I saw her, she always had a smirk on her face, as if to say, 'I know something you don't.' I guess she was right.

But one memory about the case – apart from the deputy assistant commissioner's commendation which we all received – still stays with me. We had arrested Allison, and her son was in the car with us; we'd made arrangements that he would be cared for by one of her relatives whilst she was being interviewed. As we drove along, the boy suddenly asked, 'Where are these people taking you, Mummy?'

'Oh, don't worry,' she replied, blithely. 'They're hoping to pin something on me, so they can send me to prison for two or three years!'

I was aghast at such a crass answer. So was the kid, who gasped, '*What!*'

'Don't mind me,' chuckled Allison. 'You know my crazy sense of humour!'

I told her that I thought her sense of humour was inappropriate.

Or, at least, words to that effect.

Cracking a Crib

Different crimes go in and out of fashion. Do thieves still take part in 'jump-ups', where the victim's lorry is followed by a van load of thieves, and when it stops in traffic, the thieves jump up on to the lorry, throw the goods down to their mates who quickly secrete it in their van? The lorry driver then drives off, totally unaware that anything untoward has happened. Perhaps not. I witnessed a jump-up a few years ago in Sidney Street. What happened when the jump-up team was subsequently ambushed is quite an amusing little story in its own right, with the villain whom I was pursuing coming to an abrupt halt when he erroneously believed he was about to be shot, and I myself was buried under a pile of blue serge, when members of the Divisional Support Unit mistook me for one of the gang. So perhaps jump-ups have gone out of fashion, much like smash-and-grabs, so prevalent in the 1930s and 1940s, where Billy Hill, the self-styled 'Boss of Britain's Underworld', elevated them to an art form, using two and sometimes three cars as getaways. During the 1960s, raids on banks and building societies, where the perpetrators armed themselves with clubs, became fashionable. Coinciding with the abolition of the death penalty sawn-off shotguns soon replaced the clubs and staves. Prior to that, if one of the team had injudiciously discharged his firearm, causing fatal injuries to a passer-by, the whole team stood the risk of getting topped, not merely the member of the team who possessed an itchy trigger-finger. If you think criminals have a code of conduct, and want to find out about it, then read some detective stories written by middle-aged, middle-class women who've never met a real criminal or a real detective in their life: you won't find it anywhere else.

The Flying Squad, which was formed in 1919 to combat serious crime, became so accomplished at smashing gangs of armed robbers that they were in danger of being victims of their own success. With the statistics of armed robbery diminishing, loud noises were made by senior uniformed officers for the Squad to be disbanded and for the Squad personnel to be dispersed to divisions. In that way, they added brightly, if armed robberies suddenly began again, they could form their own little, you know . . . sort of mini Flying Squad. The trouble with imbecilic ideas such as this is that, to be successful against any type of specialist criminals, intelligence about them must be kept right up-to-date, using surveillance, informants and every other type of information-fed initiative.

One crime that does seem to have gone out of fashion is safebreaking. I expect it is because the security mechanisms of safes have become so sophisticated that it is far easier for the criminal to pursue the less baffling pursuits of drugs and funny money. But there was a time when safebreaking – 'cracking a crib' or 'screwing a peter' – was very prevalent.

Eddie Chapman was a thorn in the side of the authorities during the 1930s. A prolific Peterman, he would tour the country with his team, blowing safes with gelignite which he'd stolen from quarries. Since he used chewing-gum to tamp the explosives in the safe's lock, the Yard was initially convinced that American gangsters were responsible. Leaving a trail of plundered safes in his wake, Chapman was tipped off that his collar was about to be felt, and he fled to the Channel island of Jersey. Fast running out of money and unable to resist the sight of a seductive-looking safe, Chapman blew both the safe and his liberty, and wound up with two years' imprisonment. As the invading Germans marched in and, along with everything else, took over the local jail, Chapman was asked his previous trade or calling. '*Ich bin ein verbrecher*' ('I'm a criminal') he ingenuously replied. So he was flown to Germany to train as a saboteur, after which he was parachuted into England, where he became a double agent. He travelled back and forth between England and Germany, becoming so successful that the Germans awarded him the Iron Cross, and the authorities in England wiped clean the slate containing the outstanding matters of the cracked cribs.

It is a matter of record that between March and November 1938, no less that thirty-six safes were blown – the job of investigating these cases went to a police officer who was one of the best informed and toughest detectives of the time – perhaps of all time – Ted Greeno. If anybody – *anybody* – challenged his authority, no matter if he were at the horse track, in the pub or in the street, his jacket would come off, a ring of bystanders would be formed and Greeno would gleefully wade in to the attack. Afterwards, with his reputation as tough guy and good sport untarnished, he would shake hands with his opponent and that would be the end of the matter. On 18 November 1938, when Greeno was a detective inspector (1st class) on the Flying Squad, he received reliable information that a team of safe-blowers were going to attack the safe of a large department store in Ilford, that night. Greeno secreted himself in the darkened store with his men positioned outside, ready to come to his assistance. After hours of waiting, three shadowy suspects entered the building. Greeno waited just long enough for them to satisfy the requirements of the Larceny Act 1916 before calling out to the waiting Squadmen. It was then that things started to go

badly wrong. The outside doors jammed and the Squad officers were unable to get in. The gang were, of course, alerted
by Greeno's shout. 'It's the watchman!' shouted the gang
leader, thereby committing his first error. 'Do 'im!' he added
to his companions and, in so doing, committed his second.
The gang rushed at Greeno, who drew his truncheon and
went into action. The room resounded with the crack of
Greeno's stick, the howls of the gang and, finally, the splin-
tering of the doors as the Squad men kicked their way in.
With the lights turned on, Greeno's strenuous breathing
turned to a gasp of horror: the store's whitewashed walls
looked like the inside of a jam sandwich, splattered with the
blood of the now unconscious miscreants stretched out on the
floor before him. Equally horrified were the staff at Ilford
police station when the three blood-soaked safe breakers were
dragged in, but this was nothing compared to the shock experienced by everybody when the gang was searched. The ringleader, John Fairlie, had eight-and-a-half sticks of Polar
Ammon gelignite in his pockets; James Robertson had deto-
nators in his waistcoat and it was only by a gracious dispen-
sation of providence that Greeno's thrashing had not ended in
both he and the gang being blown up. But all was well that
ended well. Fairlie was sentenced to five years' penal servi-
tude, Robertson to three, and a minor member of the gang
was bound over to keep the peace and placed on probation.
The justices at Stratford Petty Sessions went overboard with
their commendation for Greeno, he was highly commended
by the commissioner and later awarded £10 from the Bow
Street Police Court Reward Fund. He went on to retire as a
detective chief superintendent, was awarded the MBE and
was commended on 86 occasions.

Between 1941 and 1950, over 200 post offices, banks, jewellers and council offices were entered and the contents of

their safes stolen. There was no sign of forced entry and, I'm sorry to say, suspicion fell on many innocent members of staff who possessed keys to both the front and safe doors. The person responsible was a locksmith who, during his long and blameless career, made duplicate keys when cutting the originals for these premises. Years later, he resigned and went to live in extremely modest lodgings, ostensibly on his pension; at the same time, he began to recruit a sophisticated network of expert criminals. Using the most fantastic security, the keys were distributed, the breakings carried out and the keys returned. The locksmith was never suspected and, when he died, he was still in surroundings that were so shabby no one would ever have suspected the vast wealth he had accumulated. The rest of the keys were distributed amongst the gang. Detective Superintendent Bob Lee of the Flying Squad coordinated the investigation and in an inquiry beset with difficulties (not least that the gang was being tipped off about the Squad's every move by a bent copper at the Yard), the gang was rounded up. Standing trial at Hampshire Assizes, five members of the team received sentences ranging from ten years' imprisonment to four years' corrective training.

'Johnny the Bosh' was a committed peterman and he was responsible for manufacturing skeleton keys and acquiring every kind of tool and accessory (including explosives) for breaking into premises and safes. At the time of his arrest by the Flying Squad in 1956, he had been released only a year before from a five-year sentence for office-breaking. Now, notching up his eleventh conviction for a shocking catalogue of crimes, Johnny received ten years' preventative detention. Not that this proved a reformative exercise; when the Bank of America was entered in April 1975 and anything between £8–12 million stolen from the safe deposit boxes, it was inevitable that an unfair Flying Squad would assume that Johnny the Bosh was in the frame. He was. And for his contribution to the raid, he received 22 years' imprisonment.

Which finally brings me to the case of Andy King. During his childhood, Andy had been afflicted with poliomyelitis which had affected his spine and left leg which he dragged behind him. As he limped along the Romford Road, the old East-End dears would look at him from their holly-stoned doorsteps and mutter, 'Pore little bleeder! Never do no 'arm to nobody and look at 'im!' And if he heard them, Andy would turn to them in mid-limp and give a pained, appreciative smile for their comments, hoping that he might be invited in for a comforting cuppa. The old dears rued the day if they did. Within seconds of entering the house, Andy would have stripped it of everything of value and, not withstanding his infirmity, he would have vanished at a rate of knots, not normally associated with a person suffering from such a disability. Nothing about Andy would bear close examination – his wan smile, his gammy leg, nor the fact that he frequently whined that he only stole to feed himself. With the substantial array of state benefits that he was receiving, Andy did not need to steal at all, in order to put food on the table. He stole because he was a slimy, dishonest, thoroughgoing little shit. In addition, he was an industrious peterman.

Not for Andy the keys of Johnny the Bosh, nor Eddie Chapman's gelignite: he used the skills of an old-fashioned peterman and would simply stick an old chisel into the back of a safe and rip it right off. The likes of the Bank of America had little to fear from Andy's efforts but his aspirations did not rise that high. Any little back-street business premises which possessed a cheap safe was good enough for him.

Rosie the Grass normally stockpiled her discarded lovers for me and then handed them up on a plate, together with details of their transgressions. So when she propped up Andy for a safebreaking, I was somewhat surprised, because never, in my over-active imagination, could I have imagined Andy and Rosie thrashing about in the sack together. In fact, Rosie haughtily disdained the very idea of such an amalgamation, stressing that she had far better taste than the likes of *him*; although having seen some of her past paramours, this did take some believing. No, I later discovered that one of the old dears who had taken pity on Andy and had recklessly invited him into her house was, in fact, one of Rosie's aunties, and this was how Rosie had led Andy into a spectacularly amusing ambush, details of which you may guess at, but need not enquire after.

So as Andy snuffled out his tearful excuses in which food and starvation played a prominent part, in the recently vacated CID typists' office at Forest Gate police station, he suddenly spotted my curled lip and realizing that his blandishments were having not the slightest effect on me whatsoever, dried his tears and glumly made a full, written confession. But he was a game little bugger, and just because he had failed to stretch my susceptibilities in the slightest, it did not mean that he was instructing his seconds to chuck in the towel. Not a bit of it.

Andy mournfully pleaded guilty to the lay magistrates sitting at Newham (East) Magistrates' Court, and I outlined the facts of the case, laying special emphasis on the fact that when the safe belonging to McKinnon's dress shop in Katherine Road had had its back ripped off, it had coincided with the absence of the staff and proprietor, during their lunch break, the previous Friday. Asked if he had anything to say, Andy sorrowfully shook his head. 'Anything known?' asked the clerk of the court and I proceeded to inform the bench of Andy's disgraceful amount of form, which had been acquired during a surprisingly short period of time. I gave special attention to his most recent conviction, this also being for safe-breaking, for which Andy had been placed on probation for two years by this court's neighbouring court, Newham (West) Magistrates'.

The chairman of the Bench frowned. 'This is a very recent conviction,' he muttered and then, as he consulted the desk calendar, his eyebrows shot up and he cried, 'Good Heavens – it was last Friday!'

'Quite so, Your Worship,' I replied. 'I spoke to the clerk at Newham (West) Court earlier, and discovered that the time lapse between the defendant being placed on probation and cracking the safe in Katherine Road was just 55 minutes.' '*What!*' gasped the beak. 'I believe it would have occurred sooner,' I added helpfully, 'but for the fact that the defendant's bus was late.'

The chairman was furious. 'You've been given one chance after another,' he thundered, 'and now, after the justices sought to give you one final chance to redeem yourself, you abused that trust by committing an exactly similar offence within one hour of being placed on probation. You will therefore be committed to the Crown Court, in custody under the provisions of section 28 of the Magistrates Courts Act with a recommendation for borstal training.'

What happened next was reminiscent of the first of the three title fights between Ingemar Johansson and Floyd Patterson in 1959. The first two rounds had passed fairly unspectacularly and then, early in the third, Johansson sent a smashing right-hander over the very stylish Patterson's lowered left, which effectively finished the fight. The reason why this was so surprising was because Johansson, with the odds of 5–1 against him, had been described as a no-hoper. In much the same way, Andy now came into his own, as he struggled to his feet and limped to the front of the dock.

'Borstal?' he echoed. 'I don't need borstal – I need a fucking chance, that's what I need! Something I never had before! Do you think locking me up is going to help me? I want a chance, mate, that's what I need!'

The Bench stared back at him, open-mouthed. Never had they heard such a peroration from the dock. Andy warmed to his task. 'Do you think it's fun, struggling through life with a leg like this?' he screamed. 'Having everyone taking the piss out of you? Why d'you think I go out thieving? Because I like it? No! Because nobody'll give me a job and no one, you rotten unfeeling bastards, will give me a chance! Poor little fucking cripple kid, me! I want a chance, not borstal!'

In the stunned silence that followed, a dropped pin would have sounded like . . . well . . . a safe having its back ripped off. A court reporter shook his head, dumbly. And when a probation officer, her face buried in her handkerchief, loudly blew her nose, everybody jumped.

The astonished and embarrassed chairman cleared his throat. 'Well – er – given the circumstances – the – er – quite unusual circumstances of the case,' he spluttered, 'I think that – er – two years' probation, to run concurrently with the order imposed last Friday.'

As Andy limped from the dock, a free man, he spotted the look of shocked incredulity on my face, because he grinned and winked at me as he left court. I don't know what happened to him after that; our paths never crossed and in fact, I never heard of him again. Perhaps he became an evangelist – he certainly had that sort of flair – or perhaps a member of Parliament. With his ability to make the sort of impassioned oratory that he'd made in court that day, he could have found success in just about any kind of public speaking.

The unkindest cut of all came from Rosie the Grass, when I paid her the reward money from the Informant's Fund. She'd heard of the wildly inappropriate way in which Andy had been dealt with and had erroneously come to the conclusion that there was more to it than met the eye. 'You are a big fucking softy, Dick,' she said scornfully. 'I bet you gave him a leg-up in court!'

An Ugly Pair of Customers

As Tony Freeman expertly threaded the big Rover 2600 through the East End traffic on that Wednesday morning, I felt at peace with the world. To start with, the sun was shining; for another, I'd been able to get up at a reasonable hour and breakfast with my family, unlike the previous six Wednesday mornings, when Ron Turnbull's crummy informant had told us that there was 'definitely' going to be an armed hold-up on a security van at King's Cross railway station. And how prudent it had been of our detective inspector to bring a halt to this nonsense and call off the observation. So, now, we were driving en route to the Yard with me in a happy state of mind, because I'd gained immense brownie points, having given my daughter Sue a highly unofficial lift to the tube station, and for the rest of the day . . . my thoughts were rudely interrupted as the R/T set crackled into life. 'All cars three, all cars three and any Central unit,' said the Yard's operator. 'King's Cross railway station, an armed robbery on a security vehicle. Three IC3s involved, made off along York Way in a white Ford Cortina, index number unknown. Any unit November Delta or any Central unit deal?' I groaned and nodded to Tony and as he switched on the two-tones and the Rover kicked down and roared off along the Whitechapel Road, I depressed the microphone button and replied, 'Central 923 on way.'

That DI, I thought bitterly, must have been insane calling

off the observation, especially with the information we'd got from Ron's solid-gold snout. As Tony tore into Aldgate High Street, I called up Jim Moon, who was manning Central 899, the Squad's base radio. 'Jim, we're on our way to the blag at the Cross,' I said. 'Tell the rest of the team to stand by and as soon as we know what's happening, we'll get going.'

'Right,' Jim replied and, as the car roared into Houndsditch, I could well imagine Jim shaking his head and muttering, 'Right bloody cock-up if you ask me!' and I smiled; it was about the only thing I did have to smile about, just then.

But two hours later, 12 Squad had rallied, and as the elderly door to the Victorian town house in Kentish Town gave up the ghost to a little Squad persuasion, and a bunch of grim and very determined Squad men, armed to the teeth, raced up the stairs, shouting '*Squad!*' we were, if you'll excuse a bad pun, up and running. As we ran up the last flight of stairs to the top floor, there on the landing was a horrified-looking Floyd Washington Browne. Immediately he issued the stock denial of wrong-doing. '*Fucking 'ell, man!*' he screamed at the top of his lungs. '*Me do nuffin'!*' It was clear that tact and conciliation would be needed here and I reached out a resolute hand with which to steady him. Grabbing hold of his jacket lapels, I snapped, 'Shut up, you mug – where's your brother?' Floyd's eyes swivelled towards the kitchen door, so I passed him to another qualified first-aider and ran in to the kitchen. There was Floyd's sibling, Lucas, busily attempting a hasty exit through the window and, since we were four floors up, I thought it best to pull him back in. Blimey, that was a job, what with the window being tiny and Lucas being six foot two and lumpy with it. But I eventually hauled him back into the kitchen and had a chance to have a good look at him for the first time. He was a sight. His hair was long and it stood on end, as though he were suffering from a permanent electric shock. His face was saturated with moles and his teeth were so widely spaced that they looked like individual tombstones. His nose was so wide that, viewed from behind, the sides of his nostrils protruded beyond the sides of his ears. 'What do they call you on the street, mate?' I asked, because it was important that nicknames and aliases should be recorded in the various intelligence bureaux.

'Well,' he replied, shyly, 'the guys, they call me Uggy. Sometimes,' he added, 'they calls me Uggy-Wuggy.' There was a bit of a pause.

'Any idea why?' I asked, casually.

Uggy threw back his head and laughed. As he opened his mouth, the effect was rather like looking at a cemetery on a dark night. I was glad Uggy had a sense of humour, because he was going to need it; although he and his brother vehemently denied any involvement in the King's Cross robbery, Uggy found it impossible to offer a reasonable explanation in respect of the large amount of dodgy gear, which had been found in the attic.

Uggy took his arrest philosophically and philanthropically, too, because realizing that it was on him, he rowed Floyd out of possession, both constructive and physical, of the crooked gear. "Im didn't know nuffin' about it,' he said magnanimously, and, as Floyd nodded like a mandarin, I acknowledged that Floyd had made that clear to me at the time of our meeting.

The Squad car drove off, towards King's Cross with me and Uggy in the back. 'As it goes,' Uggy said, 'I fink I can help with the King's Cross business – mind you,' he added, 'I'll need a leg-up at court wiv this little lot.'

'Uh-huh,' I replied neutrally, as though I couldn't have cared less. In fact, of course, I cared very much indeed because, right now, some solid information was what was needed.

Uggy was charged with receiving a miscellaneous collection of bent gear and, the following day at court, I had him remanded on bail for one month, so that I could ascertain the provenance of the property. And that was something that could be put on the back burner for the time being, because what Uggy had told me was this. The King's Cross job had been the worst-kept secret in North London. One team had been all set to hit the security van – then, on the morning of the raid, they all overslept. Another gang had thoroughly researched the job and had reconnoitred the area, armed with sawn-off shotguns, but when they heard about a warehouse filled up with tempting electrical goods, they did that instead. Yet another gang had put in just as much work as the second gang had done, but, the night before, one of the team had got stoned out of his brains on ganja; another met a foxy chick at a nightclub and didn't surface until the following noon; the third had turned up. Realizing that he was quite alone, he assumed that the others had set him up to the police, and promptly went on the run. And they all talked about it. They talked amongst themselves, they talked to their mates, and they talked to their girls. Ron's informant pitched in with some further information, and, within a couple of days, two of the robbers were arrested, thousands of pounds were recovered as were thousands of pounds' worth of property which they'd bought on a wild spending spree. Over the following weeks and months, other conspirators were identified, traced and nicked. 'How much did you think you'd get out of the security wagon?' I asked one of them.

'Millions,' he replied, confidently.

'Leave off,' I said, 'how much?'

'Millions,' he repeated, annoyed that I'd ever doubted his word. He really believed it, the silly twerp. So, in the end, they all appeared at the Bailey, Stuart Moore prosecuted, His

Honour, Judge Francis Petre presided, the two robbers copped ten years apiece, while the conspirators collected sixes and sevens.

Back, now to Clerkenwell Magistrates' Court to deal with the fate of Uggy, a month after our initial encounter. I looked at his form – Christ, it was a bit fierce and quite a lot of it, too – all for dishonesty, thieving and fraud and, to put the tin hat on it, he was subject of a bender (suspended sentence), too.

'Fink you can keep me out of jail, Mr K?' Uggy asked anxiously. I scratched my head thoughtfully.

'I'll have a go, mate,' I replied, 'but I can't promise anything.' Nor could I – if I was going to help Uggy, it was clear that a rabbit of mammoth proportions would have to be pulled out of the hat.

Just then, a stunningly beautiful young woman swept into court. Not only was she extremely attractive, she was also beautifully and expensively dressed in a well-cut charcoal business suit and expensive-looking crocodile court shoes. She walked straight up to my prisoner and affectionately squeezed his arm and kissed him.

'Hello, Uggy darling,' she purred.

'This me bitch,' Uggy said nonchalantly, by way of introduction.

'You must be Sergeant Kirby,' she cried, in a cut-glass accent, more reminiscent of Girton College, Cambridge, than Stoke Newington Church Street. As we shook hands, she continued, 'You do know that Uggy and I are engaged to be married, don't you – oh, please, do you think you can keep him out of prison?'

I didn't know – either about the intended nuptials, or the possibility of keeping him out of quod. Bloody Hell, I thought, how did this gorgeous creature get mixed up with a thing like Uggy? Must have hidden assets, I thought sourly.

'Can you?' she repeated, urgently.

'I'm sorry,' I replied. 'My thoughts were elsewhere. Keep him out of stir? Well, I'll do my best.' And then, I had a brainwave. 'Why don't I call you to the stand, after I've finished?' I said. 'I don't know if it'll help, but what with you going to be married . . .'

Her lustrous eyes widened. 'Do you think so?' she cried. 'Yes, of course I'll do it – I'll do anything for Uggy!'

Lucky bloody Uggy, I thought, and went off to try to work a minor miracle but, now, help was at hand: someone with a cut-glass accent to plead his cause.

Uggy pleaded guilty to receiving a quantity of knocked-off gear, in front of Joseph Childs, the stipendiary magistrate. Actually, I was pleased it was him, because I'd appeared in front of him half a dozen times before and he was a decent old stick. However, I can only assume that on this particular morning, Mrs Childs had served him cold toast for breakfast, because he was in an irascible mood. I outlined the facts of the case as briefly as possible, read out Uggy's previous convictions and then got down to the important business of mitigation. I stressed that he had admitted his guilt at the earliest possible opportunity and had also expressed remorse for his reckless behaviour.

'I'm not surprised,' grunted Childs, 'once he'd been caught!'

Oh dear; this was clearly going to be an uphill battle. Uggy looked shamefaced and repentant and I struggled bravely on about his work prospects and his genuine desire to reform. Ignoring Childs' snort of derision as he glanced once again at Uggy's form, I played my trump card. 'Mr Browne is hoping to marry in the very near future, Your Worship,' I said. 'In fact, his fiancée, who is extremely concerned about his immediate future –' ('She needs to be!' interjected Childs) '– is here in court. I feel that it would only be of assistance if you were to hear her views on the matter.'

'Oh, very well, very well,' muttered old Childs. 'Let her be sworn.' Up into the witness box stepped the ebony Venus. 'Well, young woman?' growled Childs. 'What can you tell me about this defendant?'

And with that, the bottom dropped out of my world. 'Right, lemee tell yuh sumfin'!' Uggy's fiancée snapped. 'Me geezer, 'im reely, reely lookin' 'ard for a job, right?'

Jesus Christ, I thought – why's she talking like that – whatever's happened to Girton-bloody-College? Childs' eyes almost popped out of his head.

'Seeing as how your fiancé has never had a job, Madam,' he snapped, 'I'd say that he needs to make the effort sooner, rather than later!'

'Yeah, an' me tell yuh sumfin' else, an' all!' she shrieked. ''Im reely, reely tryin' 'ard to keep out of trouble an' you gotta give 'im a chance, innit?'

I cringed and ducked my head. Had the creature gone mad? Did she want Uggy to go inside? Was this a plan to dump him? But no – it had been my idea! God in heaven, what was going on? Childs was incandescent with rage. 'Your fiancé, Madam,' he thundered, 'can hardly be considered to be doing his best to keep out of trouble, having collected eight convictions for dishonesty since the age of seventeen and particularly since he is at present the subject of a suspended sentence! That's all I need to hear from you, Madam; stand down!'

I don't know what happened; maybe Childs had seen the stricken look on my face which suggested that Uggy had been dealt with so benevolently by me because he'd stuck-up a bit of work or perhaps he thought that marriage to that beautiful harpy would be punishment enough. Whatever it was, he imposed another suspended sentence, to run consecutively with the previous one, and warned Uggy that no court would deal with him so leniently on a future appearance. The couple left the court holding hands and giggling like any other happily engaged couple – I think!

The second of the stories involving ugly characters, concerned a young villain who had far less form than Uggy – in fact, none at all. And the prize that he nicked did not, as in the case of the King's Cross robbery, net £11,000 – it came to no more than a few pence.

Dave 'Sandy' Sanderson had been born in Durban, South Africa, and served with the Kenya Regiment, where he had been engaged in mopping-up operations against the Mau Mau. In 1959, he had arrived in England where he joined the Metropolitan Police; now, as a newly promoted detective sergeant, he was posted on the 'Q' car with me, and being the possessor of a fund of humorous stories, Sandy was very good company. But there was little to laugh at on this particular Saturday night – for one thing, we hadn't had an arrest on the 'Q' car all week – bad news! In order to help readdress the balance, an informant of Sandy's had told him he'd got some red-hot information for us and this was how we'd spent the last two hours, sitting in a cheerless dump of a Dagenham pub, named The Clarion Call. The informant hadn't showed and to add insult to injury for the last three-quarters of an hour we had had to sit through a lack-lustre performance by a charmless, aging stripper. So wretchedly unattractive was this creature, that one of the audience kept shouting 'Put 'em on!', which was quite amusing the first time he'd said it, but rather tiresome thereafter.

'Let's go,' said Sandy grumpily, and we mooched outside to a dismal Dagenham landscape on which it had just started to rain. Utterly dejected, we turned up our coat collars and started to trudge towards the 'Q' car, which was parked a couple of hundred yards away; and it was then that we saw them.

Two youths, who appeared to be as bored as we were, were walking along the road in front of us, in the same direction. So bored, in fact, that as they walked along, they both leant over a garden fence and took hold of a gladiolus apiece. Snap! Snap! went the stalks and they continued on their way, oblivious, of course, to our presence.

I glanced at Sandy. 'Come on,' I said and hurried after them.

'Perhaps – perhaps we'll just show them as a stop in the street, Richard,' said Sandy as he quickened his pace which, privately, I thought was a bit soft. And then, that idea went for a burton, as the two youths opened the front door of one of the terraced houses and vanished inside. I knocked on the door. It was opened by one of the youths – the other, his brother, stood next to him. The brother who had answered my knock was tall, emaciated, and cross-eyed, with protruding teeth, and not a sound one amongst them. His nickname, he later informed us, was 'Ug'.

'No kidding?' murmured Sandy, with masterly understatement.

I told Ug who we were and what we'd seen – and suddenly realized how silly it sounded. Ug obviously thought so too, because he sneered, 'Fuck off!' and went to shut the door in our faces. Any thought that the matter might have been amicably resolved quickly went out of the window (although telling him to put the gladioli back would have been rather tricky). So I shoved the door open and in we went. Ug was furious. 'You're fucking barmy!' he shouted, as we pushed our way into the dining room. 'What flowers?'

'*These* flowers,' I replied, snatching the two gladioli from

101

the jam jar on the dining-room table. 'Those flowers 'ave been 'ere for two bleedin' weeks!' shrieked the mother of Ug, and Sandy, who was obviously blessed with second sight, read the thought that had crossed my mind about nicking the mother as well, for feloniously receiving two stolen flowers, because he hastily said to the brothers, 'Right – come on, you're both nicked.' With that, each of us firmly holding on to an Ug brother, plus the two offending gladioli in my other hand, we marched them outside to the 'Q' car.

'Those for me?' said Johnny Gray, the driver, and I gave him a piercing look.

'Keep an eye on these two,' I said. 'I'll be back in a minute.' With that, I knocked up the elderly owner of the flowers and told him what had happened.

He was hopping mad. 'Caught 'em, did yer?' he growled. 'Bloody good! Little bastards have been getting away with strokes like that for years – 'Ope they both draw a carpet apiece!'

'I doubt it!' I laughed, and returned to the car.

In the charge room at Dagenham police station Ug began seriously to push his luck, as we explained the arrest to the amused station officer.

'That right?' he asked the brothers.

'We ain't done nothin'' shouted Ug. 'We was fitted up!'

'Really?' the station officer replied dryly. 'I hope you're not suggesting that the officers planted them on you!' and the rest of the night-duty who had been listening at the charge room door burst into snuffles of strangulated laughter, before they were shooed away by the duty officer, who was as amused as everybody else.

Emboldened by this, Ug turned to me. 'Yeah,' he sneered, 'and you – you, mate. You're going to look a right prick when we go to court over a couple of poxy tulips!'

I permitted myself a thin smile. 'Shall we have a word about this,' I asked, 'in private?'

Shortly afterwards, a much chastened Ug returned to the charge room where he saw his brother. 'Better make a statement,' he said, mournfully. 'I 'ave!'

Both of the brothers were charged and I took their fingerprints. 'Ever had this done before?' I asked them. They hadn't – a fact that was confirmed by COC3 Fingerprint Branch who allocated them pristine CRO numbers.

Sandy was enormously embarrassed by the whole affair. The following Monday morning, on our way to Barking Magistrates' Court to deal with the brothers, we popped into Dagenham CID office and ran into a tidal wave of sustained piss-taking. The CID officers knew about it, because the word had spread from the uniform, like a bush fire; and that wasn't all. The rest of the Division knew about it as well, after a highly amusing entry in the log from the night duty CID had officially dubbed us 'The Flower Power "Q" car'. I got some stick as well, but Sandy, as the DS, bore the brunt of it. Sandy good-humouredly shrugged it off but it was clear that he was far from happy. Arriving at court, Sandy very nobly passed the buck to me. 'I think, young Richard, that you ought to present this case to the Bench,' he said smoothly. 'In the absence of your own supervising detective sergeant, I have to report on your progress, and I shall be most interested to see you give evidence, first hand.' I gave Sandy a bitter look and made my way into court. The genius Ug pleaded guilty to the theft of two gladioli of nominal value and I outlined the facts to the Bench, emphasizing the annoyance felt by the owner. I confirmed that neither had any previous convictions, the chairman of the Bench gave them a mild whigging and fined them a fiver each. As they left the dock, I noticed a suspicion of a grin on the faces of the Magistrates – certainly, there was one on the faces of the Ug brothers, who made no attempt to disguise it.

'I thought you did very well there, Richard,' Sandy said graciously, patting me on the back. 'Something to forget about and put behind us, Sandy,' I replied, to which he whole-heartedly agreed – which just goes to show you how wrong you can be.

This was our last week on the 'Q' car; we finished it off in style, with some good-quality arrests, some good meals and drinks, and, at the end of it, we shook hands and congratulated ourselves on a fine 'Q' car tour, in good company. Sandy returned to divisional duties at Dagenham and the ragging from his peers over the gladioli incident slowly started to diminish, which was just as well, because Sandy's patience was, by now, wearing rather thin.

The following week, Sandy received a telephone call from a pal of his, Detective Sergeant Ted Bentley. 'Sandy, the other week, you charged a couple of lads for nicking some flowers,' he began and that was as far as he got.

'*I've had enough of this!*' roared Sandy and it took several minutes for him to calm down. However, this was no wind-up. Ted Bentley was the 3 Area Fingerprint liaison officer and the reason why he had telephoned Sandy was to inform him that because the Ug brothers had had their fingerprints taken for the first time, they had been compared with outstanding fingerprints found at scenes of crime in the area. Lo and behold! they were found to match the marks left at the scene of no less than six burglaries. Well, well!

Sandy flew out of the office with the zeal of a man possessed and scragged in the brothers Ug and charged them with the burglaries. 'Now, if you've done any more, you'd better tell me, and we can get them cleared up now,' he said, sternly. 'If you've done any others and you don't admit them now, I'll find out about them and I'll be round to see you again.' The brothers denied any further wrong-doing, duly went to court, pleaded guilty to the charges and were placed on probation.

So that was that – until a week later, Ted Bentley telephoned Sandy again, with more details of crime the brothers had committed. Then it happened again – and again and again.

Eventually, just 12 months after we'd first nicked them for the gladioli, both of them were starting 18-month jail sentences.

Sandy went on to lecture at the Detective Training School and then for the last 15 years of his 34 years' service, he was one of the finest lab liaison sergeants at the Yard, dealing with suspicious deaths both at home and abroad, including three in his native South Africa, one of which was the protracted investigation into the death of Julie Ward.

Of course, Sandy dined out on the gladioli story for years afterwards; in fact, he still does. When I spoke to him on the telephone the other night, I suggested that every time he saw a bunch of cut flowers, he experienced flashbacks which required counselling. Sandy laughed – but he didn't deny it.

My Horse!

The elderly lady at the bar of the Special Forces Club in Knightsbridge had infinitely more interesting tales to tell than I; but as a former member of the Special Operations Executive's 'F' Section, who had parachuted into occupied France, she maintained a remarkable reticence about her own feats. Instead, she was badgering me to tell her about some of the things that had happened to me, during my police service.

'For instance,' she said, as Mustapha, arguably the greatest bartender in the universe, replenished our glasses, 'who was the most horrible person you ever had dealings with?'

I almost laughed out loud, thinking that the unpleasant people that I'd encountered bore little resemblance to the Gestapo toughs, Vichy police and the informers that she'd dealt with, probably at the business end of a silenced pistol. But I mentioned the exploits of one or two of the horrors I'd met – their names, of course, meant nothing to her – and her curiosity satisfied, we passed on to other subjects.

On the train home that night, I thought again about some of the unappealing people with whom I'd had dealings over the years. Robbers, not unnaturally, came top of the list, but there were pimps, wife beaters, sneak thieves, drug addicts . . . the list was endless. But then I remembered; the lady from SOE had stipulated not necessarily the most dangerous or violent, but 'the most horrible'.

I glanced idly out of the window as the train from

107

My Horse!

Liverpool Street roared through the stations. Ilford, Seven Kings, Goodmays – and then, I caught a glimpse of Chadwell Heath. Just a glance but it was enough for me to recall Old Bluey: someone I'd known well over thirty years before. Until that moment, I'd forgotten all about him but he certainly fitted the category of 'the most horrible'. I was glad I *had* forgotten him; the dignified lady from SOE would not have been amused to hear of Old Bluey's exploits . . .

Life had been spectacularly unkind to Old Bluey. He had long since been robbed of his baptismal name, so that when folk saw him walking the streets of Ilford, pulling at the bridle of his repellent, tubercular mare which dragged along his wobbly, junk-filled cart, they would nudge each other and say, 'Here comes Old Bluey.' Bluey had acquired his nickname, because following the Second World War, one of the popular criminal pastimes was stealing lead from roofs – it was known as 'blue-flying' – and it was either by stealing or by feloniously receiving a sufficiency of this commodity, that he was able to purchase the lease of a piece of ground at Chadwell Heath, where he erected a ramshackle hut for himself, a stable of sorts for his charmless mare and a dumping ground for stolen property. Many compared Bluey with another well-known receiver of stolen goods who had been immortalized in Dickens' *Oliver Twist*, a comparison that was fairly accurate! Bluey, too, was a repugnant creature: unwashed, with greasy, matted hair, and he dressed in a collection of rags. His age, beneath the crusty filth, was indeterminate. Bluey's horse and cart were a useful (although not fully convincing) cover as a totter, because when he knocked on the door of dwelling-houses on the pretext of collecting junk, he was able to evaluate whether the house was suitable for screwing within a split second, before the appalled householder slammed the door in his face.

So, usually, the most recalcitrant of children could be

brought into line when their mothers admonished them with the chill warning, 'Bluey'll get you!' because it was whispered that Bluey did ill-use children; and what's more it was quite true.

When Oliver Twist was conscripted into going out burgling, it was in the company of Fagin's associate, one Bill Sykes, but Bluey failed to conform to his Dickensian counterpart on that score. He trusted no one. So when Bluey induced children to steal for him – and I assume it must have been through hypnosis – he would accompany them to the specially selected premises. This was not out of concern for them, nor to facilitate their escape if things went awry; it was to ensure that not one piece of the loot went astray. And when the kid squirmed his way out of the freshly ransacked shop or house, Bluey would be there to snatch the proceeds, pay the child a pittance for his endeavours, dispose of the goods to a waiting outlet, and make a handsome profit.

An astonishing incident occurred when a shop's alarm was activated whilst one such child was busily plundering the contents of the premises, and Bluey, who had been hovering in the background, had been spotted by the rapidly forming crowd. With the sound of the approaching police sirens coming ever nearer, Bluey realized that his sudden departure from the scene would only consolidate the crowd's suspicions. With a terrific sense of style, Bluey decided to cut his losses and, as the child emerged from the shop, he put himself into the role of an innocent passer-by: He made a dramatic citizen's arrest which coincided with the arrival of the area car. "Ere you are, officer,' said Bluey, firmly grasping the stunned, wriggling child. 'Caught 'im bang to rights. 'E's the sort what'd nick anything what wasn't screwed down, 'e would! Lucky I 'appened to be passing,' and to the by-now completely disorientated child, 'Thieving little bastard, ain't yer?'

Disregarding the terrible, feculent stench that arose from Bluey, the officer gingerly took hold of his oil-encrusted sleeve and brought him in as well, but the CID drank bitter herbs that day, when Bluey escaped prosecution after he stuck to his wildly improbable story, and the terrified, mesmerized child refused to acknowledge Bluey's complicity.

That, then, was Bluey. Filthy, venomous and also certainly verminous. Shunned by all decent members of society, the direct cause of small, susceptible children's nightmares and bed-wetting and utterly loathed by the local CID, Bluey was surely the most unloved of all God's creatures. Perhaps his mum had once clasped him to her bosom in adoration, but if that unlikely scenario had occurred, that was long ago and nobody or nothing had ever loved him since. Nothing? Well . . .

The sight that gladdened the eyes of the crew of the Chadwell Heath area car, cruising slowly and silently past Bluey's yard, early one morning, was spotting Bluey, standing on a rickety old orange box behind his ringbone-infested mare, his trousers round his ankles and, as he rocked slowly backwards and forwards, a look of pure bliss on his face . . .

When the area car crew had managed to choke their laughter back to more manageable proportions (the driver had to sit quietly for a bit, because his streaming eyes would have made driving impossible), the luckless Bluey was led away. Contrary to anything that the RSPCA or Section 12(1) of the Sexual Offences Act 1956 had to say about his behaviour, Bluey honestly believed that ownership of this wretched animal permitted conduct of this nature. All Bluey felt was a profound sense of deprivation and injustice, because he kept repeating to the chuckling officers, 'But it's *my* 'orse!'

Sheer Coincidence

All through my career, I was plagued by remarkable coincidences. Like the time when I was a detective constable and had given Barry Howe, a fellow detective constable from Plaistow police station, a lift in my car back to his office. Barry and I were chatting. 'I've got an old boy up at court tomorrow, for criminal deception,' he said. 'Funny old bugger, he is. Do you know what he did?' And as the story of this old fellow's fraudulent tricks unfolded, I realized that the *modus operandi* that he had used, was so similar to an unusual fraud that I was investigating, that Barry's prisoner must have been the person responsible. The journey took a quick détour, my passenger and his prisoner were reunited quicker than they thought, and a terse introduction to me resulted in a confession to my previously unsolved crime. Coincidence, see? Simply because I'd given Barry a lift in my car, because his was in the garage. Try telling counsel for the defence that, or any other genuine coincidence during a contested case. 'Oh, come, come, officer! Do you really expect this court to believe . . .' they'd scoff, incredulously.

I don't know what the current state of play is, but at the time I retired from the Metropolitan Police, each reported crime was awarded points to see if it satisfied certain criteria and thus merited further investigation; and if it didn't, it was 'crashed' – or, simply not investigated. All nice and legal. Much the same thing used to happen years before, except the

111

question of points didn't come into it: we were under pressure to keep the crime figures low. One despotic old detective chief superintendent refused to accept a classification in the crime book of 'Burglary – Residential' if the value of property stolen from the house came to less than £3 – it was classified as the lesser offence of 'Theft in Dwelling'.

An attempted burglary simply didn't exist; the classification was always recorded as 'No Crime'. 'Window, broken by stone, thrown up by passing lorry', was the inevitable conclusion. One particular officer had the hell of a job explaining away a window which was situated half-way down a narrow alley which had been removed after the putty had been stripped away. 'Putty, pecked out by voracious birds,' had been his cunning explanation, a solution I might add, which was accepted without question. One mature detective constable actually classified an attempted burglary as being just that. Within minutes, the detective chief superintendent (the same one referred to above) came flying down the stairs to the CID office where, eschewing the need for lines of communication via the line manager, he launched into a full-frontal attack against the officer. 'Are you fucking insane?' he screamed, waving the errant crime book entry in the DC's face. 'Attempted – fucking – burglary! Where's your prisoner? Where's your evidence?' In vain, the DC explained about the forced skylight on the roof of the warehouse, together with the discarded jemmies, hammers and oxyacetylene equipment which had been abandoned by the burglars, after they had been disturbed. 'If you want to stay in the Department,' roared the DCS, 'you'd better get this sorted out!' The DC, who had almost as much service in the Department as the DCS, prudently did just that. The attempted burglary was crashed as a 'No Crime' and the burglar's paraphernalia went into the 'Property found in the Street' book.

Mind you, if you had a prisoner for the broken window, woe betide you if you soppily accepted his explanation that his actions had been a bit of wanton vandalism. In those circumstances, eyebrows, I assure you, would have been raised. Eyebrows were certainly raised if, when a prisoner was brought in for an unauthorized taking of a motor vehicle (known commonly as a TDA or taking and driving away) or a burglary, no TICs were forthcoming. TICs (or, to give them their full title, offences to be taken into consideration) were bread-and-butter to most detectives. The reasoning was that when a criminal was arrested for a burglary or a TDA, it was never his first time – he'd done lots of others and simply hadn't been caught for them. So when these other offences he'd committed were unearthed, the suspect would be told that he could admit them now and they'd be TIC'd. This meant they would be listed on Form 617, and he would sign the form in triplicate. One copy would be his, the next would go to the Magistrates' or Crown Court and the third would be attached to his CRO file. He would then ask the magistrate or judge to take these matters into consideration when being sentenced, and this burglary would be 'cleared-up'. This practice went out of fashion with the Police and Criminal Evidence Act of 1984, which encouraged solicitors to creep out of the woodwork and reduce the flow of justice to a snail's pace. They simply would not permit their clients to have offences TIC'd. 'If you have evidence against my client, officer,' they would say, loftily, 'pray charge him; if not, please stop this harassment.' If the suspect was sent to prison, the officer would often have amassed sufficient evidence by the end of his sentence to nick him as he emerged from the prison gates and charge him; it was something that seriously pissed-off the prisoner who was looking forward to a night out on the town. The detective, too, was not well pleased because he had another court case to deal with all over again, together with the ubiquitous paperwork, when the signing of a few forms at the previous court appearance would have obviated this. The only person who did well out of the whole sorry business was the solicitor, who would rub his hands with glee at the thought of a whole new set of legal aid fees to look forward to.

To counteract this, a new system was evolved: post-sentence prison visits. It was a ridiculous system and it was there to be abused. Two officers would visit an offender who had been sentenced to a substantial amount of imprisonment for burglary and suggest that he clear up the previously undetected burglaries which he had committed. If he did so, they would simply be written off, never to be brought to the attention of magistrates or judges, since he had already been sentenced. In this way, he could never be prosecuted for these offences. It was also broadly hinted that a word could be dropped into a beneficial ear – that of the prison authorities, who might be minded to downgrade his prisoner's category, or perhaps even the parole board. In their eagerness to assist, and working on the assumption that the more they admitted, the better the result, prisoners started admitting to burglaries which they hadn't committed, and, in some cases, couldn't have committed. This was because they were in custody for other offences at the time of the burglary, or because they were basking on a beach in Majorca or, as in one splendid case, because at the time of the offence, the prisoner hadn't yet been born.

What is the point of the wrong man confessing to a crime he hasn't committed? Certainly, the crime's been cleared up but it also means that the real perpetrator is still out there. Not that it mattered to the post-sentence officers, nor to their supervisors who were delighted at having their crime books cleared up. 'What a pair of coppers!' they'd cry. What a load of bollocks. It went on for some time until the whistle was blown on two such characters by a disgruntled fellow officer. Seriously embarrassed senior officers stammered out their excuses to a red-faced Home Office which quite properly put a stop to the whole ridiculous business. A good thing, too. But still the crime figures are massaged: whenever you read about a dramatic fall in violent crime – don't you believe it. Somewhere, someone's cooking the books.

So let's get back to the system in my day – one not without its faults. Although the procedures didn't bear too close an investigation, it was rigorously supported by the senior officers of the CID – until, that is, something went wrong.

Reginald George Grose was known and revered as being a 'character' – one of the highest accolades of the Metropolitan Police. It jostles top place, alongside the recognition of 'Sportsman' in the police, or the East-End distinction of being 'Game'. Mind you, Reggie had quite separate kudos; as a young police constable in the blitz, he had been awarded one of the eighty-two George Medals, won by police officers for heroic work in rescuing Londoners who had been trapped inside their bombed houses. Later, as a member of No. 3 Commando, he was captured during the ill-fated raid on Dieppe in 1942 and suffered terrible deprivations at the hands of the Germans. In due course, he was repatriated and demobilized from the Army and rejoined the Metropolitan Police, only to be given forged discharge papers by the Ghost Squad and infiltrated, undercover, into the post-war London gangs for some hair-raising escapades.

And then, one day, Reggie who by now was working in a divisional CID office, came an absolute cropper after an affluent member of the public reported that his expensive birds had been stolen from his garden. 'Birds flown off, and probably returned to their natural habitat', was the way that

Reggie casually wrote that one off, untruthfully showing a visit to the premises on the Crime Sheet. The very senior officers, who sat in judgement on Reggie's discipline board, were less than impressed, having heard from the furious victim that the missing birds referred to, were in fact, large valuable birds, which had been sculpted out of stone. Having found Reggie guilty of neglect of duty and falsehood in double-quick time, the examining (and let's face it, hypocritical) officers were outraged when he sarcastically asked them to take a further 249 cases into consideration, when passing sentence. Of such stuff are legends made.

My second story all began when an Asian, with very limited English, came into Forest Gate police station to report an incident. I was the officer, extracted from behind a pyramid of paperwork, who was deputed to deal with the matter, and the tale of woe that this gentleman told me, was this:

He had been walking along the road during the evening, when he had been confronted by two youths. One he had described as being white, the other off-white. The white youth had produced a knife and asked how much money he had in his possession. He produced thirty pence, which he held out to the youths. 'Go on, jump up and down,' said the off-white youth. 'See if we can hear any money in your pockets.' Obligingly, the victim jumped up and down, without producing an incriminating jingle, for the simple reason that the thirty pence which he had held out to the youths represented his entire worldly goods.

'Thirty pence? Is that all you've got? You're fucking pathetic,' said the lighter of the two footpads. 'Go on, put it away, and fuck off. And don't go to the police for 24 hours.'

'Would you know them again?' I asked him. 'Can you describe them?'

'Ah, no,' he replied. 'One is white, the other not so white.'

'If they were after your money,' I said, 'why did they give it back to you?'

'I am not knowing,' he replied.

'Whereabouts did all this happen?' I asked.

'I am not knowing that, either,' he replied.

'Well, when did it happen, then?' I enquired.

'Last night,' came the answer.

'*Last bloody night?*' I shouted. 'Why didn't you tell us before?'

'Well,' he replied, 'they say not to. Do not go to the police for 24 hours, they said.'

H-m-m! I thought. Let's have a think about this. When had this happened? No real idea. Where had it happened? No idea at all. Who were the people involved? No one who could be identified by any stretch of the imagination. Had the Asian been hurt? No. Had he been threatened with the knife or threatened verbally? No and No. Had they demanded money from him? No, they'd asked him how much money he'd got with him. Had they taken the money? No. So was this an attempted robbery at all? Well, it's all a matter of interpretation really, isn't it? And the way that I interpreted it was that it was probably a practical joke on the youths' behalf and, because of his limited English, the Asian had failed to detect the humour in it. All right then: a 'crasher' if I ever saw one, and adding my signature with a flourish to the crime report, I returned to my awesome pile of paper which merited my full attention.

Several weeks later, on a Sunday morning, I received a phone call from a detective constable at East Ham police station. 'Grab your Crime Book, and get over here, quick,' he said. 'We've got one in for burglary, and he's admitting some on your patch.'

Now this, as I've said, was a splendid way of clearing up previously undetected crimes, so I hurried over to East Ham, and there, in the CID office, I met an affable young Afro-Caribbean of mixed race. We went through the Crime Book together and he picked out and admitted four or five burglaries.

'Now look,' I said. 'You'll have to do better than that. You've done more than *that*.'

'I ain't,' he replied. 'I can't admit to something I ain't done.'

'OK,' I said. 'Forget burglaries. What else have you been up to? What about a nice flashing?'

'Leave off,' he laughed.

'All right, what else?' I said. 'How about a robbery?'

He hesitated and frowned. 'Robbery's about hurting people, ain't it?' he asked.

'Well, not necessarily,' I replied. 'Robbery can be where you threaten people, without hurting them.'

He paused. 'Well,' he said, slowly. 'There was this geezer we had, one night. I remember, we made him jump up and down.'

I groaned. 'He wasn't an Asian, was he?' I asked.

'Yeah!' he laughed. 'How'd you know, man?'

'Just a shot in the fucking dark,' I muttered and, with a skill born of self-preservation, feverishly started looking for the crime report.

This young man and the rest of his associates, who were implicated in a whole string of robberies and burglaries, were committed for trial to the Central Criminal Court, together with a welter of allegations of police misconduct, made on their behalf by a well-known and thoroughly poisonous East End solicitor.

Strange, how on the morning of what was intended to be

118

the start of a bitterly contested trial of a dozen wholly innocent and brutally abused young men, that these allegations of
a police conspiracy evaporated, when it was discovered that
one of the Old Bailey's barmiest judges was going to try this
case. A plea of 'Guilty', all round, was presented to this judge
(who really was as mad as a bag of bollocks), and he ensured
that the full weight of the law, in the form of a two-year probation order, came crashing down on the shoulders of these
young thugs.

They, of course, were delighted, and whooped with joy.
We, of course, were bamboozled and off we went to 'The
Feathers' to drown our sorrows.

Even less impressed than we, were the elderly victims, who
were disgustingly tortured and murdered by two of the worst
of the gang members, a few months later. I harboured the
unworthy thought for years afterwards – in fact, I still do –
that if they had been sentenced to an appropriate term of
imprisonment for the crimes that we had arrested them for,
the murders wouldn't have occurred.

Well, that's me. Biased as buggery.

A Square Peg in a Deep Hole

In a nutshell, the Flying Squad exists, as it has done for the past 85 years or so, to arrest top criminals. It is therefore reasonable to assume that the detectives best suited for the task should staff and also lead it. In the majority of cases, this has been so; but there have been police officers posted to the Squad who have been utterly unsuited to the work or, indeed, any type of work. Totally unaware of criminals and their activities, demonstrably useless at any type of investigation, pitifully unable to run informants and downright dangerous when putting pen to paper, they represent dead-weight; all the more infuriating when nothing is done to get rid of them and also when so many competent Squad officers know excellent, keen detectives out on Division who have been passed over for this worthless crew.

A classic case in question arose when I was approached by an extremely worried detective constable on the Flying Squad. A certain officer had been selected for the Squad, he told me, and was only waiting for a vacancy to appear before he was posted. 'He's a wrong'un, Dick,' said the DC, and I gave a sharp intake of breath when he added, 'He's selling drugs and middling in stolen jewellery. If he comes up here, I'm off – there's no way I'm getting involved in any jobs with that bastard.' I went and saw a senior officer – a notoriously weak individual – and told him what had occurred. In addition, I too had heard nothing good about the officer who was, to all intents and purposes, on

his way to the Squad, so I added my two penn'oth, as well. The
senior officer helplessly shrugged his shoulders. 'What can I
do?' he wailed. 'Now he's been accepted for the Squad, I can't
undo it . . . he'll just have to come up, that's all . . . we'll have
to – you know – just keep an eye on him.'

I thought I was going to throw up. 'What can you do?' I
echoed. 'You can go to the Commander and tell him what I've
just told you; the DC and I will come with you. The lad who
told me this is as sound as a bell and if he says an Old Bill's
dodgy, then believe me, he is. We can knock this on the head,
right now – we need a wrong'un on the Squad like we need a
dose of the clap.' Privately, I thought to myself, 'Keep an eye
on him? Christ, with Squad-work, you need eyes in your arse
to keep the armed robbers from having one over on you, let
alone having one of your own who's bent!' This, I felt, would
have been lost on the senior officer, who flapped his hands
around for a bit and all but chewed the edge of his hankie. 'I
don't see there's anything we can do . . . can't go to the commander with something like that . . .'

I stood up. 'Well, there's something that I can do,' I said.
'I'm going back to my desk and I'm writing an account of our
conversation in my pocket book. If chummy comes up and the
wheel comes off – and it will – your head's going to be on the
block.'

Now, the senior officer could have got round this and saved
face at the same time, by saying, 'All right, Dick, all right. I
can see this is something you really feel strongly about. Come
on, we'll go and see the commander together.' But he didn't.
Not because he was dishonest himself, because he wasn't. He
simply didn't want to cause waves by addressing the problem
head-on and hoped that if the bent copper did come up on the
Squad, he'd have a change of heart and – er – you know –
behave himself.

Well, the rogue officer never did come up on the Squad. Before his posting could be implemented, he was suspended from duty. His next move was to the Old Bailey and thence, to serve a substantial period of imprisonment for dishonesty. We all sighed with relief. The loudest exhalation came from the senior officer who was posted elsewhere, on promotion.

One person who did disastrously serve on the Squad, long before I did, was the officer I shall call Detective Constable Brian Huggins. It was not so much astounding that he served on the Squad; what was amazing was how he was ever accepted into the Metropolitan Police in the first place . . .

Huggins had scraped through his two-year probationary period as a police constable, with the absolute minimum of work. His successes – and they were few and far between – he elevated out of all proportion. His catastrophic cock-ups – and they were many – were minimized and, to a certain extent, hushed-up by his reporting sergeant, who wanted nothing more than a quiet life. When this was not possible, Huggins would endeavour to turn these bloomers to his own advantage by putting the blame on others. In common with many inadequates, he sneered at and belittled his contemporaries and was cordially disliked.

He became an aid to CID – there was an acute shortage, at the time – and relied on others to produce results. When they did, he was quick to claim them, overtly, as his own; when they did not, he was first in line for the jeering and finger-poking. To the astonishment of all who knew him, Huggins was appointed to the CID.

Stepping from being a police constable to detective constable is not promotion, no matter what some bumptious and insecure CID officers might tell you; but it is a large step, none the less. Huggins could have capitalized on it. He could have knuckled down, listened to the advice of his peers, kept his mouth shut and his eyes and ears open, and, one day, he might have made a competent, although not a great detective. Since he possessed less common sense than God gives to an average goat, he did not. He blundered through the Crime Book entries that were allocated to him, not having the slightest ability or, let it be said, desire to solve the crimes through sheer detective work. Informants might have helped him, but his inability to promote confidence in criminals, or anybody else for that matter, blocked this particular avenue of success in the world of criminal investigation. Many officers – and I was certainly one of them – were helped enormously by tips and advice from the Uniform Branch. But Huggins, who had only recently left their ranks, decided that he was now definitely a cut above them and his idea of interdepartmental cooperation was to patronize them mercilessly, earning himself their profound contempt. In short – and I hope I am not putting the matter too high – practically everyone regarded Brian Huggins as being a 22-carat prick.

But not everybody. During the internal investigation that followed Huggins' demise, it was earnestly desired to discover who it was who put his name in 'The Book' – that unofficial notebook, kept in the Flying Squad's divisional office, in which Squad officers entered the particulars of their protégés for appointment to the Squad. Unfortunately, the page containing Huggins' details had been neatly and mysteriously removed and, rumour had it, burnt, and the ashes surrendered to the four winds. Nevertheless, what was not in dispute was that in *Police Orders* was an entry which revealed that PC (CID) Huggins was transferred from 'J' Division to COC8 – the Flying Squad.

Huggins had carefully researched the way in which he considered a Squad officer should speak, whilst he was still a divisional officer. He peppered his conversation with phrases such as, 'grab some wheels' (acquire a car) 'get a brief' (procure a search warrant) 'give 'im a spin' (search a suspect's premises) and most annoying of all, to refer to his fellow CID officers as, 'Handsome'. This wearisome practice continued until one of them demanded to know if he'd like to be known as, 'Broken-nose'.

Thus, Huggins came to the Squad. He continued his she-nanigans and was promptly sent to Coventry; he was excep-tionally lucky to avoid serious bodily injury. Ostracized by his fellows, Huggins longed for 'A Big Job' – one that would push him to the forefront of the Flying Squad and one which would cover him in laurels. Given his inability to put together the simplest of cases, plus the fact that he was ignored by the other Squad officers, this appeared to be highly unlikely. And then one day, this happened . . .

Huggins was sitting alone in the Squad office, when one of the switchboard operators stated that a caller wished to provide some information. His ears pricked up and Huggins asked for the caller to be transferred to his extension.

If Huggins had possessed even the slightest knowledge of the criminality of the East End of London, when the pro-fessional informant whom I shall call Herbie Watkins asked Huggins if he had ever heard of him, he would have replied, with a laugh, 'Get lost!' and slammed the telephone down, thankful that he had not provided him with his name. But of course, he did not. In fact, he arranged a meet with him.

The name of Herbie Watkins was known and reviled by every active CID officer throughout East London. Watkins' stock-in-trade was to carry out a crime, usually a burglary, and get the best price possible for half the proceeds. The other half would be planted on a fellow criminal who had incurred Watkins' displeasure. His next step would be to inform the police that stolen property was to be found at the other crim-inal's address. When the address was raided and the property discovered, the criminal would naturally deny all knowledge, but who would believe him? Watkins would then receive a reward from the Yard's Informant Fund plus the ten per cent reward from the loss adjusters who were dealing with the insurance claim in respect of the stolen property. Not only that, but Watkins had got a rival criminal out of circulation and had gained a valuable contact in the CID, one who hopefully could come to his aid if he were compromised. This disgraceful behaviour soon became common knowledge and any self-respecting CID officer gave Watkins a definite miss.

Upon their first acquaintance with Watkins, many people came to the conclusion that they were addressing a child molester, because with his laboured breathing and a permanent leer which revealed crooked, discoloured teeth, Herbie Watkins did have a certain nonce-like air about him. In fact, child molestation was one of the very few offences which did not appear in his bulging CRO file. But Brian Huggins could not have cared less. As the two men sat at the stained table in the Canning Town café, Huggins was almost beside himself with excitement, having secured a real, live informant.

Talking during the exercise period in prison had, as an offence, gone the way of the cat-o'-nine-tails, but Watkins still persisted in talking out of the corner of his mouth, in rather confusing cockney shorthand. 'Do the job – bosh – get the gear – wallop – put it on 'im – give you a bell – spin the gaff – sorted – a right nice drink. Right?

Huggins had caught about one word in four but he was fairly unconcerned; he only knew that the big job he had longed for was on its way to him. Giving Watkins his home telephone number, he rushed back to the Yard and interrupted his detective inspector who was in the middle of compiling a rather complicated report concerning the activities of a team of safe blowers.

'Guv, how do you get a reward for an informant?' he asked, breathlessly.

The DI frowned and put his pen down. Surely this obnoxious young man must know something as fundamental as *that*? But he was a patient man and he told Huggins that which every working detective knows: an informant puts up some work, such as where stolen property is stashed. A search warrant is procured, the premises searched, and if the property is there, the arrest is made and the prisoner charged. Then a report is submitted outlining the circumstances, a sum of money is granted which is handed over to the informant who signs a receipt for it using his pseudonym. The informant's real identity, in those days at least, was known only to his handler.

'Thanks, Guv,' replied Huggins and raced out of the office. The DI shook his head. The types they were getting on the Squad, these days! What he had *not* said, purely because it was such common sense, was that when an officer received the information, he checked it out as much as possible to try to corroborate the information before ever applying for a search warrant. And, also, the person who was found to be in possession of that property was *not* automatically arrested and charged; he was questioned about how the property came to be there. But, for now, the DI picked up his pen and resumed the compilation of his report and forgot about the matter. Later, when the senior officers from the investigating team questioned him about the conversation, he blandly replied that *of course* he had mentioned those points to Huggins.

Later the same evening, Watkins pulled up in his van in north-west London. He had never been to the address before but he knew that that slag, Ronnie Davis lived in Church Road, NW4. It was high time that he was paid back. He peered at the street sign. Yes, that was it. He drove slowly along the road until he came to the house. It looked a pretty posh sort of drum for that slag Davis; he must have come up in the world after cheating him out of that gear, mused Watkins. It took only a minute for his skeleton keys to open the garage door and slip the gear inside; then he was in his van and away. As he reached the road junction, he peered left and right to ensure that the traffic was clear and then he saw the name of the road more clearly; in fact, he had visited an address in Church Row, NW3. He cursed under his breath – he could hardly go back and retrieve the stuff. It had been dodgy enough putting it in there. Then he grinned. So what? Whatever happened, he would get his reward money and Ronnie Davis could be sorted out another day. He drove to the nearest telephone box and dialled Huggins' number.

The following morning, the occupier of the house in Church Row was awakened by knocking at his front door that was so thunderous that he shot bolt upright in bed. He looked quickly at the bedside clock – 6.40 – thrust his feet into a pair of Fortnum & Mason's monogrammed slippers, pulled on a silk Sulka dressing-gown and as the deafening pounding continued, he padded downstairs. Pulling open the front door, he was confronted by five rather tough-looking and resolute men. The annoyed and, by now rather apprehensive, householder got as far as, 'What the devil do you think –' before the person who appeared to be the leader of the group – and reader, you will not be astonished to know that his name was Detective Constable Brian Huggins – pushed his way past him and into the hallway. 'All right, handsome, relax. It's the Squad, see? Got a brief to turn you over.' And Huggins pulled back his jacket to reveal a folded piece of paper protruding from his inside pocket which might, or might not have been a search warrant. He made no attempt to produce it.

Huggins was quite unaware of the identity of the householder who, in fact, was a highly respected surgeon. Not only had he received one of the very few Military Crosses awarded to officers serving with the Royal Army Medical Corps in Korea for coolness and courage under fire whilst carrying out a delicate operation, but he had also been knighted for his services to neurosurgery.

As the rest of the Flying Squad officers trooped into his hallway, Sir Donald McKenzie trembled with rage at the insolence of the young man who had dared to speak to him in such an insulting manner and, at that moment, he was joined by Lady McKenzie, who swept imperiously down the staircase. 'Donald, what on earth – who are these –' she began, before being interrupted by Huggins. 'All right, Darlin', all right. No drama. It's the Squad, paying you a little visit, that's all. Tell you what, be a good girl and put the kettle on – mine's two sugars.'

Lady McKenzie, who had recently been appointed OBE in recognition of her tireless work with a charity helping Third World orphans and who was also distantly related to the royal family, simply gaped at Huggins; like her husband, she was completely unused to such studied insolence. As her jaw dropped lower and lower, Huggins turned to Sir Donald. 'Come on, Handsome, let's see what you've got in your garage.'

One of the other Flying Squad officers looked nervously around the hallway. He was unaware that the painting of the sleepy-looking woman with the funny-shaped head was by an artist named Modigliani, nor would the name have meant anything to him; similarly, he did not know that the matching Chinese vases came from the T'ang Dynasty but what he did know was that all this spelt class, and trouble, and he wished he'd never volunteered for this operation with that little prick – Higgins? Hawkins? Whatever. He gave a significant glance to another Squad officer who was thinking exactly the same. The two remaining Squad officers were several jumps ahead of their colleagues; they *knew* something was well and truly up and they were muttering contingency plans for when the wheel came off, as it was now inevitable that it would. The thought that was at the forefront of all their minds was when that idiot Hickling, or whatever his fucking name was, failed to find anything in the garage, they would firmly discourage him from searching the rest of the house, make their apologies and push off.

Meanwhile, Sir Donald had unlocked the garage and the oiled door slid smoothly upwards. Inside, was a highly polished Bentley, a row of gleaming tools on the wall and, on the floor, a grubby sack. Huggins whooped with delight, snatched it up and returned to the house, the thoroughly bemused neurosurgeon trailing along in his wake.

In the drawing-room, in front of the fireplace, with Sir Donald and Lady McKenzie and the four other Squad officers forming a semi-circle, Huggins tipped out the contents of the sack. The items which now reposed on a rather expensive seventeenth-century Damascus rug were as follows:

A quantity of silver ornaments, which would later be identified as being the part-proceeds of a smash & grab at a jewellers at Gants Hill, a couple of days previously.

A .45 Webley revolver, which was so rusted that any attempt to fire it would have caused the user's hand to be blown off.

A small but sickening collection of child pornography and, as the cherry to top the cake, a block of cannabis resin.

As the couple stared goggle-eyed at the items on their rug, Huggins roared with laughter, born of relief; for a time, he had feared that Watkins had given him the wrong address!

'Who's a naughty boy, then?' he chuckled. 'Ever been in trouble before, Handsome?' Sir Donald dumbly shook his head. 'Bleedin' are now, though, ain't yer?' commented Huggins and, then, turning to Lady McKenzie, 'Come on, Darlin', where's that tea?'

It was this last remark that provided the final straw. Lady McKenzie's head jerked up and a steely look came into her eye. She stated that she was going to make a telephone call, and, no, in answer to Huggins' question, she was not going 'to give her brief a bell'.

If a rogue asteroid had burst through the Earth's atmosphere and landed in The Wash, effectively taking out much of Norfolk, Lincolnshire and Cambridgeshire and causing much of the surrounding countryside to become rather damp, it would not have matched the catastrophic effect that the result of Lady McKenzie's telephone call would have.

Lady McKenzie's father, a Gloucestershire landowner and an MP, who up until that very moment had been a passionate advocate of law and order in general and the police in particular, was irritated at having to answer his telephone so early in the morning. Within seconds his petulance turned to rage. Telling his daughter to 'leave it to him', he immediately telephoned the prime minister, who was staying at Chequers. The furious prime minister telephoned the home secretary; in turn, he called the commissioner of police at his home. The head of London's finest hit the roof – then he telephoned the assistant commissioner (Crime) who actually stood to attention by his bedside; he then bellowed his displeasure down the phone to the commander of the Flying Squad.

Several of the residents of the quiet residential side-turning of Bexleyheath who had started out to work were appalled to hear the torrent of blasphemous filth that was emitted from the commander's open bedroom window; in fact, his wife

spent the rest of that day and some of the next, apologizing
to the neighbours for her husband's immoderate language.
His mind made up, the commander picked up the telephone
again, dialled the home number of his personal driver and
told him to bring the car round; no, not at 9 o'clock – *right
fucking now*!

Back at Church Row, it was now abundantly clear to all the
Flying Squad officers – with the exception of Huggins, that
is – what had occurred. One was already murmuring apologies to the incensed householders and was not particularly
surprised when his generous offer of two places at the top
table of the forthcoming Flying Squad dinner and dance was
curtly refused.

Meanwhile, another had taken Huggins to one side and
told him that it would not be a good idea to drag the householder off and charge him with receiving stolen goods, nor
would it be prudent to pull in his stuck-up old tart of a wife
as well, and charge her as an accessory. Far better, he suggested, would be for Huggins to make his way to the local
nick, make a report of the search and then return to the Yard.
The rest of the team would not, unfortunately, be able to
accompany him, since they had a pressing engagement elsewhere. In fact, the other two Squad officers had already left.

The seething Squad commander stepped out of the lift at
the fourth floor of the Victoria Block at New Scotland Yard.
He was as certain as he could be that his half-promised
Queen's Police Medal for distinguished service was about to
be hoiked right out of the Honours List – he was right – and
as he emerged into the passageway, the first person he saw was
Huggins, who had arrived only moments before. 'Get in my
office,' said the commander, through gritted teeth.

Nobody knows what was said in the commander's office
during that short and exceedingly one-sided interview; the

commander never mentioned it and Huggins certainly did not. But within five minutes, Huggins erupted from the office, close to tears. Not only was he off the Squad, he was out of the CID, as well. He went straight to his second fitting of the day, at Lambeth clothing store, where he was given an itchy, and not particularly well-cut suit of blue serge; his next port of call was the divisional headquarters of 'L' Division.

The uniformed commander of the division, who had been fully appraised of the disgraceful circumstances surrounding Huggins' departure from the CID, welcomed him to Brixton police station with a wintry smile. He was a man well-known for his sardonic sense of humour.

'I should think,' he said smoothly, 'that you must be extremely pleased with your posting here for what remains of your career, which, I feel sure, will be a short one.'

Huggins, who had been contemplating the enormous amount of travelling time from his three-bedroomed semi in Hornchurch to here, thought his new boss must be potty.

'You see,' continued the commander, 'from what I've been hearing about you, I was convinced that your next posting would certainly be to Brixton but I was under the impression that it would be to the prison, rather than the nick!'

Neatly Wrapped Up

The case which follows was probably the most unpleasant of my career and the arrest that I made in respect of it was one that was personally the most satisfying. I've got a lot of hard things to say about quite a number of people who feature in the story and I've changed the names of everybody concerned, especially the victims who, although I doubt very much if any are still alive, would not care to be reminded of their ordeals. Included in this anonymity are the identities of the two criminals who, the newspapers later reported, spread 'a reign of terror'. Without doubt, Brown and Black, as I shall call them, were the most spineless, cowardly pieces of garbage that I ever had to deal with. Out of the thousands of criminals with whom I had dealings, even in the most hard-boiled of cases, it was possible to find some spark of humanity and decency. But Brown, particularly, was the only criminal whom I ever met who possessed not one single redeeming trait. Cunning, vicious, vindictive and manipulative, it came as no surprise to me to learn that he was loathed in prison as much as he was during his periods of liberty.

It began in September 1979. It was the first of five attacks on elderly people, the youngest of whom was seventy-four and the eldest, eighty-three years of age. Each of the robberies followed the same brutal pattern. Brown and Black, carrying a parcel, would knock on the pensioner's door, which was always situated in a prosperous area. Explaining that they had

135

a parcel for delivery, the pensioner would take possession of it, and Brown and Black would seize this opportunity to rush into the house. Having gained entry, they would subject their victim to a sickeningly brutal attack, bind and gag them, ransack the house, stealing their victims' most sentimental possessions, and leave totally unconcerned as to the fate of their victims who were still tied up.

So the area was chosen carefully for its prosperity, as were the victims for their age and frailty. Not only would they be unable to put up the sort of resistance expected from a younger person, but should this cowardly pair have the misfortune to be arrested, identification might prove difficult owing to their victims' deteriorating eyesight.

Take, for example, the case of Mrs Jones. An hour before she was attacked, she had taken medication for her heart condition. It was this one factor that she attributed to surviving her ordeal. She later told me that having been attacked and tied up, she begged her assailants not to restrict her breathing by taping her mouth, having explained to them the seriousness of her heart condition. Brown, the piece of tape outstretched in his hands, extended towards her mouth, paused, and then put the tape down. Mrs Jones sighed with relief – at least she would be spared that. Her comfort was premature. With a look of near-imbecilic pleasure, Brown took a thicker, wider piece of tape and covered her mouth with it. It was hardly surprising that her condition deteriorated substantially after the attack.

The next victim, Mrs Smith, had a nervous disposition even before the robbery; her terror following the attack can be well imagined. Sleep was denied her for months afterwards.

Mr White had a box of coins stolen and, most upsetting of all, his gold, folding eye glasses . . .

The most cowardly attack of all was on Mr Green. He had

already suffered a serious stroke which had left his speech impaired and one side of his body partially paralysed. He was treated to even more callousness than Brown and Black had meted out to the rest of their victims. Following the attack, Mr Green's health deteriorated to such a degree that he was confined to a wheelchair for the rest of his life.

'They've done it again,' said the detective chief inspector, who had called me and another sergeant into his office. 'This morning, they were at Hornchurch – the same M.O. Drop all your current cases and reassign them to somebody else. Get out and nick these two bastards before we've got a murder on our hands.' The DCI wasn't being over emotive, either; the fact that nobody had been killed so far was nothing short of a miracle.

We retired to a vacant interview room and read and re-read the statements. We had reasonable descriptions of the pair. And just one lead. At the scene of one of the robberies, one of the neighbours had seen a white hire van nearby. We made a list of the rental company addresses who leased white vans. The following morning, we would start with the nearest, to see if they could help. If not, go to the next one – and then the next . . .

The next morning, we booked out to the hire company in the Duty Book. As we went to leave the office, the DCI stuck his head round his office door. 'I've got the list of property nicked from the Hornchurch job,' he called, waving the scrap of teleprinter message. 'And listen! One of the items stolen was a loaded revolver – watch yourselves!'

As we drew up outside the rental company, so a man walked out of the office. He bore a strong resemblance to one of the robbers. In fact, he proved to be Brown. He hung about and appeared to be waiting for somebody. Eventually he was joined by another man and he, too, bore a strong resemblance to the

137

second robber, who it transpired, was Black. Both of them went to an old van parked nearby and got in. Although we were unaware of it at the time, this van had been stolen that morning.

We stopped them, got them out of the van, separated and questioned them. I spoke to Brown – what an unpleasant creature he was. Short, dark-haired and stocky, he was evasive and oily. I later noticed that he spoke with a marked Jewish accent when he was trying to promote credibility – his accent was very pronounced, right now. If he was indeed Jewish, as he asserted he was, I can only think that the whole Jewish community must have reviled him. I told him to open the back doors of the van. Very slowly and unwillingly, he did so. There, in the back of the van, were three boxes containing valuables and quite a lot of silverware and also rubber gloves, tape and ropes, and immediately the suspicions that I had been harbouring were confirmed. I grabbed hold of his wrist to stop him escaping.

Over the years, I've often thought about that arrest and I find it difficult to put what happened into words. Brown, when he had been engaged in lawful employment (it had not been often) had been a scaffolder and his wrists were thick and muscular. But as I grabbed hold of him, his wrist seemed to deflate and it was as if any pluck or resolution that he possessed was pouring out of the ends of his fingers, as though a tap had been turned on. Bizarre, I know; I'm afraid I can't explain it any better than that. 'All right, mister,' he whined in that almost guttural accent. 'I von't be no trubble.' That, I can assure you, was to be the understatement of the year.

The revolver was recovered from a jacket Brown had in his possession: a stolen jacket, naturally. En route to the police station, he unsuccessfully attempted to dispose of the remainder of the cartridges, because both robbers were later to admit firing off two rounds, following the robbery.

Neatly Wrapped Up

Brown confessed to everything. Not only did he admit the robberies, he confessed to stealing cars, dumping them and stealing others nearby. We checked this out: the stealing, dumping and fresh stealing of the cars agreed completely with everything he'd said. Everything in their possession was examined and checked. Brown said that a clip-board which we found in the van was stolen from a goods yard: it was. He told us that he'd tried to sell some of the gear to the son of a notorious gangster – we checked, and the gangster's son confirmed that this was so.

Black denied everything. At the time of the robberies, he said, he had been in the company of a friend, who would verify this. We took him to the friend's house and put the matter of the alibi to him. The friend angrily repudiated it and Black's denials collapsed; he too, admitted everything.

All the stolen property was identified by the victims. Brown's fingerprints were found on one of the bogus parcels, left at the scene of one of the robberies. They were charged with a whole range of offences and appeared at the Magistrates' Court and were remanded in custody. A nice job, all topped and tailed? Don't you believe it. The fun was just about to begin.

Black had one very minor conviction; Brown had a lot more. By now, it had obviously percolated through to them that they were in a lot of trouble, and it was on the cards that they were going to cop quite a bit of porridge, even on a guilty plea – in front of the right judge, that is. Brown instructed a solicitor whom he'd used before; it was widely held in police circles that they were as crooked as the people whom they represented. I'd had dealings with them for years – it was a view with which I fully concurred.

Did they really think they could bluff their way out of these very serious charges to which they'd confessed? What I think is indisputable is that they were going to cause as much upset for everybody concerned. With the police, in particular, so much shit was slung that they felt that some of it must surely stick.

The first intimation of Brown's sordid behaviour was when he instructed a woman barrister in the cells at the Magistrates' Court. In fact, I knew her: a very attractive young woman, she had been part of the defence team at a protracted trial of mine, which had finished a year or so previously, and I'd got on well with her. Now, she emerged from the cell area, shut her eyes and shuddered. 'Never,' she said through gritted teeth, 'will I ever appear for that disgusting creature, again!' I couldn't really ask what had transpired and she wouldn't have told me if I had. So I simply asked if she fancied a drink. 'No, thanks,' she smiled and as she turned and walked off, she called over her shoulder, 'What I need, right now, is a bath!' I sympathized; Brown brought out that reaction in people.

Because of the seriousness of the charges, this was a case where the prisoners had to be tried before a judge and jury at the Crown Court. In order to arrive at the higher court, they first had to be committed from the Magistrates' Court. All the prosecution statements were served on the defence, and if they agreed that there was what was known as a *prima facie* case – a case where the allegations were sufficiently supported by evidence to call for an answer – the matter could be dealt with by what was known as a Section 1 committal. It meant that the prisoner would be formally committed to stand his trial at the Crown Court, either on bail or in custody. By accepting that there was a case to answer did not necessarily mean that the prisoner was going to plead guilty; that was something that would be dealt with at the Crown Court.

If, on the other hand, either the prosecution or the defence felt that a case was weak, they could ask that the evidence be tested by the prosecution witnesses giving evidence at the Magistrates' Court. There, their evidence would be taken down in longhand by the clerk of the court and the witnesses could be cross-examined. If the magistrates decided that there was a case to answer, they would then commit the prisoner to the Crown Court; if not, he would be discharged. This was known as a Section 7 committal.

But as you will already have realized, the case was not weak; indeed, it was very strong, but a Section 7 committal was what Brown and Black demanded, and what they wanted, they got. It was a way of dragging out the proceedings and, as they appeared, week after week, a source of tremendous fun for Brown especially, screaming abuse at both police and the magistrates.

They demanded identification parades, which necessitated their frail (and often quite ill) victims attending the line-ups; and when those victims came to the Section 7 committal to give their evidence, it was the perfect opportunity for Brown and Black to jeer at them and insult them. They knew this behaviour wouldn't endear them to the magistrates but so what? They weren't going to be granted bail in a thousand years, so they might as well have a little fun as they stretched out proceedings more and more and their solicitors got richer on the legal aid contributions. At one of the Friday remands, Brown suddenly leapt to his feet, shouting, 'Mister! Mister!' to the Bench. Adopting his thick accent, he cried, 'I vant to apply to have the remand changed to another day – see, I'm Jewish and the prison bus gets back so late and I can't start observing the Shabbat!' With that he sat back down in the dock and the magistrates went into a huddle to discuss this dilemma. As they did so, Brown was doubled up in the dock, almost pissing himself as he rocked backwards and forwards,

shaking with silent laughter. I looked at the Bench, still in
their tight, concerned huddle. 'Why can't you clowns look up
right now and see he's taking the piss out of you?' I thought,
sourly.

During another remand, Black attacked the other officer in
the case, and he and Brown both attacked other police officers; it was the one occasion on which, to my infinite regret,
I was not present. They were charged with these assaults on
the police and demanded trial by jury, so that no doubt the
proceedings could be dragged out even longer. But this was
an offence which only the prosecution could elect trial by jury
and they decided it should be dealt with at the lower court.
They now demanded to be tried at another Magistrates' Court
on the grounds that the present one would be partial towards
them. They got their wish, and Black eventually was sentenced to two months' imprisonment and Brown to three
months. Both immediately appealed against conviction to
Snaresbrook Crown Court; the appeals were dismissed.
Finally, they were committed, in custody to stand their trial
at the Old Bailey on the robbery charges.

And I said the fun had begun. It hadn't really started.

The prosecuting barrister at the Bailey decided that the
indictment should be split into three separate trials; a jury
could not be expected to understand the intricacies of a case
as complex as this, he said. This was vigorously opposed by
the other officer and myself; we knew full well that by split-
ting the indictment, an enormous amount of evidence would
be lost and, what was more, the thought that a jury would not
be able to comprehend this case in its entirety was absurd. It
did no good – we were overruled.

The trial opened at the Bailey, with Brown and Black
charged with just two of the robberies, possession of a firearm
and taking a vehicle without consent. Almost a year had

elapsed since their arrest, such were the delaying tactics they'd employed and, doubtless, in the expectation that some, if not all of their elderly victims had died. I was not impressed in the slightest with prosecuting counsel and even less with the judge. Nobody had ever heard of him before; I believe that this was the first criminal case he had tried. Prior to this, I believe he specialized in bankruptcy cases. By comparison, the defence team were heavyweights.

The defence put forward by Brown and Black was this. Everything the police said was a lie. All the incriminating evidence, including the fingerprints found at the scene of one of the robberies, was planted. The confessions had been fabricated. Black had signed his confession, it was true, but he had been forced to do so. Brown had not signed his notes, but evidence was given that he had initialled them. This, Brown denied. The initials, said Brown, were not his; obviously Kirby had forged them.

'Right,' said prosecuting counsel, during an adjournment. 'Get a handwriting expert up here to prove they're his initials.'

'But with that minimal amount of questioned handwriting, it simply can't be done,' I protested. I explained how I had just finished a long trial where handwriting and its analysis had played a crucial part in the case and, believe me, I knew what could and couldn't be proved by handwriting experts. 'The very best a handwriting expert can say is that it might be Brown's handwriting,' I said. 'It's not going to take us any further forward.' It was bad enough that I'd argued with the barrister about the indictment; now, with this business about the handwriting, it was too much. He drew himself up to his full height and looked at me sternly.

'Get him here!' he commanded.

It was the beginning of the nightmare. God knows where the Forensic Science Laboratory had dragged up this specimen from, but he was the defence team's dream. 'I have examined the questioned initials, together with the samples provided by the defendant Brown,' he said, 'and I have come to the conclusion that the samples bear no similarities to the questioned writing.' (Hardly surprising, I thought!) 'There is also the possibility that the defendant might have written the initials and then disguised his handwriting when he provided the samples, but I do not give much credence to this. I also examined the handwriting of the alleged confession and it is not disputed that Detective Sergeant Kirby wrote this. He could have written the initials as well, in a clumsy attempt to forge them!' My jaw dropped – Jesus Christ, what was going on! I glanced at the jury – some furious looks were coming my way. I was seething; I saw the prosecuting counsel shortly afterwards. 'Let me know if you have any more fucking brilliant ideas like that!' I snapped.

'If we hadn't have called a handwriting expert,' he replied, snottily, 'the defence could have said that we'd something to hide.'

'Oh, well that's all right, then,' I said, sarcastically. 'Now that the jury's convinced that I'm a fucking forger!'

'Nonsense!' the barrister said, although I detected a look in his eye that suggested that he was fully convinced of my alleged duplicity.

Next came the matter of Brown's fingerprints on the parcel, which he and Black had abandoned following their brutal attack on the disabled Mr Green. We'd planted his fingerprints on it: easy. (This was a common, if desperate ploy used by criminals; but how do you plant fingerprints on an item? I'm buggered if I know.) In fact, it was not so easy. You see, the box had been submitted to the Fingerprint Department at the Yard, prior to the arrest of Brown and Black. Even so, the civilian van driver who had picked up and conveyed the exhibit to the Yard was brought to the Bailey and rigorously cross-examined about the times he had picked up and deposited the item – in fact, every step of that exhibit was accounted for, with every person who dealt with it being called and cross-examined until it was proved beyond any doubt whatsoever that the fingerprints were well and truly on that box, prior to the arrests. Do you know, the poor old civilian van driver was so traumatized by the cross-examination, that every time I saw him after that – and I'm talking about seeing him at Chigwell Sports Club, after I'd retired – he would drop his eyes, jump into his van and drive away. Apart from planting the fingerprints of someone I didn't even know existed, I expect he'd heard that I was a forger of signatures, as well. So that was the planted fingerprint theory kicked into touch. Something a bit better than that would have to be concocted. Something was.

Brown was in the witness box, giving evidence. As usual, he was adopting his Jewish accent, still in the belief it would give him credibility. Because he had attacked the characters of the prosecution witnesses, his previous convictions had been exposed to the jury. Since they now knew he was a criminal, he thought he had best adopt a different criminal lifestyle. He therefore put forward a daring defence. 'Me? I ged my money by dealing drugs vith liddle kids,' he whined. 'Bud robbery? Nah. Nod my scene.'

'How, then,' asked the barrister, 'did your fingerprints get on to the box?'

'The day before the robbery,' replied Brown, 'this geezer comes up to my place with that box with a load of silver and stuff in it. Course, it was nicked wasn't it? So I had it, didn't I? Took the box off him, so that's how my dabs got on it. When he went, he takes the box with him, didn't he? He must have done the robbery the next day – and, of course, all the other robberies. Course, if the police had charged me with receiving stolen property, I wouldn't have had a leg to stand on.' He gave his imbecilic look of delight to the jury. 'But they didn't, did they?'

Of course, I knew that Brown wouldn't be able to supply the man's name; except that he did. I did some checking and discovered that he was inside, doing twelve years for armed robbery. We went and saw him and told him what Brown had said. The robber's reluctance at assisting the police with their enquiries was overtaken by his loathing for Brown and, in fact, he was a pretty impressive witness at the Bailey. He made no attempt to conceal his contempt for Brown and was unwisely tuned-up by the defence counsel who sneered, 'Of course, you're a highly respectable armed robber, aren't you?' This caused the robber to lose his rag and he roared, 'At least I don't go around wrapping up geriatrics!' which went down quite well with the jury.

Brown and Black put up alibis for their whereabouts at the times of the robberies of such a nebulous nature that it should have been impossible to have proved or disproved them; in fact, we were able to demolish them, completely.

They were both found guilty of the robberies and I gave their antecedents. 'Who, in your opinion, was the ringleader?' queried the judge. 'Brown, without a doubt,' I answered shortly, anticipating a mouthful of abuse from Brown. He didn't disappoint me.

Brown got eight years and Black, four years. I thought the sentences were risible. Well, now for the rest of the charges. Perhaps when they'd been dealt with, they'd get a more realistic sentence. But on the advice of the prosecution barrister, no further trials were forthcoming. We were furious, but worse was to come. Instead of allowing these very serious outstanding robbery charges to remain on the file, not to be proceeded with, without leave of the court or the Court of Appeal (Criminal Division), two months later, the prosecution acceded to an application made by the defence and allowed the entire remainder of the indictment to be quashed. Well, you might say, so what? The prosecution wasn't going to proceed in any event, so what did it matter whether the outstanding charges were left on the file or completely dropped?

Quite a lot, actually. Brown still had one more card up his sleeve.

One month after the indictment had been quashed, I received a letter from Brown's solicitor. In it, they had the blatant impudence to demand the return of all the outstanding silverware and jewellery to Brown. It was his property and, after all, he was innocent of any charges in respect of that property. In fact, they reminded me smoothly, the prosecution had dropped all the outstanding charges.

Now, what normally happened in circumstances where there was a dispute as to the ownership of property in a criminal case, would be that the property would be retained by the police and both parties concerned would be invited to sue the police under the provisions of the Police (Property) Act 1897. The case would be heard at a Magistrates' Court, both parties would put their claims forward and the magistrate would decide who the owner would be.

But of course, there was no dispute. Brown, despite what he now said, had admitted obtaining this property by robbing the rightful owners of it. The property had been correctly identified by the losers. And if that useless prat of a barrister had done his job properly and proceeded against Brown and Black for all the robberies, this matter couldn't have arisen. Naturally, this was further evidence of Brown's twisted vicious personality. What fun it would be to have a few days – well, weeks, if he could stretch it that far – out in court, jeering at his victims at their pathetic attempts to get their treasured possessions back. Those that made it, of course. Remember Mr White, who had had his gold, folding eye glasses stolen? Well, he'd died. If proceedings had been taken on that robbery charge, perhaps there'd have been a case of murder that could have been brought against these two heroes. Not now, of course. Not now that the prosecution had allowed the indictment to be quashed.

So do you know what I thought to myself? Fuck that for a game of soldiers, I thought, and gathering up all the stolen property, I rushed around to all of the victims and restored the property to them, against receipt. And I told them all – Mrs White especially, as I handed her her late husband's gold spectacles – that they were not to give them up to anybody and to inform me, if anybody tried. Then I returned to the police station, filed the receipts and told a senior officer what had happened. 'Ah!' he said, nervously. 'I hope you told them that they'll have to hand them over if there's a court case?'

'No,' I replied. 'In fact, I've told them not to, not under any circumstances. That's it, as far as I'm concerned.'

I wrote a thoughtful, three-page report. It found its way to the Metropolitan Police Solicitors Department and I later heard that they sent a rather sharp little letter to Brown's solicitors. In it, they advised them that it would be prudent for them to tell Brown to drop the matter. You see, Brown had stated under oath that he had received the property, believing it to have been stolen and that if he persisted with this claim, there was every likelihood that Brown could end up in the dock again, charged with attempting to obtain a quantity of silverware and jewellery by means of criminal deception. And that being the case, there was also the possibility, they added, that the solicitors would be joining him in the dock as well, for aiding and abetting him.

We heard not one more word on that matter.

So, what happened after that?

At the time of his arrest, Brown was on bail for inflicting grievous bodily harm – what happened to him in respect of that or, indeed anything else, I don't know.

Black came out of prison and went on a spree of building society raids. He was nicked by the Squad, confessed everything and went away for ten years, still complaining that 'Kirby had stitched him up.'

I next saw that prosecuting counsel some five years later; it was again at the Bailey. I'd arrested a man for murder: he'd stabbed his victim through the body with a sword and skewered him to the floor. When the defence asked him to accept a plea to manslaughter on the grounds that the killing was not premeditated, the prosecuting counsel readily agreed and then, spotting me, sneered, 'Oh, providing Mr Kirby doesn't object, of course!' Carrying a sword about with you doesn't amount to a premeditated murder. Oh, sure.

'Why ask me?' I said. 'Please yourself. You normally do!'

So the swordsman got five years for manslaughter. It didn't bother the prosecuting barrister. However, it did rather bother the prostitute that the killer picked up, following his release, because when he took her back to his flat, he tried to throttle her. After she escaped and went to the police, they discovered another prostitute at his flat. I expect she had been quite bothered as well, because her decomposing body was discovered inside a bin liner.

Detective Superintendent Geoff Parratt asked him if he'd like to comment about this state of affairs. 'Not likely!' replied the swordsman. 'The last time I made a comment, that bloody Kirby got me five years!'

Which, with hindsight, he might have thought to have been a drop in the ocean. The judge at his subsequent trial told him he thought he was too dangerous ever to be released and sentenced him to a total of 40 years.

Of course, if he'd been sentenced to life for my murder, where there was an abundance of evidence on which he could have been convicted, one poor old brass wouldn't have been throttled and another wouldn't have been murdered. Still, my murder wasn't premeditated, was it? No more than Brown and Black were guilty of the other outstanding offences.

That prosecuting counsel is today a High Court judge.

I bumped into Brown's barrister a little later, again at the Bailey. 'My dear chap!' he cried, wrung my hand so much I thought it'd fall off, said lots of complimentary things about me and then rushed off to court, leaving me standing there with his instructing clerk. 'He wasn't as affable as that, the last time I saw him,' I commented, ruefully. The clerk nodded; he knew the case that I was referring to. 'He'd come back to chambers, every night after being in court with that case,' he said. 'I'd never seen him in such a filthy mood.'

'I rather thought he'd got the upper hand of me,' I remarked, mildly.

The clerk shook his head. 'What he was so furious about was the instructions that Brown was giving him. He had to act on them, you see. He was furious that he had to keep on attacking your character!'

Well, well. A penitent brief. Five years later, the 'N' Division Crime Squad and I nicked an unpleasant little gang for conspiracy to rob – punters who had been lured into having sex with prostitutes and then being robbed. I entered court to give evidence and who should the judge be, but Brown's defence counsel. Before I could get to the witness box, he cried, 'Good Heavens, members of the jury – it's Detective Sergeant Kirby! Now we'll see some fireworks!' The case was robustly defended, so see them we did; and at the conclusion, the judge gave them some very respectable sentences and me a lovely commendation for leadership and detective ability; perhaps it was his way of saying sorry.

I was commended by the commissioner for the Brown and Black case, and what else? Oh yes – the loaded revolver. The owner didn't want it any more, so it ended up in the Yard's Black Museum, because it had a bit of history attached to it. The owner's father had purchased it in 1888 to help hunt down Jack the Ripper. Remember him? He preyed on defenceless people, too.

Fagged Out

Sammy was an informant whose intelligence input could be categorized into three sections: (1) good, reliable information; (2) a name, which with considerable digging might hold the promise of some kind of police action in the possibly foreseeable future, and (3) absolute drivel, bordering on complete and consummate bollocks. Into this latter category came Sam's mum, the current state of his verrucas, the Benefits Agency who, Sam stated categorically, 'had got it in for him' and his girl friend, Katie, with whom he had enjoyed a two-year relationship.

So when Sammy requested a meet, it was all rather debatable whether he was going to present me with a little gem of information or drone on about his wearisome domestic circumstances. It was all a lottery; and if he phoned me, it would have been inadvisable to say, 'Look, Sam – I'm busy, so if all you want to do is whine on about your rotten mum or the state of your feet, don't bother!' because if I had, it's sod's law that he would have replied, 'Well, I *was* going to give you the name of a bloke who was part of the Great Train Robbery, who's never been caught *and* who wants to give himself up *and* hand back his share of the loot – but if *that's* how you feel . . . !' and then I should have had all the embarrassing rigmarole of having to give him a grovelling apology.

But not this night. The moon careered through the clouds overlooking Highgate cemetery and, although it was cold, I

let the car window open a little wider to release a little of
Sammy's decaying pong. His foetid breath came in short
gasps, because Sammy was beside himself with excitement.
'There's snout all over the place, Mr Kirby!' he kept exclaiming and after I'd calmed him down, I managed to discover the
names of the gang of young tearaways who had broken into a
tobacco warehouse and made off with a large amount of stock.
The swag had been divided into individual shares and since
they'd had a hard time getting rid of it, the loot now reposed
in their respective living-rooms. Thanking Sammy, I dropped
him off and, with the car windows wide open, I drove
through the night to Holloway police station and checked
out the names and addresses of these young rascals. A telephone call, followed by a visit to a friendly magistrate who
greeted me with a large schooner of sherry and a Bible,
resulted in me acquiring four search warrants. I telephoned
the members of the 'N' Division Crime Squad for an early
morning meet.

At 6 a.m. next day, the front doors of four council flats were
bashed in and four surprised and sleepy young men were
escorted to Holloway police station. Accompanying them was
a very large amount of cigarettes, cigars and cigarillos which
had been found in each and every one of . . . three of the
addresses.

Bobby Cooper was an up-and-coming young boxer, as well
as a persistent burglar with whom I'd crossed swords before,
and I quite liked him. However, upon searching his flat, not
one packet of cigarettes, not even a dog-end was found.
Therefore if he was involved – and Sammy, who said he was,
had been right about everything else – everything depended
on a confession. He turned to me, as he was being booked in.
'I hope this won't take too long, Mr Kirby,' he said.

'Don't fret yourself about that, Bob,' I replied with an as-

surance I didn't completely feel, 'because you ain't going anywhere.'

'I am, actually,' he replied. 'I'm due up at Snaresbrook
Crown Court for sentence at 10 o'clock, if you want to know.'

I strolled over to Detective Constable Clive Jamieson.
'Better interview this one first, mate,' I muttered. So we did.
Clive (who later went on to do good work in the shadowy
world of surveillance) and I got stuck in and we tried all our
combined skills to get Bobby to crack – all without success.
Eventually, we chucked the towel in and told him to push off.

The 'N' Division aids had fared far better. Their three prisoners, faced with the indisputable evidence, put their hands
up to the burglary and were duly charged and bailed. I tried
to tell myself that three out of four wasn't bad, that we'd got
most of the gear back and a not unimportant burglary had
been cleared up, but I did wonder if the smirks of the aids
were aimed at their own success or at Clive's and my discomfort. The tale, however, did not end there.

The following morning, I picked up the ringing telephone
in my office to hear the chuckling of the station officer. 'Better
come down, Dick,' he laughed. 'There's a bit of a treat for
you.'

There, in the front office was a sorry sight. Bobby Cooper
had gone to Snaresbrook and had been conditionally discharged, instead of receiving the stretch that he had half
expected (and which he richly deserved) for his transgressions.
Elated at his good fortune, he eagerly sought out the company
of his three sorrowful companions who had, by then, been
charged with the burglary. They, too had thought that Bobby
faced an inevitable custodial sentence – when they discovered
that, in addition, he had not been charged with the burglary,
they came to the immediate (although erroneous) conclusion
that (a) Bobby was the snout and (b) I had stepped smartly

into the witness box to say a few mitigating words to the judge, on Bobby's behalf. Their rage had boiled over and now Bobby, his swollen face reflecting both misery and the considerable amount of punishment meted out by his accomplices, demanded that he be allowed to make a full confession to his part in the burglary. This, he admitted, was to regain some form of credibility amongst the young toughs of Holloway, since graffiti artists were already proclaiming that he was 'Kirby's Grass'.

'Anything to oblige, Bob,' I said, as I put my arm round his shoulders and escorted him to a vacant interview room, 'and I hope this teaches you a lesson.'

Puzzlement screwed up the corners of Bobby's battered eyes. 'What, not to go out screwing?' he asked.

'No, to keep your left up!' I replied and while Bob had a short sense of humour failure, Clive and I had a quiet chuckle – and Sammy the Snout lived to grass another day.

The Dalston Defence

Sometimes, divine providence intervenes. If I hadn't gone into Tom Lamont's office that day, I wouldn't have been posted to Barkingside police station. I wouldn't have met Gerry Wiltshire, who wouldn't have asked me to go to the Flying Squad. And I wouldn't have crossed swords with the Seymour brothers. But, as Errol Flynn once said, 'There's no use telling a story arse-backwards.' Let's go back to the beginning.

I'd spent five productive years with the Serious Crime Squad and thoroughly enjoyed myself. I had been taught the mechanics of investigating large, complex cases and, just as important, how to put them together afterwards to present them to the Court. Apart from working all over the British Isles, I'd conducted inquiries in France, Holland, Germany and Switzerland. I had dealt with major criminals from all those countries, as well as from Italy, Malta, Hungary, Israel and Hong Kong – plus, of course, the home-grown variety.

Naturally I was flattered when I was asked if I would like to stay on for another five years: flattered . . . but not tempted. First, I had the feeling that I was getting a little stale. Next, I wanted to get out and use the skills I'd acquired. And last, I was one of the officers who had been seconded for duties at 2 Area Headquarters at Portman Square. There, the late Commander Len Gillert QPM was planning a massive offensive against crooked coppers.

Now, I don't like dishonest police officers any more than

the next bloke; similarly, I don't like the idea of blocked drains or an infestation of cockroaches, but it doesn't mean to say that I want to volunteer to eradicate them – far better to leave it to someone who likes doing that sort of thing.

So having made my mind up, I went and knocked on the office door of Detective Chief Superintendent Tom Lamont, the officer in charge of the Serious Crime Squad. I liked Tom very much. He was a good old copper who'd helped me out once or twice, particularly with regard to a deeply unpleasant deputy assistant commissioner who was intent on doing me a mischief. I told Tom that my wife had been nagging me about my long working hours; since I had discovered Gillert's intentions by slipping into his office and giving his correspondence the once-over, I thought it imprudent to tell Tom the real reason!

Tom picked up his telephone, dialled and within a couple of minutes, left me in no doubt as to exactly why he was a good guv'nor. Speaking to an officer of equal rank he smoothly paved the way for me to begin duty at Barkingside police station the following Monday.

I think that Barkingside was the happiest divisional posting of my career. The drive from home, across country, was a joy and the area itself was interesting. In the smarter houses lived the affluent, mainly Jewish community; there was a busy shopping centre, many commercial properties and large council estates, housing a miscellaneous selection of ne'er-do-wells. Best of all were the senior CID officers. The late Gerry Wiltshire was the detective chief inspector and his deputy was Detective Inspector Frank Rushworth. I admired them both for being great investigators; I never heard a cross word between them and the general CID office, and they were responsible for harmony between the CID and the uniform branch.

The Dalston Defence

I enjoyed a modest success with the teams of burglars from the East End who would periodically jump on to a tube train and head east on the Central line until they reached Woodford or Loughton. I spent as much time in their part of the world, searching premises, retrieving stolen property and making arrests, as I did at Barkingside.

The Seymour brothers' saga began when a uniformed police constable was called to the scene of a burglary in progress, at a house in a cul-de-sac in Loughton. As he arrived, a black youth shouted, 'Run for it, Hicksey!' The officer grabbed him, but was unable to stop a white youth, who raced away across some fields. Although a search was quickly organized covering that and the surrounding area, of 'Hicksey' there was no sign.

I turned up at the station to interview the prisoner. Since it was clear that he had driven his car to bring the white youth to the premises and had not actually entered the house himself, I decided that the prisoner would either say nothing at all during the interview, or he would use the Dalston Defence.

To those of you who don't know what the Dalston Defence is, let me enlighten you. In the East London suburb of Dalston (and in the areas surrounding it) there live a number of young men who possess a variety of cars – Rovers, Jaguars and BMWs. All these vehicles are in an advanced state of decay, none are in a roadworthy condition, and their owners have found it convenient to leave the vehicle registered in the name of the previous owner, from whom they purchased the car, for cash. They also consider it unnecessary to insure, obtain an MOT certificate or tax the vehicle. Many of the owners even baulk at the thought of paying for the car's petrol too.

Arising at noon, these young men indolently drive their

cars around their natural habitat until such time as they meet a complete stranger, whom they would be unable to recognize again. The stranger takes them into his confidence, that the previous evening he met a desirable young lady and is keen to continue the relationship. For the payment of a fiver, for petrol money, the driver readily agrees to convey the lovelorn swain to the young woman's address. Inevitably, she resides in a smart suburb.

Upon arrival in the Barkingside/Chigwell/Loughton/ Woodford area, they drive slowly through the streets until the passenger excitedly points to the address where his *inamorata* resides. The driver stays with his car; within ten minutes or so, the passenger returns, and the driver expresses mild astonishment at the young lady's beneficence. Given their remarkably short acquaintance, she has generously provided the passenger with a television set, a video recorder, an assortment of silverware, some expensive-looking jewellery and some cash. Warmly congratulating the stranger on his good fortune, the driver roars away from the scene, as fast as he can go, eager to return to his own territory. With the absence of any directions whatsoever, he then drives straight to the stranger's address which, for the life of him, he is unable to recall thereafter.

There are variations on this theme. Sometimes, he picks up a stranger who has found a chequebook and cheque card on the pavement. Courteously, he drives him to a bank so that he can reunite the owner with his missing property. It is not unknown for a driver to pick up a whole group of anonymous magicians. At their request, he will drive them to a parade of shops where, following their subsequent departure, the store owners shake their heads in bewilderment at the way their stock has substantially disappeared. In this, and in many other cases, it is not unknown for the driver of the car to be so pleased at his passengers' good luck, that, as he drives away, he repeatedly sounds his horn and gives what appears to be a victory salute out of the window.

Now, if in the course of one of these odysseys (or perhaps afterwards), the driver is stopped, he will activate the Dalston Defence. And should an unfeeling police officer have the temerity to query his account of how he came to be driving a car full of thieves, who are groaning under the weight of the stolen property they have recently acquired, and actually arrest him, the driver will exercise his right, at the police station to demand vociferously the attendance of a rat.

Upon the rodent's arrival – he is sometimes referred to as a solicitor – his first objective is to get his client to sign a green form. The effect of obtaining this signature is sufficient to open wide the purse strings of the Legal Aid fund. Not only is the solicitor handsomely recompensed for turning up at the police station, he is now in a position to acquire the services of a former public schoolboy, who is a complete stranger to the truth. This is a defence barrister and, apart from honing and polishing the Dalston Defence to suit the circumstances of the case in question, his initial objective is to arrange bail for his client from the vacant-faced Muppets on the Bench at the local Magistrates' Court. This, given the bovine stupidity of the representative from the Crown Prosecution Service, does not normally present a problem. In both releasing the driver and committing him to the Crown Court for trial, the Bench have tacitly acknowledged that in the intervening period, of anything up to a year, the driver will resume his chosen profession.

However, it sometimes happens (not very often, certainly) that the magistrates may display reluctance at the thought of granting bail. The seasoned defendant immediately activates the codicil of the Dalston Defence, and, eschewing the services of his barrister, he loudly reveals to the Bench the existence of his estranged child, whose name, inevitably, is Chanel. This luckless infant ('wot me luv more than *anyfin''*) is trotted out to gain the sympathy vote, and as the Muppets snuffle loudly into their handkerchiefs, it does provide a measure of success. I imagine that it will continue to do so until the day comes that a plucky CID officer enters the witness box and respectfully informs the Bench that little Chanel is a product of the defendant's over-active imagination, rather than his loins.

When his trial is called, the driver may well decide to attend Snaresbrook Crown Court. There, he sees a dozen prime examples of local pond life. They are called jurors. Before lunchtime arrives, the jury will have unanimously acquitted the driver. It is not unknown for them to join him in 'The Eagle' for a celebratory drink afterwards, because about twenty-five per cent of them are the driver's near-neighbours, friends and relatives.

So *that*, my friends, is the Dalston Defence; and if you think I've been just a teeny bit cynical, then you are not a police officer who has taken a copper-bottomed and watertight case to Snaresbrook Crown Court, as I have on many occasions, only to see it chucked out with the bath water.

Wearying of listening to all this assorted nonsense, I locked the driver up and went off to search his car for anything that would give me a clue to his passenger. Nothing. Then I searched his home. Upon my return, the driver found it difficult to pinpoint the provenance of the bent gear I'd found there, so that formed the basis of the first charge, and the burglary, the second. His brother, who had admitted me to the family home, accompanied me back to the police station and I charged him as well. It was fortunate that their mum hadn't been at home when I called.

Now for Hicksey. I contacted the Yard's Criminal Records Office (CRO), gave them the probable surname of Hicks, an approximate date of birth, his height and the fact that he was a white male. I also provided his nickname and his *modus operandi.* The nominal method and miscellaneous indices at CRO had been fruitful to me in the past but not, alas, on this occasion.

Next, I checked the CRO file of my prisoner. No trace of an associate named Hicks or Hicksey to be found. I sent an 'All Stations' teleprinter message to the whole of 3 Area – the quarter segment of the Metropolitan Police District where I worked and, hopefully, Hicksey resided – asking for assistance in tracing him, giving the very good description provided by the arresting officer. Nothing. Not a bite. So I sent a further teleprinter message, this time to include 2 Area, as well. That meant that the whole area north of the Thames had been covered. Still nothing. During my short stay at Barkingside, I had acquired a couple of informants. I pressed them to identify Hicksey, but they were indigenous to the Barkingside area and were unable to help.

A forensic examination had been made at the scene of the burglary at Loughton. When Hicksey had broken in, he had gashed his finger on the broken glass and had helpfully left a bloodprint behind. About a week later, telephone calls started coming in from the Yard's Fingerprint Branch. They had what they called 'a series' – Hicksey's fingerprint matched those found at a number of burgled premises in the area – quite recently, too. The question that was starting to consume me was: who was Hicksey – and where was he? Well, I might not have known who he was, but I knew what he was doing; he was taking the piss by going round the manor, screwing houses left, right and centre. *That* was going to stop.

I checked the crime book for the burgled premises, trying to work out some sort of pattern, something that would help, ·

anything . . . Then came my first big breakthrough. A witness had seen a white Rover leaving the scene of one of the burglaries and had noted the registration number. Of course, the vehicle was not registered to the current owner, but I circulated the details of the vehicle on the Police National Computer with instructions that if it were seen, it should be stopped, the driver detained and me informed. My next port of call was Gerry Wiltshire's office. A CID man through and through, he immediately struck me off all my other duties and gave me *carte blanche* to round this gang up. I split up Woodford, Loughton, Chigwell and Barkingside into sections and put every available police officer to work, scouring the area for the vehicle and its occupants. The following night, the driver of the Rover was stopped and arrested by police from King's Cross, for drink-driving. It was when they were carrying out checks on the vehicle, that my message came to light.

The following morning, I had to attend Court, so I sent Peter Kingston, a young but very talented Crime Squad officer to interview the driver. It immediately became apparent to Kingston that the driver, whose name was Alan Seymour, bore not the slightest resemblance to Hicksey nor, at that stage, could he be connected with the burglaries, but due to his record and criminal connections, Kingston asked to search his address, and Seymour agreed, telling Kingston that, 'he had no worries on that score.'

In fact, Kingston thought he might have had when he discovered two bags full of costume jewellery, but Seymour replied that this property had been seized when the Regional Crime Squad had arrested him and his brother. It had been checked out by the RCS who had discovered that the property was not stolen and had returned it to them; hence, said Seymour, the 'Metropolitan Police' printed on the bags. A telephone call to the RCS revealed this to be the case.

And just when Peter Kingston was about to give it all up as a bad job, the front door opened and in strolled a youngster, looking for all the world like a cardboard cut-out of Hicksey . . .

David Michael Hicks was just sixteen years of age and had been a promising amateur boxer – so many of them are! – until he by-passed training for a more lucrative pastime. And lucrative it was; as I later discovered. During a six-month period, Hicks' burglaries had netted him property valued in excess of £30,000.

I checked at CRO and found to my delight that Hicks already possessed a CRO number; this meant that at some stage his fingerprints had been taken and were still on file. I got straight on to Fingerprint Branch, gave them Hicks' details and told them to get cracking.

I interviewed Hicks in the presence of his parents. As the questions and answers were contemporaneously recorded, Hicks denied involvement in every burglary that I put to him. A telephone call came in from Fingerprint Branch. 'Have you still got him?' I had. 'Keep him there!'

The hours drifted by. Tea was offered and accepted. More questions. More writing. And more denials. And, then, the telephone call from Fingerprint Branch. 'It's definitely him!'

Maybe Hicks thought he'd called my bluff, but when I charged him, he cracked and admitted all the offences I'd put to him – all the offences I knew about, that is. Over the next three days, Hicks came out and from the back of a nondescript police car, he pointed out to us all the burglaries that he remembered committing. There were . . . quite a lot! But there were two matters that Hicks refused to discuss: where the stolen property was and who his associates were.

Peter Kingston, who had now been permanently co-opted on to the inquiry, and I had a laborious task in front of us.

Hicks had admitted a large number of offences but was unable to recall when he had actually committed them, so we had to trawl through many months of reported crimes, contained in the crime books of several police stations. The details of every identified burgled premises, I transferred on to a chart, showing date, time, place, method of entry, property stolen and value. And then divine providence stuck her foot in the door.

As we looked through one of the crime books, we came across a 'red inker'. The red ink denoted that an arrest had been carried out and this one was in respect of the Seymour Brothers, Alan and Johnny, by the RCS. Peter and I rushed downstairs to the front office and found the relevant entry in the Charge Book, together with a list of the property which had been brought in with them – an enormous amount, especially costume jewellery. We compared the property shown on the charge sheet and the stolen property contained on our chart – there were a great many similarities. And the RCS had restored it to the Seymours, not because it was theirs but because they had circulated a description of the property to ascertain if it was stolen, without success. The RCS had been searching in the dark; we, however, had the edge, because now we had a pretty shrewd idea of where this property had originated. And now we also knew who had been Hicks' accomplices – especially since we had discovered that the Seymour brothers were Hicks' uncles.

A search warrant was obtained and in came the brothers Seymour, as well as the restored property, and the searchers were saved an onerous job, since the goodies were still in Metropolitan Police property bags. The brothers made full signed confessions, in which they detailed their parts in the burglaries and the manner in which they had disposed of the property, stolen by their nephew during the course of other

166

burglaries. They also admitted something else to me: this was the first time in their chequered criminal careers that they had ever given the police signed confessions.

Wouldn't it be nice, once the arrests have been made and the prisoners charged, if you could put your feet up? It's then that the real work begins, putting together all the evidence to bring about a conviction at court. Over the weeks that followed, apart from the enormous amount of paperwork that was being generated, I had six large tables set up in a room that had been specially set aside at Barkingside police station. On these, I set out all the property which we had re-seized and, night after night, the occupiers of the burgled premises turned up to try to identify their possessions. Mrs Green was one such loser, an elderly, infirm lady and her next-door neighbour had kindly driven her to the police station. Telling her to take her time and wishing her the best of luck, I sent Mrs Green and the neighbour on a circular tour of the tables. I was delighted when, twenty minutes later, Mrs Green returned, triumphantly holding three items, which she positively identified as being hers. I was astonished when her neighbour showed me a couple of items. 'These are from my burglary!' she said. 'What burglary?' I replied. 'My house was broken into, the same day as Mrs Green's,' the neighbour said and a check of the Crime Book entry, right next to Mrs Green's, showed this was indeed the case. What had happened was that when Hicks was indicating the premises that he'd broken into, he had pointed to Mrs Green's address and said, 'There.' I had made a note of the house number and we had pressed on to the next address. He had completely forgotten that he had also broken into the house next door. I pointed out this deficiency to him, the next time I saw him. 'Sorry, Dick,' he grinned. 'Forgot that one. Stick it down on the list and I'll sign it!' It was one of six burglaries that he pleaded guilty to, asking the court to take thirty more cases into consideration. He was sentenced to borstal training. Alan Seymour pleaded guilty to three cases of burglary and asked for another case to be taken into consideration. Johnny Seymour pleaded guilty to four cases of receiving stolen goods, one offence of burglary and asked for eleven other cases to be taken into consideration. Both brothers were each sentenced to four years' imprisonment. The driver? Hicks let him off the hook, saying he knew nothing about the burglary – the Dalston Defence had triumphed again! – but at least he went down on the other charge. Peter Kingston and I were commended by the trial judge and later, the commissioner.

After that, things went swimmingly. I was posted on to the 'Q' car, 'Juliet one-one' and I asked that Peter be the aid. We had a busy tour, including the arrest of four burglars from Hackney who had embarked upon a Central Line 'Awayday'. After that, I took over the running of the Divisional Crime Squad and we had a number of high-profile cases. We arrested another uncle-and-nephew burglary team and their nine receivers. Following a tip-off, we recovered a cache of priceless 2,000-year-old Judaean coins and arrested the five burglars responsible for their disappearance. A gang who robbed an off-licence and another who robbed a filling station were wiped up; so was a gang who had terrorized a housing estate. We kept observation on an off-licence, when I heard it was going to be broken into. It wasn't. Instead, right out of the blue, a car-load of fraudsters from Stoke Newington arrived and started acquiring goods from all along the shopping parade with a chequebook which they'd stolen in a house burglary earlier that day. The driver used the Dalston Defence; it worked, of course. Later he sued us for unlawful arrest and false imprisonment. He won, of course.

But we were on a roll. We were commended for practically

every case and our photographs and reports of our derring-do appeared in the local newspapers, almost on a weekly basis.

Gerry Wiltshire had gone to the Flying Squad; now, he asked me to join him. However, the unpleasant deputy assistant commissioner with whom I'd previously crossed swords (and would do so again) blocked my transfer, saying that I had only fifteen months' Divisional experience. Really, I wasn't bothered; I was having the time of my life. But Gerry persisted and eighteen months after leaving the Serious Crime Squad, I was on my way to the Flying Squad.

As a member of 12 Squad, I had more than enough work on my plate, although we had an agreement with 10 Squad that we would help out on some of their larger cases where extra manpower was required and *vice-versa*. On one particular occasion, 10 Squad's Detective Sergeant Tom Bradley had received some excellent information about an East-End gang who were planning to rob a rent collector and 12 Squad's aid was enlisted to help out. At the briefing, Tom mentioned the names of the participants in the proposed robbery and when I heard the name of Alan Seymour, I laughed out loud. 'Bloody hell, Tom, he must have only just got out!' He had, too. We all took up our positions and, at the appointed time, when the gang were about to pounce on the unfortunate rent collector, Tom gave the order to attack. We leapt from our cars and rushed them. My enduring memory of that case is seeing Alan Seymour running at full pelt down Shoreditch High Street and me sprinting after him, only to be overtaken by the late Detective Inspector Cam Burnell. Cam, an exceedingly useful member of the second row in the Metropolitan Police rugby team, gave a roar and launched himself at Seymour, bringing him crashing to the ground with a perfectly executed tackle.

As I ran up, I was perturbed to see smoke rising from

Seymour's inert body. Had Cam shot him – and if so, why hadn't I heard the report from his revolver?

In fact, the mystery was quickly solved. It was a cold winter's day; the shock of sixteen stone Cam landing on him, had caused Seymour to evacuate his bladder. What I had mistaken for smoke was steam rising from his nether regions. Exhibiting all the classic symptoms of combat fatigue, Seymour was dragged to his feet, still steaming. I couldn't help laughing. 'Wotcher, Alan,' I said, cheerfully. 'Bit chilly today, ain't it?' His shock and misery intensified as recognition dawned. The look on his face seemed to say, 'Every time I get nicked, fucking Kirby's there!'

Memories

Just a word or an action can trigger off a memory: in *The Three Hostages*, John Buchan refers to it as 'the cross-bearing', and whatever it was that prompted the memory is often quickly forgotten as the memories come flooding back; or, as in my case, they appear as a scratchy, badly cut film. I often get these flashbacks at reunions. Of course, by the time I come to write them down, so much alcohol has been consumed in the interim period that not only can I not remember what it was that triggered off the memory, I often forget the actual recollection.

So when I bumped into Dave Morgan the other night (and because I see him so seldom) I suddenly recalled how Dave had given me a hand with a robbery case. Both of us had been sent to Holloway as detective sergeants, Dave from the Stolen Vehicle Squad, me from the Flying Squad, and I'd been saddled with the case of a young girl who alleged that she'd been robbed of her expensive leather jacket by a female juvenile delinquent, who was known to her. So off we went to the Islington council flat where the suspect lived, together with her mother. Now, I was to find out later that the mother's former husband, who sounded an eminently sensible sort of fellow, had tired of his wife's stupid, liberal posturings, and reaching the irrevocable conclusion that she was as wet as a dripping tap, had dumped her and gone off to find a little happiness. Eventually, she had found her way to these insalubrious surroundings together with her similarly abandoned offspring – a bored, vicious child named Emmaleez. It was the mother who answered the door. She was dressed in the sort of outfit that a slim and very beautiful nineteen-year-old could just about have got away with; but when a woman is pudgy, faded and forty-ish as indeed Emmaleez' mother was, the effect was preposterous.

What follows is a summary of our conversation. My questions are superfluous, so really this becomes her monologue.

'Oh, hi! You're who? Great, big deal . . . what is it now? Emmaleez? No, she's not here . . . how should I know? Round the streets, I guess . . . how should I know what she's doing? Yes, Sergeant Whatizface, I am concerned and don't take that tone with me, OK? No, I don't know who she's with . . . I expect she's being screwed by some black kid, she's really into ethnic relationships . . . yes, I do know she's fourteen, is that a crime or something? Oh, I knew you'd say *that*!'

Eventually, Emmaleez, her thin, pinched face bearing an expression of utter contempt, was brought in and, as she sprawled in her chair, she sneered at my questions and denied the whole thing. Dave and I had to have a chuckle afterwards. 'This is ridiculous,' I laughed. 'You've smashed international gangs of car thieves, I've broken up gangs of armed robbers and between the two of us, the cream of Scotland Yard couldn't get a confession out of a fourteen-year-old schoolgirl!'

The Juvenile Bureau decided to charge Emmaleez and she was told to attend Holloway police station at a given date and time, purely to be formally charged. She duly turned up in the presence of a barrister – yes, you heard me, not a solicitor, a bloody barrister – and a social worker, and she was then charged and cautioned to which (and to nobody's surprise) she made no reply. 'I do think it's a bit over the top,' I said, mildly, 'having a barrister and a social worker present, purely to hear her make no reply to the charge. Easy way to make a living, ain't it, pal?' I added to the barrister, who blushed a glowing pink. Emmaleez scowled at me and, after a cursory inspection, crammed her already torn fingernails into her mouth and began hungrily gnawing them.

'Emily's mother –' the social worker began, before she was promptly interrupted by the ghastly kid, who, wrenching her grimy fingers from her mouth, screamed, *'Emma-leez!* That's my fucking name! Get it right, bitch!'

'Emmaleez' mother,' the social worker went on, hastily correcting herself, 'would have been here herself, but for a prior engagement.'

I took a step backwards. 'Really?' I replied, feigning interest. 'And what, pray, was that?'

The barrister thrust his hands into his trouser pockets and as he strolled off down the charge room, he began to whistle tunelessly, giving the impression of a man who wished he was a long way away. Emmaleez sneered and resumed her nail-gnawing. The red-faced social worker looked down and studied her shoes as she shamefacedly muttered, 'She's attending her African Dance Class!'

On another occasion, a barrister also featured. I'd arrived at the Magistrates' Court with a prisoner who was charged with a number of high-value armed robberies – the prisoner himself had been a household name at one time. This was his first appearance at Court and he was going to have a lay-down. To ensure that this was the case, I approached the representative from the Crown Prosecution Service and told her that I, not she, would make the application for the remand in custody. This, I should mention, was in the early days of the CPS, when their untrained representatives could be treated rather like naughty children in a kindergarden although, in fairness, I never treated them any other way.

Just then, I was approached by a tall, smartly dressed chap with an extremely pleasant manner, who introduced himself as the prisoner's barrister. With him was a small, rodent-like individual, who turned out to be the instructing solicitor. The barrister courteously introduced me to the solicitor as well, but I ignored the little runt because I'd met him once before when he'd made a cheeky remark to me and he'd been extremely lucky to walk away unmolested from the encounter.

'Will you be applying for a remand in custody, Sergeant Kirby?' asked the barrister.

I conceded that I would.

'I see,' he said, nodding solemnly. 'Would you mind telling me what your objections will be?'

'Certainly,' I replied. 'Firstly, due to the gravity of the offence, I believe that if granted bail, he will abscond and, secondly, I believe that he will commit further offences.'

The barrister nodded again and now, the solicitor, unable to contain himself any longer, launched himself into the attack; just as I hoped he would. 'On what do you base your assumption that my client will abscond?' he snapped. 'And what's more, I should very much like to know how you have come to the conclusion that he will commit further offences. My client can provide substantial sureties and I should like to know what possible grounds –'

And now, I'd just run out of patience. 'Stop,' I interrupted and laid a steadying hand on his shoulder. The solicitor stopped in mid-sentence and gaped at me. 'Now, let's get something straight, shall we?' I said. 'First of all, I am under no obligation to speak to you out of court at all, let alone give you reasons as to why I'm objecting to bail. I did so on this occasion, because this gentleman,' indicating the barrister, 'has far better manners than you'll ever have and because he was courteous to me. Next, never presume to cross-examine me or any other police officer out of court. I for one won't stand for it and furthermore, it's a wasted exercise, because you're not very good at it – got it?' With that, I turned to walk away and then stopped, turned back and added, 'And please cover yourself up – you're making a bit of a spectacle of yourself!' The solicitor gasped and clutched at the family jewels with both hands before realizing his fly buttons were quite secure, and he hardly had time to start spluttering with indignation, when suddenly I heard my name called. I turned and rushing towards me was a woman with the sort of voluptuous figure that Renoir would have drooled over. 'Dick Kirby!' she cried again and crushed me to her ample bosom. 'I haven't seen you in fifteen years – what a lovely surprise!' I emerged, inhaling deeply from this asphyxiating encounter and greeted the clerk of the court. 'Janice!' I gasped. 'You look ravishing – are you in this court, today?'

'Yes, of course,' she replied. 'Oh, let me look at you – now, what're you doing here?'

'Just a remand in custody,' I admitted, carelessly.

'That'll take all of two minutes,' she scoffed and putting her arm around my waist, she led me away. 'Now, what about a drink afterwards?' As we strolled away, out of earshot of the defence team, I made a slightly salacious remark which caused her to throw her head back and shriek with laughter.

A colleague later told me that as we sauntered away, the barrister leant towards the small solicitor, who was still seething with rage, and murmured, 'I think we'll give the bail application a miss this week!'

Time Gentlemen, Please!

Excessive drinking has always been a problem in the Metropolitan Police. On 29 September 1829, William Atkinson was the first police constable to be sworn in and was allocated Warrant Card No. 1. Almost immediately, he (together with the holder of Warrant Card No. 2) was kicked out for drunkenness. They would not be the last by any means.

As a young man, I spent my formative years indulging in a variety of sports and chasing crumpet. I didn't drink because that went against all the rules governing sport training and also, because given the meagre wages I received as an apprentice in the printing industry, I simply couldn't afford it. My abstinence continued when I joined the Metropolitan Police; married with a young family, the money was going out as fast as it was coming in.

But when I joined the Criminal Investigation Department, I discovered that regular drinking was mandatory. It was a popular misconception that if you spent a lot of time in pubs, you'd be swamped with information from the manor's criminal fraternity. 'You gotta get out among 'em!' was a popular cry. Out amongst whom? Other pissheads? Because many of the CID officers who went to the pub became so blotto that if anyone had approached them with information they'd have been incapable of making sense of it. I met informants in pubs, of course I did; but I also met them in other places – cafes, parks, churchyards, the Circle Line and even police stations.

As a new detective constable, I wanted to make a name for myself by nicking villains, not spending a whole evening in a pub, getting smashed.

When I did have a drink, my favourite tipple in those days was scotch and ginger ale; a couple of them, which I really enjoyed, was quite enough for me. If I stayed any longer, I'd just have a succession of ginger ales. This, I discovered was not acceptable to a number of CID officers, who regarded prudence in drinking with the same sort of scepticism as they treated ballet dancing or poetry.

This matter was raised one evening when I joined a group of detectives in a pub, who had been ensconced there for some considerable time. One of them staggered over to me, with the offer of a drink. 'Just a ginger ale, please,' I said. Now in these enlightened times, a request for a ginger ale, a Perrier water or a cup of coffee would fail to raise any eyebrows, but that's now – and this was then. 'Ginger ale?' echoed my inebriated workmate. ''Ear that?' he remarked, as he turned to the others in the group. 'Bleedin' ginger ale!' 'Ginger beer, more like!' replied an unknown voice and as the others sniggered and giggled, my provider called over the barman. 'Harry, give 'im a big scotch,' he ordered, and sorrowfully shaking his head, he muttered to nobody in particular, 'Ginger ale!' As Harry turned towards the optics, glass in hand, I said firmly, 'A ginger ale, please Harry.' Harry duly lowered his outstretched arm, which was en route to the optic, turned, and picked up a bottle of ginger ale. 'Oi, oi, 'arry,' interjected the sozzled 'tec, 'never mind 'im, give 'im a scotch!' Harry turned towards the optics again before being halted by me with my renewed request for ginger ale. This silly scenario went on for several minutes, before I lost patience and realized that severe measures were necessary. I put my arm round my companion's neck and gently pulled him towards me. 'Listen,' I said quietly, so softly that he leant towards me in order to catch my words. 'Now, do you want to fuck me?' I asked. As my query sunk in, a look of shock spread over his face. 'Wot?' he gasped. 'You see,' I explained, 'you're so intent on pouring scotch down my throat, I reckon that you must want to give me one. So, come on – just set my mind at rest; do you or don't you want to fuck me?'

He took an unsteady step backwards. ''Ere, fuck off!' he muttered nervously and returned to his resolutely heterosexual cronies. I was able to pick out extracts from his ensuing mumbled conversation. '. . . Fucking bloke . . . bleedin' queer, if y'ask me . . . only wanted me to give 'im one!' . . . and then the rejoinders from his compatriots, '. . . Ain't surprised . . . dunno what he's doing in the Department' . . . (and best of all) 'Never trust a bloke what don't drink!' Details of our little encounter reached the ears of Detective Chief Inspector Randall Jones, that tremendous detective for whom I had the most wholehearted admiration. Randall loved a drink himself; the difference between him and the others was, he was tolerant of those who didn't. 'I don't see why I should be expected to go out on the piss night after night, Guv'nor,' I protested. 'I've got a lot of work to do and I can't do it if I'm spending all my time down the pub, doing something I don't even like.' I could also have mentioned that now my young family had increased to four, I couldn't afford it – in fact, I couldn't afford to have my car regularly serviced. Randall puffed ruminatively on his pipe. 'I know what you mean,' he said quietly, 'but look at it this way. One of these days, you're going to be a DI on the Squad.' As I started to scoff incredulously, he held up an admonishing hand. 'And when your team has a good job off, you're going to want to congratulate them, aren't you?' I nodded, slowly. 'And how are you going to do that?' he asked rhetorically. 'By buying them a drink, of course.' Again, I nodded. 'There's no need to get at it,' said Randall, 'just a glass now and then. You could start now,' he added with a grin. And of course, Randall was quite right; it was just a matter of keeping a sense of proportion. I saw what happened to some who didn't.

During the middle of the night, a couple of drunks had jumped out of a car, which had crashed into a parked car. The unattended vehicle was the property of an off-duty Traffic Patrol officer, who had been roused from a deep sleep at the noise and had rushed downstairs, where he remonstrated with the occupants of the other car. During the ensuing row, a neighbour called the police, and my 'Q' car was one of several of the police cars which drew up. Both of the drunks were arrested, put into separate cars and taken to the local police station. One of the men who had been brought in was an off-duty uniform inspector, who was promptly told to push off. The other man, who had never seen so many police officers in his life, immediately admitted that not only was he pissed and had also been driving the car at the time of the crash, but that he was also disqualified from driving, to boot. Because he didn't want to get anybody else (i.e. the police inspector in the car) into trouble, he then elected to make a written statement, admitting his transgressions. So all would have been well, had the drunken inspector not returned to the nick, and demanded to make a statement under caution, stating that *he* had been driving the car. And the result? Eighteen months' imprisonment.

I knew a young detective who would regularly arrive at the Magistrates' Court with a prisoner (not necessarily his) and repeatedly ask the gaoler to get his case heard quickly. Now, it's been my experience that most gaolers were happy to accommodate an officer's request, but if there was a heavy list, matters had to be prioritized. Drunks who were pleading guilty were disposed of first, swiftly followed by the cases of officers who were on night-duty. Then remands on bail were followed by remands in custody, simple committals to the Crown Court, pleas of guilty and then disputed charges. Now, this officer would become more and more agitated as 11.30 a.m. approached – coincidentally, pub opening time – but if his case hadn't been called by then, he'd ask the gaoler to 'put his case back', because he had (with a broad wink) 'an informant to meet'. Eventually, he'd return to court, reeking of drink and deal with his prisoner and then retire back to the pub for the lunch-time session. And all this happened over thirty years ago; you can imagine the state he's in now.

So some officers allowed drink to take over their lives. When I first met Detective Constable Joe Matthews (that's not his real name), alcohol had already laid a heavy hand on his shoulder. Prior to this, I'm unaware if Joe had ever been a productive detective, but after seeing him in court, I was appalled. Joe had just outlined the facts of a case to the sti-pendiary magistrate, who then asked if anything was known – if the defendant had previous convictions. Joe nodded and handed a form to the beak, who quickly scanned the paper and I watched as his expression changed to one of incredulity, before he snapped, 'I don't want to see this!' and handed the form back. I was surprised to say the least, because in common with every other officer, Joe would have had the defendant's previous convictions neatly typed out on a Form 609, which was the accepted medium at both Magistrates' and Crown Courts.

'Something wrong with your 609?' I asked Joe afterwards, adding, 'because the Beak obviously thought so.'

'It wasn't a 609,' answered Joe, apprehensively checking his wrist watch, to see how much valuable drinking time had been lost.

'Not on a 609?' I replied, completely mystified. 'What was it, for Christ's sake?'

'A photocopy of his collator's card,' Joe muttered.

'*What!*' I gasped. To those of you who don't know, the details on a collator's card were not only strictly confidential for police eyes only – they also contained matters that were certainly not evidence and were not necessarily strictly accurate, either. Details of associates, sightings and suggestions as to what sort of criminality the subject might be up to were matters contained in these records and this drunken idiot had photocopied the cards and presented them to a magistrate! 'You bloody fool!' I burst out. 'Why the hell didn't you get his convictions from CRO in the normal way and have them typed on a 609?'

'Didn't have time, did I?' mumbled Joe, before making a speedy exit in the direction of the nearest pub. This explanation I knew was blatant bollocks. The prisoner had been arrested weeks before, giving Joe more than ample time to get his paperwork right. The furious magistrate had a word with the court inspector – in turn, he informed the uniform chief superintendent who, with acerbic words of wisdom, passed the news to the detective chief inspector, who, by now, had just about had enough of Joe's antics. 'Right, that's it!' he snapped. 'He's out!'

For all his faults, I did like Joe. 'Guv'nor,' I said, 'let me take him under my wing. Perhaps he just needs pointing in the right direction. What d'you say?'

The DCI pinched his lower lip. 'Hmm!' he mused. 'Give it a try, Dick, but if it doesn't work, he'll have to go; he's fast becoming a fucking liability.'

The following day, I had a salutary word with Joe and left him in no doubt that if he didn't shape up, he'd be shipped out. I'd deliberately caught Joe at a rare moment of sobriety and he nodded, knowing what I'd said was right.

That afternoon, I received a telephone call from a woman who introduced herself as Mrs Janice Allen. 'I want to come in and see you,' she said.

'Sure,' I replied. 'Can you give me some idea of what it's about?'

'Yes,' she replied, slowly. 'It's my husband – he's a bigamist.'

Blimey, I thought, that's one that you don't get saddled with every day, so I made an appointment for her to come in the following day; in the meantime, I grabbed hold of my ten-year-old Detective Training School course notes to find out what was required to prove a bigamous marriage, because I certainly didn't know.

Bigamy was (and probably still is) an offence, contrary to Section 57 Offences Against the Person Act 1861, punishable on indictment with a maximum seven-year gaol term. So what I had to do first was to prove the celebration of the lawful or first marriage and identify both parties. Whilst the legal spouse was competent to give evidence, he or she was not compellable and therefore witnesses would have to be traced to give evidence of the ceremony and be able to identify both parties. I would have to obtain a certified copy of the entry in the marriage register. I would then have to prove that the lawful spouse was alive at the time of the bigamous wedding. Next, I'd have to trace witnesses from the bigamous marriage – get wedding photographs if possible – and get a certified copy of the entry in the marriage register for the bigamous marriage, as well. And if the bigamous marriage had taken place abroad, I'd have to find witnesses who could state that the ceremony was a lawful form of marriage, even though the marriage itself wasn't – but if the lawful marriage had been conducted abroad, a witness from the consulate of that country would have to give evidence as to the lawfulness of the ceremony. But supposing the suspect could show a mistaken belief that he reasonably thought his spouse to be dead at the time of the bigamous marriage? This was a lawful defence to a charge of bigamy, as was a reasonable belief that one's first marriage was void, as was an honest belief that at the time of the second marriage, the first had been dissolved by divorce. Oh dear – what a can of worms! Well, lucky I'd kept those old Detective Training School notes; luckier still I'd actually attended the Detective Training School, because a decade or so later, a reckless commissioner, acting, no doubt on sycophantic advice, closed the school, in the honest (but mistaken) belief that young detectives could learn their trade out on the streets and sort of . . . you know . . . pick it up as they went along.

So the following day, at the appointed hour, in walked Janice Allen with a glum-looking weasel. This turned out to be her solicitor and he had every reason to be miserable; he could sense that, somehow, this case wasn't going to be an 'earner'. We sat down and I said, 'Now, as I understand it, you want to report your husband for bigamy, because he's gone and married another woman while you were still legally married to him?'

Which just goes to illustrate the inadvisability of having preconceived ideas, because she replied, 'No – he was already married when he married me.'

'When did you find out that he was married?' I asked.

'Oh, I knew he was married before he married me,' she replied. 'We've been living apart for some time and now, I've met someone that I do want to marry. My husband's found out and he's been blackmailing me, by saying that if I don't stop seeing my boyfriend, he'll expose me as a bigamist.'

'Ah!' I said, quickly setting aside a witness statement form which I'd intended to use and replacing it with one more suitable for confessions.

I took a long and detailed statement from her, which included the most minute details about the bigamous wedding ceremony and as many details that she could provide about the lawful one, and released her on bail.

The errant husband, Steve Allen, lived in County Durham so, having filled in the Crime Book entry, I called Joe over. 'Right, Joe, we've got a trip to Durham to catch a bigamist and a blackmailer but before we do, we've got a lot of groundwork to put in.' Joe displayed enthusiasm, so I handed him a photocopy of Janice Allen's statement. After he'd read it, I pointed out names and locations that I'd highlighted. 'This woman, April Jenkins, was matron of honour at the second marriage. You can see that Janice doesn't know her address, just the area, but we can find that out through the telephone directory or the electoral roll; failing that, perhaps the local beat copper will know and, if she's moved, maybe some of the neighbours can point us in the right direction . . . Harry Ponsford was Steve Allen's best man at the second wedding – this is the street where he was living, so finding the number will be a piece of cake – he's also important, because he arranged for the wedding photos to be taken. If he hasn't any of the photos himself, perhaps the photographer will still have the negatives . . .' This was all bread and butter stuff, but it was the framework of the case against the Allens, so it was vital to get it right. Joe seemed a bit overawed by this but all I was doing was utilizing the major enquiry skills I'd learnt on the Serious Crime Squad and scaling them down a bit. I got the distinct impression that Joe's past investigative enquiries had been conducted on a wing-and-a-prayer basis but, within a few days, Joe and I boarded a train at King's Cross and headed north. We were met at Durham railway station by the local CID and, after an enthusiastic welcome, we were booked in at a local hotel with instructions for the local liaison officer to pick us up from there, early the follow-ing morning. The evening that Joe and I spent together was completely 'dry' – not my idea of fun, but what was the point of me trying to have a sensible drink if Joe was going to end up arseholed? The next morning, we were driven away to the east, to Shotton Colliery and at 6.30 a.m., I was knocking on the peeling front door of a shabby terraced house. Sometimes, it's difficult to know how best to approach a tricky situation like this one, but since I'd discovered that Steve Allen had got form for violence, I decided the direct approach was best. The door was opened by a dishevelled, tousle-haired Steve Allen who was still rubbing the sleep out of his eyes when I grabbed hold of him, introduced myself and informed him that he was under arrest for bigamy and blackmail. 'Get dressed,' I said, shortly. 'You're coming with me.' Allen simply stared at me and then suddenly burst into tears – goodness, what an unhappy bigamist he was! At the local police station, he strenuously denied blackmail (and in fairness, perhaps Janice had been gilding the lily just a bit) but admitted the big-amous marriage in great detail.

Released on bail from the police station, 'and don't think you're out of the woods yet, because you ain't!' the tearful big-amist began the slow trudge back to Shotton Colliery. During the next couple of days, Joe and I made ourselves busy, tracing and obtaining statements from the witnesses at both wed-dings and obtaining the photographs from both occasions. It had been an interesting, if boringly sober trip and, returning to London, I prepared a comprehensive report for the Director of Public Prosecutions. I also reported to the DCI that, off the sauce, Joe had behaved quite well; indeed, he had made quite a substantial contribution to the case. The DCI choked on his morning coffee stating, quite rightly, that I was larding up the facts and sourly adding that he didn't believe a word of it.

The docket returned from the Director of Public Prosecutions and he agreed with my view that there was insufficient evidence to proceed against Steve Allen on a charge of blackmail. He decided that little would be gained by prosecuting the Allens for bigamy, so he instructed that both should be cautioned under the provisions of the attorney general's guidelines. In fact, it turned out well for everybody. He praised my investigation of the case, complimenting me for 'tenacity and ability' and, although it certainly didn't merit further commendation, it was nice to receive a pat on the back, as opposed to a kick up the arse. The Allens were pleased too, because now, having received the most humane of knuckle-rapping, they were free to get on with their separate lives. And Joe was happy, because he'd received a stay of execution and had been retained in the CID – for the time being.

Funnily enough, the next case which involved Joe (and which occurred just days after the Allens' bigamous antics) was another blackmail investigation; and a pretty nasty one it was, too.

Adam Gray was a fourteen-year-old kid with a couple of minor convictions for dishonesty. He had shacked up with a nineteen-year-old girl who similarly had form and who, after she had begun foaling at an alarming rate with a multiplicity of indifferent partners, was rewarded with a large, high-rise flat, courtesy of a grateful Islington Council – hence her and Adam's cosy arrangement. Adam looked older than his fourteen years and, persuading a local shopkeeper named Ikhbal Siddiqui that he was eighteen, he obtained goods to the value of £11 on credit. When Siddiqui discovered that Adam was, in fact, four years younger than his assumed age (and therefore not in receipt of Social Security benefits with which to repay his benefactor), he demanded immediate repayment,

187

and if this was not forthcoming, he threatened that Adam would be 'stitched-up' for a robbery. Adam prudently vanished and this was when I appeared on the scene: to investigate the allegation of robbery at Siddiqui's store. Siddiqui told me a dramatic story of how he and his brother had been confronted by a knife-wielding raider, who had snatched money and cigarettes to the value of £70 before running off, with the brothers Siddiqui in hot pursuit. Listening to them, you'd have thought that their gallantry would have been recognized by an immediate award of the Binney Medal. They provided a detailed description of their assailant – so much so that I felt that, if I saw him, I could not fail to recognize him.

A few days later, I received a telephone call from Siddiqui, who told me that he had received an anonymous tip-off that a person named Adam Gray had been responsible for the robbery. I made a few enquiries and discovered that a minor tearaway by that name lived just off the manor and that he certainly appeared to fit the description given by the Siddiquis. The following morning, I scooped him up and interviewed him at the police station in the presence of a social worker. Adam strenuously denied the robbery and explained what had happened, in just the way I've described it. I didn't believe him and told him so, quite forcefully, too, which caused the Social Worker to huff and puff. His story, I told him, was incredible: nobody would invent such a story for the sake of eleven measly quid. 'Siddiqui did,' Adam retorted. So locking him up, I strolled off down the Hornsey Road to Siddiqui's shop and told the brothers what Adam had said. They were shocked, they said, and outraged, too. Sticking firmly to their story, they indignantly repudiated these claims and reinforced them with written statements, in full knowledge that an innocent boy had been locked in the cells at the local police station, accused of a crime which they knew he had not committed and which had not even occurred.

But I still disbelieved Adam's story, so I returned to the police station where I tried to arrange an identity parade. I was unable to assemble the required number of participants so, eight-and-a-half hours after his initial incarceration, Adam was released on bail, until such time that an identification parade could be held.

So far as I was concerned, Adam was as guilty as sin. I spoke to a police officer who had previously dealt with Adam and told him the details of the crime of which Adam had been accused. 'Robbery?' the officer queried, shaking his head. 'No, I wouldn't have thought so. Adam's not the sort of kid to be violent.' Drip, I thought, that's all you know!

Because, as I'd said to Adam, nobody would invent such a thing for the sake of eleven quid; especially when they'd been challenged about it. But, all the same, I took a closer look at friend Siddiqui; and what do you think I found out? A year previously, somebody else had owed him money and he, too, had refused to pay. So Siddiqui anonymously telephoned the police and told them there was a bomb in the debtor's office. When the police arrived and evacuated the rival's office, Siddiqui used the cover of the ensuing panic of the fleeing office workers to creep into his opponent's office and search his briefcase for the money. He got six months for that.

Well, well. I dug a little deeper. I traced the nineteen-year-old slattern, and although Adam had foresworn her bed and company, her sentimentality for him overcame her natural abhorrence of grassing and she confirmed that everything Adam had told me was true. From her, I obtained several more leads and over the next weeks and then months, I tracked them down and started amassing quite a lot of solid evidence against Mr Siddiqui and his equally dishonest sibling. My biggest break came when I unearthed a witness who described a conversation that he had previously had with Siddiqui who had told him precisely what would happen to Adam if the owed money was not forthcoming. It was at that point that I grabbed hold of Joe Matthews and said, 'Come on.'

The brothers Siddiqui were brought in and, after a token denial, cracked and admitted everything. I told Joe to send the SPECRIM message on the teleprinter to the deputy assistant commissioner 'C' Department (Operations) to inform him and a number of other agencies of an arrest for a serious and interesting crime, and poor Joe became quite overcome when I told him to ensure that one of the arrests was shown as down to him. 'But I didn't actually do anything . . .' he protested. 'All I did was write the notes . . .'

'Joe,' I said quietly. 'Now listen. I hope I don't have to impress our senior officers that I know how to arrest criminals. However,' I added, 'you do!'

Ikhbal Siddiqui pleaded guilty to a charge of blackmail and both brothers pleaded guilty to conspiracy to pervert the course of public justice. Fortunately for them, the judge at the Bailey was the same deaf, irascible, daft old bugger that both Peter Connor and I had crossed swords with several times before. So bearing in mind that the maximum penalty for blackmail is fourteen years' imprisonment, that the elder Siddiqui had a very recent previous conviction for almost exactly the same sort of offence and that the victim was a fourteen-year-old boy, the judge sentenced him to 6 months' imprisonment. With the time he'd spent on remand, I should think Siddiqui had about five minutes of his sentence left to serve. His brother, for his part in swearing an innocent kid's life away, was fined just £75. So much for British justice.

I was later personally commended by Deputy Assistant Commissioner Mike Richards OBE for 'diligence and detective ability' in cracking the case, so I was quite pleased; I was about the only one who was.

Adam was so seriously affected that he attempted suicide and was placed into permanent care. The Siddiquis returned to their store and to their dismay discovered that every window in the place had been smashed and particularly unflattering remarks had been sprayed over the frontage of the premises. They, too, left the area. And Joe fell by the wayside once too often. By now, I'd moved on to another police station and, without me to champion his cause, he had made the mistake of coming on duty one morning still pissed from the night before. He was kicked straight back to uniform and, as he spiralled downwards, out of control, his wife left him, their home was sold and Joe made another disastrous and very short-lived marriage.

The last I saw of Joe was a few years later at an armed siege. Following a security van robbery, one of the participants, who was armed with an automatic shotgun and had been separated from his colleagues, had been chased through the streets; he had used a couple of passers-by (including a seventy-one-year-old widow) as human shields, tried to hi-jack a car, fired shots at anything that moved and held police officers at bay, before bursting into a council flat and taking a pensioner hostage. I'd arrived at the scene to discover the repellent young protagonist screeching his illogical demands to an unfair world, the pensioner's distraught wife, just returned from a shopping trip and attempting to find out what had happened to her husband, and a gaggle of very senior uniform officers who were rushing about like headless chickens. As I attempted to take charge of this scene of orchestrated chaos, I felt my sleeve being urgently tugged. 'Anything I can do,

Sarge?' an eager voice said – a voice I knew well. Turning, I looked into the excited face of the uniform officer who was plucking at my sleeve. I shook my head. 'Sorry, Joe,' I replied. 'Not this time!'

Rough and Tumble

There are times when there isn't any back-up. Then you have to be resolute. This is particularly the case with undercover men and women whose courage takes my breath away. Thank goodness I was never asked to participate in anything like that because I've been scared more times than I care to remember. On one occasion, I was involved in an arrest which developed into a huge riot.

It had started out as a routine arrest – for possessing an offensive weapon. And after my prisoner had wrenched himself free it developed into a chase, which culminated in my re-arresting him, surrounded by a howling mob of his chums. One of the group was an enormous youth, who loudly professed to be an authority on karate. He attacked Police Constable Dave Castle and as Police Constable Dennis 'Buck' Ryan came to his aid and pushed the youth down on the bonnet of the area car, he savagely bit Buck in the shoulder. An elderly bus inspector tried to intervene and was kicked in the groin by this young man, who finally met his match in a police constable, by then no longer in the first flush of youth, who was not at all fazed by the news that his opponent was a Karate expert. 'Are yer?' he replied, grimly. 'Well, I'm a Graeco-Roman expert – come 'ere!' And with that, this violent thug was seized in what is known in wrestling circles as a side chancery and was dragged off shrieking to the local nick. Meanwhile, I was pushed into the back of an area car with my prisoner, another prisoner swiftly joined us and as I was fighting with both of them, I looked out of the car window. We were in Ilford High Road, but I could see neither shops or vehicles in that busy thoroughfare; all I could see were men fighting, and I devoutly wished that I was elsewhere. With my two prisoners trying to get out, it occurred to me that some of their mates might well try to get in, to rescue them – and my worst fears were confirmed as the front passenger door was suddenly wrenched open and a figure launched himself towards us over the front seats. As he did so, I punched him hard on the nose.

'And did this unfortunate gentleman say anything, as a result?' the defence barrister enquired silkily, in court some months later.

'Well, yes,' I replied, feeling rather abashed. 'He said, "You fucking idiot, I'm CID!"'

The barrister nodded, sagely. 'Quite so,' he replied. 'A bit handy with your fists, weren't you?' he added.

You weren't there, you little wanker, I thought to myself, but the point I'm trying to make is this – the police officers who were there that night were tough and brave and they weren't going to turn away from a colleague in trouble. It didn't happen on every occasion.

The officer who I shall refer to as PC Bloggs was a few years older than I and had established a reputation for cunning and column-dodging to black-belt standards. On one occasion, he was the station telephonist and during the first half of his tour of duty he kept coughing and spluttering. 'I'm ill,' he whined. 'I think I'm coming down with flu – I don't reckon I'll be in for the next few days.' If he said this once, he said it half-a-dozen times. At last, it was time for his meal break and as he shuffled off to the canteen, the rest of the reserve room breathed a sigh of relief for this welcome break from his coughing and whimpering. As he returned, the relief telephonist who had mercifully been spared Bloggs' snivelling, stood up and prepared to go for his own meal break. 'Oh, by the way, Bloggsy,' he said, as he walked towards the reserve room door, 'your wife phoned up. She said all the wallpaper and paint has arrived, so could you start the decorating tomorrow, like you said?' The others in the reserve room roared with laughter at Bloggs being caught out, but, true to form, Bloggs didn't turn a hair. It also didn't stop him going sick for the next three days, either.

Very early in my career, I gained considerable court experience, although it was the sort of education that I could well have done without, since I found myself standing in the dock. While out walking my beat, I had discovered a van parked on the pavement. I had traced the owner and asked him to move it and he had refused. I was joined by another police constable who also told him to move the vehicle. Again the owner refused, then punched the other officer in the eye. During the ensuing struggle, the man grabbed hold of the van's wing mirror to stop himself being placed into the police car. I took hold of his thumb to release his grip and, in so doing, broke it. Now, at the nick, he made all sorts of malicious allegations against us, and the very nervous duty officer, having charged him, promptly bailed him, after the man had refused to provide his fingerprints. If he had been kept in custody until his court appearance when an order to take his fingerprints could have been obtained from the magistrates, it would have revealed that he had given a false name, was a criminal who had served a term of imprisonment, and who, deciding that prison life was not for him, had arranged a little unofficial parole of his own: he had been on the run for two years. In addition, he was also on bail for offences of obtaining credit by fraud, forgery, false pretences and fraudulent conversion.

Still, all that and the charge against me for actual bodily harm which was ultimately slung out was all in the future. At the time I was extremely worried. Here I was, accused of a serious assault. I felt sure that I had acted properly: the man had assaulted a fellow officer, he had been arrested for doing so, he had struggled violently and tried to prevent his arrest by hanging on to the wing-mirror, so I was entitled to use reasonable force to effect his arrest – wasn't I? It wasn't as if I'd set out to break the wretched man's thumb, and now I wished I'd never clapped eyes on him, but that's what had happened, and by the time I reached the canteen for a much-needed cuppa, the nick was full of it. In the forefront of the canteen cowboys was Bloggs. 'Did you give him a verbal?' he sneered, slyly. I hadn't a clue what he meant. 'Well,' I replied, 'I was going to give him a verbal warning if that's what you meant,' and led by Bloggs, who had never verballed anybody in his life, the entire canteen roared their appreciation of my naïveté.

Let's leave Bloggs for a moment. Remember the fight in the High Road? Because a yob element was steadily advancing on Ilford, my fellow probationer, Dick Miles, and I decided to approach our duty officer for permission to work a plain-clothes' patrol for rowdyism. We backed up our request with an impressive list of arrests which we'd both made for this sort of anti-social behaviour and assent was finally, albeit grudgingly, given. Dick and I were delighted, until we were told that we would not be allowed to work together: the memory of how Dick and I had been involved in a pub fight which had taken on the proportions of a Wild West saloon brawl was still sharp in the minds of our senior officers and we were given different partners.

Instead, my fellow officer was a useful young PC named Ron Turnbull. Ron, I seem to remember, was enamoured with a young woman who specialized in exotic Balinese dancing and we both shared a taste for adventure and mischievous behaviour. Ron's slight eccentricity was displayed when we chased and arrested two young low-lifes whose idea of fun was to terrify old-age pensioners by throwing fireworks at them. Ron's prisoner was dragged by the scruff of his neck to a nearby telephone box where Ron muttered terse instructions to him. I watched in wonderment as this piece of refuse picked up the telephone receiver, dialled 999 and said, "Allo, is that the police? Can you come and take us down the nick – me and my mate've been naughty!' 'Blimey, Ron,' I said afterwards. 'That's style!'

The Ilford Palais was a lucrative venue for bad behaviour – yobs came from all over London to cause trouble amongst the dozens of teenagers who'd gone there just to have a good time. Ron and I spotted five such characters, who'd come from Notting Hill, Kilburn, Forest Gate and Holloway and who were intimidating the harmless youngsters who were entering the Palais. One of the group was asking them for money, and getting it, too, and was whooping his success to his chums. Of course, we swiped up the five of them and, the following day at Barking Magistrates' Court, the ringleader, who was informed that he could be facing a charge of blackmail, gratefully tendered a plea to begging. A couple of nights later, Ron and I were patrolling the High Road when we saw three rather drunk young men set fire to a rubbish bin which they then solemnly proceeded to dance around. Ron and I stepped in and nabbed them and – goodness – what a fight ensued. We later discovered that this group had been fighting as mercenaries in Angola and upon their return to the old country had been letting off a little steam. The five of us rolled around on the pavement, punching, kneeing, elbowing until – thank heavens! – a Panda car drew up. This was a welcome sight because, if the truth be known, Ron and I had been getting the worst of this encounter and both of us had taken considerable punishment. I wondered why my prisoner had not been pulled off me and flung into the back of the police car – and then I looked up and saw the smirking face of the driver. It was Bloggs. He simply looked at us, gave a short laugh and drove off. Fortunately, the van came along and we received some proper assistance. As the van roared off with our prisoners, Ron and I dusted ourselves down. Across the road, the Palais had just emptied and the crowds had stopped to witness the fight. Now, Ron was furious that we'd been bashed-up, and was even more furious at Bloggs' attitude, so when one youth who was part of the audience displayed considerable mirth at our plight, Ron's rage boiled over. Stepping smartly across the road, he furiously suggested to the grinning youth that it would be in his interests to shove off, before harm befell him. Difficult to say what might have happened next, because a steadying hand was placed on the cheeky youth's shoulder. It belonged to our erstwhile client, the beggar of the Palais. 'Come on, man,' he said, sadly. 'Let's go. It no use arguin' – they stitch you up!' And with that slanderous comment, the situation was defused and we were able to return to the nick, where I sought out the company of Bloggs. 'Thanks for your help back there,' I said, furiously.

He shrugged. 'You looked so funny, rolling about there,' he said blandly, 'that I was laughing so much, I couldn't have helped, anyway.'

'I hope I can return the favour one day,' I shouted to his retreating back, but, as I said it, I knew it was an empty threat. Bloggs had never put himself in that sort of situation, and for the rest of the time that I knew him, he never would.

On the last night of our patrol Ron and I excelled ourselves. A dozen young men had enjoyed a drunken celebration and had now got out of control, as they spilled out of a pub in Ilford Lane. It was the sort of behaviour that could degenerate into smashing shop windows and attacking passers-by, instead of being frightened as they now were, so Ron and I stepped in and nicked the lot. We lined them up against a wall and I quickly phoned Ilford police station. Dick Miles was the telephonist. 'Milesy, we've got a dozen prisoners down here and it looks like things could get out of control,' I said, nervously. 'Be a pal and get the van down here, sharpish!'

'Right!' answered Dick, and, just then, Bloggs, the van driver, walked past the reserve room. 'Just the man!' cried Dick. 'Bloggsy, get the van down to the Broadway, quick – Dick Kirby's got a dozen prisoners down there!'

Bloggs looked at him blankly. 'Dick Kirby?' he echoed. 'I ain't getting the van out for him – that bloke's trouble!' '*You fucking coward!*' roared Dick, and bare-headed, he ran out of the nick and sprinted down to the Broadway, where, stick drawn, he helped usher the prisoners into the nick. Dick later received a bollocking from the duty officer for leaving the station helmetless and the telephones unmanned, whilst Bloggs got away with it scot free. I should like to be able to report that Bloggs eventually received his come-uppance but, alas, it would not be true. He drifted through the rest of his service, ducking his responsibilities and unmolested by criminals or senior police officers alike, he now is enjoying a long, stress-free retirement.

Pity, really.

A Question of Corruption

Since its inception, the Flying Squad has always been in the public eye. It was accurately identified as the top crime-busting arm of the Metropolitan Police and, if the men who staffed it were described as being hard-faced, incorruptible detectives who always got their man, the press, who were responsible for this slightly inflated hyperbole, had pretty well got it right. But when people are put in a position of great trust, there are always those who will abuse it and, when that happens, because of their position and the betrayal it involves, it is eminently newsworthy. When a police officer is convicted of corruption, the Police Service is embarrassed because of the adverse publicity, but when that police officer is a member of the elite Flying Squad, it is catastrophic.

Ever since it began in 1829, there have, inevitably, been bad apples in the Metropolitan Police, and the same applies to the Flying Squad. During the 1970s, the Squad was dealt a crushing blow when past and present members of its ranks were sentenced to various terms of imprisonment for corruption. Since then, there have sadly been other instances of criminality in the Squad. When it happens, it not only tarnishes the reputation of this elite band of thief takers, it also infuriates the vast majority of its members who are a hundred per cent straight.

In order to combat corruption in the ranks, the police police themselves. This brings howls of derision from the dissident groups who loathe the police and everything they do. In their eyes, every internal investigation is a whitewash: something I, and indeed most officers who have had their conduct scrutinized, can categorically state is bollocks. Mind you, I've always thought it highly amusing that those who have chosen to live outside the law, who despise the police and display their open contempt for law and order, go straight to the police when they want to complain about an officer's conduct. This has happened frequently with terrorists in Northern Ireland. So can investigations into what are often very serious allegations of misconduct, be conducted by anyone other than the police? It is difficult to think of a viable alternative.

Traditionally, internal investigations were carried out by two arms of the Metropolitan Police. If the allegation made was one of faulty discipline – rudeness to a member of the public, for example – it was usually dealt with by a uniformed chief inspector. If the offence alleged was more serious – an assault, for instance – it was often investigated by someone of detective chief inspector rank. He would also deal with any matters of discipline arising out of the allegation. The second arm came into play with far more serious and damaging allegations, such as corruption. This was dealt with by officers from COC1 department, originally known as 'Central'. They were nicknamed 'the OGPU', after Stalin's secret police in the 1920s and 1930s, which committed terrible atrocities. Many of the officers investigated by the Scotland Yard equivalent expressed their conviction that there were certain similarities with their Russian counterparts. Sometimes, the officers charged with investigating these allegations of impropriety were known as 'Rubber-heelers' on account of their predilection for creeping up silently behind you and stabbing you in the arse. Not every officer in that situation was guilty of this:

many were thoroughly decent men, who had been appointed to investigate their colleagues, and thought the whole matter distasteful, but they did a thorough job, got it out of the way and returned to other investigations. No, those officers who volunteered for these duties were the ones dubbed 'Rubber-heelers'. Often, they were failed detectives, or detectives who were largely ineffective against proper criminals, and, as such, despised by their contemporaries. Therefore, to sit in the interrogator's seat and have someone sitting opposite them who, they hoped, would soon be squirming with dread at the thought of being 'sent back to the big hat' was, to them, the pinnacle of their career. On one such occasion, a uniformed chief inspector went to incredible lengths to screw me down. He investigated a complaint which had been received from a woman who accused me of going to her address on more than one occasion to arrest her husband who was wanted for a serious offence, despite her having told me that he wasn't there. On the second occasion that he wanted to interview me, I prudently took 'a friend' – the CID's Federation representative with me, who knew the rules rather better than I and silenced this piece of garbage when he tried to threaten and bluster again. The chief inspector later became a commander, having spent several triumphant tours on CIB2; the Federation Representative got nicked, and chucked out of the job. I'm sure there's a moral here somewhere.

Later still, Divisional Complaint Units were formed, usually headed by a uniform chief inspector and a sergeant, so this was a full-time posting. And, in addition, there was A.10, which later became CIB2 – let me tell you how all this came about . . .

In 1968, the future commissioner, Sir Robert Mark GBE, QPM, had been appointed deputy commissioner of the Metropolitan Police. As such, he controlled all matters of discipline and he immediately stopped the practice of allowing officers, who were suspended from duty whilst lodging an appeal against dismissal from the Force, to be on full pay. And where the Director of Public Prosecutions had declined to prosecute officers, simply because there was insufficient evidence (or if the officers had been acquitted at court), Mark now wished to consider the case papers to see if there were sufficient grounds to bring disciplinary proceedings against them.

Mark criticized the way that Metropolitan Police CID officers had investigated each other in the past which, in his opinion, seldom led to disciplinary proceedings, let alone a court appearance, and the commissioner, Sir John Waldron KCVO, told him to go ahead and start A.10 – the police complaints department. This Mark filled with a mixture of CID and uniform officers and some – certainly not all – were a collection of some of the most cowardly, vindictive characters it has ever been my displeasure to meet.

Be that as it may, it appeared to be not a moment too soon. An exclusive in the *Sunday People* revealed that none other than the commander of the Flying Squad, Ken Drury, had been on holiday with his wife to Cyprus with Soho businessman, Jimmy Humphries and his ex-stripper wife Rusty. It was an imprudent move by Drury, to say the very least. Humphries had had a chequered criminal career, which included a six-year sentence in Dartmoor. He had also paid for Drury's holiday, and when Drury sold his own story to a rival tabloid, *The News of the World*, he desperately tried to suggest that the reason he had gone to Cyprus was to search for the Great Train robber, Ronnie Biggs, who had escaped from prison some six years previously. This was a bit too much for Humphries who, realizing the dangers of being labelled a grass, gave an alternative version of the tale. It was a disaster for Drury and, indeed, for the whole of the Flying Squad.

A Question of Corruption

Allegations were made by a Flying Squad resident informant (or supergrass) that gangs had carried out three armed robberies, with the assistance and connivance of City of London police officers. The Squad commander, Don Neesham, informed Assistant Commissioner Kelland and, as a result, 'Operation Countryman' was formed, manned by West Country provincial police officers. They were swiftly nicknamed 'The Sweedey' by their London counterparts, not only because of their lack of sophistication but also because of their naïve eagerness to believe anything said by armed robbers who were desperate to be let off the hook. As the allegations drifted into the Metropolitan Police in general and the Flying Squad in particular, the staff of 'Countryman' complained that they had been blocked at every turn by the Yard. This was strongly denied by the Squad commander, who, it will be remembered, had been responsible for instigating the inquiry, but Neesham was shifted from the Squad and later resigned. He died a few years ago; how bitter he must have felt at this shabby treatment. He was not alone. More shoddy treatment was meted out to a number of Squadmen, past and present, who were suspended on the flimsiest of evidence. One such was John O'Connor who, at the time, was a detective chief inspector. Ten years after the event, he told me, 'I was suspended for eighteen months on the word of a blagger, who I'd never met, who said he'd bunged me. I think they must've realized their mistake, because after I was reinstated, they couldn't stop promoting me!' He was right: at the time of our conversation, he was commander of the Flying Squad – not an appointment given to someone whose probity was in any doubt.

After four long years, Countryman ground to a halt. They had secured just three successful prosecutions of police officers. Two of them were from the City of London police force, from whence the inquiry had originated. The cost, in the region of £3 million, was enormous, both to the public purse and to the morale of the Flying Squad.

In spite of being knocked sideways, by the immensely damaging allegations that had been made and the non-existent leadership from above, the Squad continued to make tremendous inroads into the detection, arrest and successful prosecution of organized, sophisticated gangs of armed robbers, but then, as now, a wave of Flying Squad hysteria swept across the Metropolitan Police district. The following story, in which the names have been changed to protect the vacuous and the intransigent, and which occurred, oh, 20 years ago or more, serves to illustrate the sort of hysteria which many police officers felt about the Squad.

George Collins was a grey-faced uniform inspector who, during his 29 years and nine months' service with the Metropolitan Police had done absolutely nothing of any merit. He looked with something akin to longing for the next three months to pass as quickly and uneventfully as possible so that he could grab his pension and retire to nurse his ulcers. During his career, he had passed the necessary couple of examinations to bring him to his present rank but, in so doing, practical police work had never interfered with his studies. His last appearance in court was now no more than a dim and distant memory. He had never been commended but, due to his sedulous inactivity, his conduct had never been complained of, either. His police work was a vacuum, with his days spent dotting the i's and crossing the t's of station trivia. In short, George was a complete and utter drip.

And then, one spring morning, to spoil everything, who should turn up at his police station but a Flying Squad team, having arrested a local villain, together with forty-nine cartons of tea which he had feloniously received. George shivered as he beheld the unscrupulous, piratical-looking bunch of scoundrels who were littering up his tidy charge room. Several of them were unshaven, since they had been up before dawn in order to plot up the receiver's address, and George briefly toyed with the idea of finding someone to whom he could report their scruffy appearance, but dismissed the idea as quickly as it had been formed, for fear of reprisals. In comparison with George, all these Squadmen had been commended, not once but many times; similarly, all had been on the receiving end of malicious but damaging allegations of impropriety made by desperate criminals. The only common denominator was that they all possessed warrant cards; otherwise, they were as alike as beings from different planets. This, thought George, was the stuff that nightmares were made of. He knew, of course, that it was an irrefutable fact of life that the CID were bent; and now, the worst of the bunch, the Flying Squad, were here at his station. Right, George resolved that from now on everything would be done strictly by the book. Nobody was going to interfere with *his* pension. And so, while the Squadmen waited, sighed, tapped their feet impatiently and looked up at the sky, George counted the cartons of tea *eight* times to ensure he'd got it completely right. He was only stopped from repeating the process for the ninth occasion, after the Squad's detective inspector loomed ominously over him and growled menacingly, "'Bout time you sorted out your fucking arithmetic, ain't it?'

So it was 49 cartons of tea that George dutifully and personally recorded on the receiver's charge sheet, and it was he who personally stowed the tea into the station's bulky property store. And as George, the perspiration running down his face, pushed the last carton inside the store and locked the door, his ulcers gave a small twinge of protest. But it didn't matter, thought George, as he walked back across the station yard. Everything was tip-top.

A Question of Corruption

The superintendent at the station was Frank Bruce. A tall, overpowering, bombastic man, he knew, as sure as the sun would rise in the east and set in the west, that the CID were bent, and he hated them. Not that the CID were a particularly endangered species, because Frank Bruce hated *everybody*. And according to rank or status, everybody hated, despised or feared Frank Bruce.

Two days after the Squad arrest, Bruce returned from leave and was checking the station's books, looking for some discrepancy, no matter how small, so that he could identify and then publicly humiliate the person responsible. Suddenly, his eyes fell upon the receiver's charge sheet and he quickly scanned the details. The Flying Squad! In *his* station! And that idiot Collins had failed to notify him of it immediately. Right, thought Bruce. What's this? Charged with receiving 49 cartons of tea, the property of Albert Cross and Sons, Manchester? We'll see about that. And off went Bruce to the bulky property store, unlocked it and counted the cartons of tea. Forty-seven! Christ, I can hardly believe my luck, thought Bruce, and then, just to be sure, counted them again. Forty-seven it was. Carefully relocking the bulky property store, Bruce spotted Inspector George Collins walking across the yard.

'*Collins!*' Bruce bellowed, and George started, since he had thought that Bruce was not resuming duty until the following day. He trotted over to Bruce, the steel claws of the crabs inside his stomach nipping him ferociously.

'Yessir?' he panted, looking up at Bruce. He was as short, as Bruce was tall.

'Was it you who checked in that tea that those bent Flying Squad bastards brought in the other day?' he demanded.

'Yes, I did sir and I counted them, every one,' gabbled George. 'Eight times,' he added.

'And were there 49 of them?' Bruce asked, softly.

'Yes, that's right, sir. Forty-nine,' George confirmed. '*Well, there fucking-well isn't now!*' screamed Bruce. '*There's two fucking missing! You're involved with those bent bastards, aren't you!*'

'No! No!' cried George, his worst fears realized. Goodbye pension!

'What was the deal, Collins?' Bruce snarled, bringing his face down close to George's. 'One for you and one for them? *Is that it?*'

'No! No!' George sobbed, sounding very much like a Victorian stage heroine, about to be rogered by the wicked scoundrel.

By now, the station's civilian staff had given up all pretence of typing and filing and were craning their necks from the second-floor windows to view the spectacle in the arena below. One elderly lady who, as she was passing by in the street, heard the commotion and actually went into the station yard, was absolutely flabbergasted at the sight of the two police officers, both in full uniform, who were facing each other. The taller of the two, who had a lot of scrambled egg on his cap, was screaming into the face of the shorter one, who had started to sob loudly and was being sprayed with saliva. Fearfully, the pensioner crept away, unable to comprehend what was going on and as a thin finger of pain began to creep across her chest, she unsteadily headed towards the front office.

'Right!' snapped Bruce. 'Stop that crying and get A.10 down here, *right now!*'

'Yessir!' George stuttered, and saluting so badly that he gouged a trough above his right eyebrow with his thumb nail, he turned and scuttled across the yard towards the front office, pausing only to collide spectacularly with a passing constable, who was carrying a tray of teas.

Rushing into the front office, George snatched the only telephone from the hand of a woman police constable who was frantically trying to inform the ambulance service about the plight of the blue-faced pensioner who had just collapsed with chest pains in the waiting-room and, in a voice shaking with emotion, demanded to be connected with A.10, the police complaints branch.

Impatiently pacing up and down in the yard, waiting for what would be his finest hour, Bruce was suddenly accosted by old Norman Bell. Norman had served his country with distinction during the Second World War and had been decorated for his conspicuous gallantry. Upon demobilization, he had joined the Metropolitan Police with a chest full of medal ribbons and had conscientiously served it for 30 years. To supplement his pension, Norman was now employed as a civilian storeman, one of his duties being the safe custody of prisoner's property. And Norman who, in truth, had never been a respecter of rank, didn't give a rat's-arse about *anybody*.

'Wot's all the bleeding noise about?' he protested to Bruce. 'You bleedin'-well woke me up!'

Bruce was tempted to put a flea in the old bastard's ear, but he wasn't too sure about his status in bollocking a civvie. And what's more, as storeman, old Norman was going to be a prime prosecution witness, when those Flying Squad thieves were brought to trial. Better be civil to him, Bruce thought.

'Two of those cartons of tea are missing from the bulky property store,' he said, impressively. 'I have reason to believe that the Flying Squad have got them.'

'Quite right, they have,' grunted Norman, through the stem of his pipe.

'*What!*' shouted Bruce. This was wonderful news!

'Yep, took them yesterday, they did,' continued Norman. 'One to go to court with the prisoner and the other to take up

210

to the owners in Manchester, so's they could formally identify it. Ah!' he cried, his eyes settling on the charge sheet that Bruce was holding. 'So *you're* the one who's got it!' And taking the charge sheet from Bruce's hands, he turned it over. 'There you are,' Norman said, showing Bruce the 'disposal of property' section on the reverse of the sheet. '"Received two cartons of tea." All signed for by the Flying Squad. I wondered where this had gone! No wonder I can't keep my books straight,' he said, 'with people like you about,' he added, darkly.

Bruce trembled as the staggering proportions of his *gaffe* sank in and then, as he saw Inspector George Collins emerge from the front office, realized the implications of the terrible course of action he had instigated.

'*Collins!*' he screamed.

'Don't worry, sir,' replied George with a sunny smile. 'They're on their way!'

'ilda 'arris Went to Paris

Or at least, I should think she did. Hilda was an intrepid traveller and, because she was a born romantic, I should think it impossible that she never visited the City of Lights; but whatever the case, it's a good reason for a snappy piece of alliteration. Hilda was also an authority on the work of Dickens, possessed a tongue that a viper would have died for and was a brilliant detective. As a young CID officer, I knew women detectives who were truly excellent – Hilda Coles, Thelma Wagstaff, Joyce Cashmore, Mo Dennison and many more besides. Was the reason why they were so good because there was only a limited number of women in the police force at that time and only the best were selected to serve in the department? At the risk of seeming uncharitable to the women of today's Metropolitan Police, I suppose the answer is yes.

Hilda Jean Harris was born on 20 January 1936 in Bromley-by-Bow – a true East End girl. Just after her twenty-first birthday, she joined the Women's Royal Army Corps and there she served for seven years, achieving the rank of sergeant. After working for eight months as a clerk for the London County Council, she joined the Metropolitan Police on 5 April 1965 and began her career at Notting Hill. Within three years, she was appointed to the CID and worked at police stations on both sides of 'K' Division. As I moved in to Romford police station, Hilda had just moved out, to Leyton on promotion as detective sergeant. Still in that rank, Hilda was posted to the Yard's Serious Crime Squad, where she spent two-and-a-half years, and it was there that we met and worked together – a thoroughly enjoyable experience. She was instrumental in cracking the 'Hungarian Circle' case, which earned her her fifth commissioner's commendation and me, my first. We travelled all over the country during the course of our investigations, one of which was to Bournemouth, to keep tabs on a violent thug who had been persuaded to become a witness for the prosecution in a blackmail case. We met his girlfriend who was a poor, simpering creature, who, I could tell, immediately got 'ilda's back up – however, Hilda realized that kindness and sympathy were the order of the day, in order to keep things sweet. 'Oh, Miss Harris,' the girlfriend wailed. 'My Johnny ain't been the same since he was interviewed by that Superintendent Jones at Limehouse.' She was referring to Detective Superintendent Randall Jones, a very tough customer indeed and one who was hugely disinclined to search for the possibility of finding redeeming traits in violent criminals. I coughed discreetly and caught Hilda's eye.

'Oh, dear,' Hilda said, comfortingly.

'He can't sleep properly and his hair's been coming out in clumps on the pillow,' went on this thug's paramour. 'I've got to change the pillowcases every day!'

'Oh, you haven't, have you?' soothed Hilda.

'You don't know the worst of it, Miss Harris,' said this worthless trollop, convinced that she'd found a confidante for life. Leaning forward in a conspiratorial manner, she added, 'The worst of it is, he's started shitting the bed!'

'Oh, no!' cried Hilda. 'How awful!'

The woman priest who conducted the service at Hilda's funeral remarked that Hilda didn't suffer fools gladly. I've got news for you, dear, I thought. She didn't suffer them at all, because as we walked off down the wretched woman's front

214

path, Hilda boiled over. '"He's started shitting my bed, Miss
Harris,"' she mimicked. 'The dirty bastard! If any man
started shitting in my bed, I'd kick his fucking arse right out
of it!'

Hilda left the Serious Crime Squad in early 1977 having
been promoted to detective inspector and after three years
working on 'E' Division, returned to 'K' Division and later
still, upon promotion to detective chief inspector, to the
Detective Training School. Women officers, over and above
the rank of DI are habitually referred to as 'Ma'am' (which
either rhymes with 'harm' or 'spam', according to one's protocol) – but, to Hilda's delight, she was invariably referred to as
'Guv' – she was respected as a woman, a detective and a
bloody good Guv'nor. She had compassion and common
sense, was highly knowledgeable, backed her staff to the full
and was impossible to fool; and I saw the tattered remains of
the very few people who did try to take advantage of her good
nature. Following her retirement on the day before her fifty-
fifth birthday, Hilda worked for Social Services, but the cancer
that had first visited her sixteen years before, returned and she
died on 23 January 2001, just three days after her sixty-fifth
birthday.

I and many others were left with some wonderful memories of Hilda – some amusing stories, as well. My favourite
story was when she and I attended the Old Bailey. We arrived
just prior to the resumption of a case, following the lunchtime adjournment. As we approached the court, there were
double doors leading into a short passageway and at the end
was another set of double doors, which led directly into court.
Hilda and I each opened one of the doors at the beginning of
the passageway and were about to enter when a barrister and
his instructing solicitor entered the passageway from the
other end. Four people in that area was two too many, so

Hilda and I, still holding our doors open, stepped back to let the two men through. The barrister was a tall flabby man, whose sole exercise was restricted to wrestling with alibis and manipulating defences and, as he strode down the passageway, his robes streaming behind him, he looked like a galleon in full sail. His rodent-like solicitor bobbed along in his wake, like a bum-boat, sporting pernicious wares. The barrister swept past us, without a word of thanks. Rude bugger, I silently thought to myself and I was about to enter the passageway when I heard an almighty roar. *'What's your fucking game!'* Hilda had shouted. The barrister and the solicitor were frozen to the spot and stood there, quivering, like pointers who've discovered a fairly interesting scent. Hilda strutted over to them, adopting her bantam cock walk that she used when she was really angry and faced the shocked barrister. 'Why'd you think I was holding that door open?' she snapped. 'For a fucking bet, you fucking rude wanker?'

'Oh, Miss Harris,' gasped the barrister, 'I'm so sorry!'

'Yes, so you fucking should be,' seethed Hilda. 'I've never seen such bad manners. All right, that's it, then. Piss off!'

'Yes, Miss Harris,' the barrister stammered, 'and I'm so, so sorry!' And with that, they scuttled off. I was pretty shell-shocked myself and as we walked into court, Hilda linked her arm in mine. 'I'll tell you what dear,' she chuckled, 'It's just as well I'm a lady, otherwise I'd really have given them what-for!'

You were a lady, all right, Hilda – and a great one, too.

A Hard Taskmaster

The late Detective Superintendent Allan Cheal was never referred to as anything other than 'Charley'. I knew him for over fifteen years and on a number of occasions we worked together. I learnt an enormous amount about criminal investigation from him. He could be a hard taskmaster, it's true, but you knew that when you worked for Charley he'd back you to the hilt. He was also the possessor of an explosive temper and, when it came bubbling to the surface, it was prudent to don a steel helmet, shout, 'Incoming!' and duck.

Charley had served for ten years in the Royal Navy, joined the Metropolitan Police in 1957 and served as a detective constable on the Flying Squad for three years; later, as a 1st class detective sergeant, he served twice on the Regional Crime Squad. Charley spent over three years on 'K' Division; in fact, on the day I moved into Forest Gate police station as a brand new detective constable, so Charley moved out, to West Ham. A year later, he was promoted to detective inspector and was still retained on 'K' Division. 'Morning, Charley,' one of his colleagues called out cheerfully on the first morning of his promotion.

'Sir, to you!' Charley snapped back.

I remember being in court when Charley had requested that one of our prisoners be remanded in custody. Rising to his feet, the defence barrister said smoothly, 'When you say that you fear that my client would commit further offences if granted bail, that is merely your own opinion, is it not?'

Now, if that had been said to me, I expect that I would have stared down at my shoes, shuffled about and muttered, 'Yeah, I s'pose so,' or something equally inane. Not Charley, who firmly replied, 'It is.' He then turned to the magistrate and added, 'and as an experienced detective, I do not give my opinion lightly.' I saw the magistrate nod vigorously and I thought to myself, 'when I grow up, I want to say something like that. And in the fullness of time, I did – very successfully, too. As a word of caution, this rejoinder should not be attempted by anyone with less than eighteen months' service.

Charley rose through the ranks to become a very fine detective superintendent, serving on C1 Department twice and collecting fifteen commendations along the way. Aged 56, he retired in May 1988. Cruelly, his retirement lasted a matter of months before he succumbed to a massive heart attack. I was shocked and upset when I heard of his death.

Detective Sergeant Peter Connor and I had just finished lunch on that Friday afternoon over twenty years ago when we received a summons to see Charley. We walked down the stairs of the old married quarters at Limehouse police station, which served as the headquarters for the Serious Crime Squad (part of the Yard's COC1 Department) for almost ten years, and entered his office. Charley came straight to the point.

'I want you two to go to Bath straight away,' he said. 'There's a man named Ernest Jones that I want you to trace. He's involved in a fraud that I'm looking at and he holds the key to everything. I don't care how long it takes, but you've got to find him.'

Actually, Peter and I were pretty miffed, because we'd only recently returned from Lanarkshire, Uddingston and Bishopbriggs in an unlikely (although fruitful) quest to trace some

Triads and we could have done with some time off. 'Right, Guv,' I replied. 'This Jones character – what's his address?'

'He's cased-up with a woman who runs a bookshop,' Charley replied.

'Well, what's her name?' I asked.

'No idea,' Charley replied.

'Whereabouts is her bookshop?' I said cautiously, because I suddenly sensed that things were going seriously boss-eyed.

'I didn't say it was *her* bookshop,' Charley said, testily. 'I said she runs it. How do I know where it is? You're the detective, aren't you?'

I swallowed and tried a different tack. 'Right, if I find this bloke –'

'*When* you find him,' Charley cut in.

' – *When* I find him,' I continued hastily. 'What do you want me to do? Nick him? Question him? What about? What's he done?'

Charley stepped forward, fixed me with a piercing look and laid a heavy hand on my shoulder. 'Dick,' he said, quietly. 'I know I can leave it to you; I know you won't let me down. Lean on him, that's all. Just . . . lean on him.'

And with that, a thoroughly bemused Peter Connor and I slowly climbed the two flights of stairs to our office and shut the door. 'The man's impossible!' Peter exploded. I slumped into a chair. 'What'll we do?' I wailed. Peter, ever the pragmatist, replied, 'What about tearing the arse out of the overtime, for a start?' I brightened up immediately. 'Good idea!' I exclaimed.

Hastily packing our suitcases and skilfully avoiding the accusing looks from our wives, we rushed to the Yard and made a sizeable incursion into the imprest belonging to the commander of COC1. I put my foot down to try to beat the usual Friday afternoon exodus from the capital and by 6 o'clock, we were drawing on to the forecourt of a prestigious hotel in the magnificent city of Bath, famed for its Roman baths – and its booksellers. After a shower and a change of clothes, Peter and I met in the hotel bar where, over a large drink, we toasted 'loose change' – a reference to all that was left in the Commander's imprest. We strolled into the restaurant and I remember that venison was on the menu and *Vosne-Romanée* was on the wine list – we consumed generous portions of both.

The next day, Peter and I compiled a list of the bookshops in and around the area of Bath and when we had finished we viewed the itinerary with dismay: it contained dozens of names and addresses. With heavy hearts, we stepped out in the direction of the first booksellers on the list. Fortunately, the God who looks after small children and lunatics decided to smile benevolently upon two young detectives.

'Me? A boyfriend?' giggled the fifty-something and generously endowed bookshop owner, who had fallen prey to Connor's massive charm offensive. 'Paul Newman, if he's not too busy!' As we all had a chuckle, she added, 'No, the only person I can think of is Eileen Hawkins. She's got a live-in boyfriend – Ernie, Ernie Jones, his name is.' Peter and I looked at our list. Hawkins Bookshop was shown at fifty-eighth on our list. By the normal process of elimination, it would have taken a week to have got there.

Ernest Jones didn't look anything like Paul Newman. He was short, untidy, with a sprinkling of dandruff on the collar of his tweed jacket which sported leather patches on the elbows. He was also understandably perturbed when two fiercely resolute-looking young men brandishing warrant cards strode into his lover's shop. 'Right, Jones,' I snapped. 'I'm not taking any buggering-about from you – you know why we're here, so you'd better come clean!'

Jones bowed his head. 'I knew you'd find me,' he said quietly. 'I'd better make a statement and tell you everything.' Trying, with great difficulty to mask my astonishment, I wrote down an extremely lengthy statement in minute detail in which he outlined his probably unwitting involvement in a fraud, and implicated all the ringleaders. The statement, by the way, was taken under caution; those of you in the know will be aware that if a person isn't going to be prosecuted, it's a relatively easy matter to transcribe a statement under caution into a witness statement. Trying to do it the other way round can lead to, er, complications.

After this exhausting day, Peter and I tottered back to our hotel for a much-needed glass after which, we sauntered into the restaurant. The *Maître d'hôtel* took our order for *bécasse* with *salade Japonaise* and then suggested a bottle of *Gevrey-Chambertin* to accompany the woodcock. We replied that it would be rude not to.

The next day – Sunday – I telephoned Charley at home and gave him a précis of the statement I'd taken. Charley whooped with joy. 'That's just what I wanted!' he cried. 'I knew you wouldn't let me down, Dick – bloody-well done! Oh, and by the way,' he added, 'I don't want to see you and Peter back in the office before Wednesday.'

He didn't!

But whilst I could tell a host of stories about that admirable man who was also one of my mentors, this particular story belongs to former Detective Sergeant Neil Wraith. Neil joined me on the Flying Squad in the late 1980s and went on to be awarded a commissioner's commendation after making a considerable contribution to the Security Express robbery investigation, which netted a number of prominent criminals who had sought the warmer shores of Spain.

Neil had been serving on 'N' Division, and, one day,

Charley who was the detective superintendent at King's Cross, sent for him and asked him to be his 'bag carrier' – a euphemism for an assistant on investigations into murder and other serious crimes. Before Neil could reply, Charley added, 'I've got to tell you that I'm not liked by a number of people – you see, I don't wait to knock on the door of opportunity; I kick the door right in and grab whatever opportunities are going.' Gosh! thought Neil. This could be interesting.

There was just one nondescript van for the whole of the Division, so it was kept at King's Cross and was jealously guarded by Charley, who saw it as the property of the CID.

To the uninitiated, a 'nondie' is a plain van, used by police officers for observation purposes. In the back of the van is a radio, a number of seats, spyholes, perhaps even a periscope. There is also a small flap in the floor so that the observers, who are often encased in that claustrophobic atmosphere for many hours, are able to take careful aim and void their bursting bladders. Synchronized urinating is, for obvious reasons, discouraged.

When a couple of uniform police constables requested to borrow the nondie, Charley was clearly unhappy. Eventually, after a lot of cajolery, he relented, but had the two PCs attend his office, where he issued unequivocal directions. The van was to be used for one night only, Charley stated firmly. In addition, it was to be driven the short distance to the area of observation, parked up and, the observation complete, returned to King's Cross with the interior in a pristine condition. The two officers unhesitatingly agreed with these conditions and, with a curt nod of dismissal, Charley handed over the keys and the log book.

Three days later, the van had still not been returned and Charley was furious, the more so because the two PCs had ignored repeated requests to contact him. Eventually, the van turned up. The log book had not been filled in, but a check of the milometer revealed that the vehicle had travelled hundreds of miles. The petrol tank was bone dry. Worst of all, the interior of the van was cluttered with discarded chip papers and the remnants of half-consumed meals from some of the more exotic of the Cross's takeaways. The fact that the officers had badly mismanaged their aim during their ablutions added to the stench and Charley went apoplectic with rage. He demanded that Neil trace the two offenders and bring them to his office immediately. Neil did so and was present when Charley carpeted them. He had wound himself up into top form and, Neil told me, did not repeat himself once. As the furious tirade progressed the two PCs wilted and, with a final roar, Charley slung them out of his office. Exhibiting all the symptoms of combat fatigue, they tottered off into the direction of the canteen and the solace of a cuppa. There was silence in the office for about five minutes and suddenly Charley said quietly, 'Neil, I shouldn't have spoken to those two like that.' Neil reeled with shock and vainly searched his brain to say something in response to the remark that had truly taken his breath away. 'No,' continued Charley. 'I shouldn't have done that.' His brow was furrowed with concern. 'Neil, go after them, please. See if you can find them. Ask them to come back here.'

'Right, Guv,' an astonished Neil replied and scurried off to the canteen, where he spotted the two shell-shocked PCs, nursing a cup of tea. As Neil rushed up to them, they flinched and showed the whites of their eyes, like disobedient dogs who are expecting a clump for their misbehaviour. 'It's all right, fellas!' Neil said excitedly. 'Mr Cheal knows he's made a mistake talking to you like that. He just wants a word with you, to put things right. Finish your tea and get back to his office, sharpish!' Neil scooted back to the office and there was a glum Charley, hands in pockets. 'It's OK, Guv,' Neil said, triumphantly. 'I've found them — they're on their way back!'

Charley nodded thoughtfully. 'Oh, good,' he replied. 'Yes, Neil, that should be a lesson to us both. I shouldn't have spoken to them in that fashion.' Neil nodded wisely. 'No,' continued Charley. 'It's clear to me that I let them off far too lightly!'

Neil gasped and at that moment there was a tap at the office door, which opened to reveal the two smirking and now fully confident PCs. In one supple, practised movement, Neil slid round them and into the corridor. 'Would you excuse me, Sir?' he said politely. As he pulled the door to, he added, 'Something's just come up!'

Juvenile Behaviour

One of the many rewarding aspects of working on the Flying Squad and the Serious Crime Squad was the absence of juvenile offenders – or 'juvies' as they were widely known.

As a patrolling police constable and later, as an aid, if I spotted juveniles (i.e. youngsters under the age of seventeen) up to no good, I arrested them. I would have been foolish indeed if I had not; quite apart from being guilty of dereliction of duty, I would have failed to swell the number of arrests in the back of my diary, which were so important in order to become a permanent member of the CID. In my very early days, juveniles were considered to be a bit of a pain because there were one or two extra forms which had to be filled in when they were arrested, but once that was done, they were charged and either bailed or kept in custody until the next sitting of the juvenile court. Then, in 1968, along came the Juvenile Bureau system. This meant that officers were taken off the beat to deal exclusively with these young offenders, once they'd been arrested. They liaised with Social Services, the Probation and After Care Service and the local education authorities, and, once the arresting officer had submitted a full prosecution bundle of statements and documents in order to prove the case, they would then be in a position to decide whether the kid should be cautioned or prosecuted. I really don't think it worked from the word go. Many of the youngsters saw a caution as a weakness on behalf of the authorities and went on to re-offend. And with the tremendous amount of paperwork that was being generated – really, it was the forerunner of the Crown Prosecution Service – it fast became a bureaucratic nightmare.

Then, in 1984, the Youth and Community Section (referred to as 'YACS') was formed and this cottage industry took off like a rocket. It provided social and educational contacts with youth and school groups and monitored children at risk of offending, as well as those who appeared at court. The YACS officers liaised with social workers at meetings and case conferences, received recommendations from local authorities' juvenile panels and consulted with parents about their offspring's behaviour. All of which removed even more police officers from the streets. Undeniably, there were police officers who were deeply committed to the care and welfare of children and young offenders – Police Constable Dennis Tuff, who drove me in the 'Q' car Kilo one-one, was a splendid example – but YACS was also regarded as a safe-haven for work-shy, column-dodging officers who saw it as a welcome break from shiftwork, and an opportunity, as one repellent woman police officer grandly informed me, to do her shopping, pick up her kid from school and, for Christ's sake, to organize darts' matches for retirement homes.

Kieron Douglas rightly regarded himself as Cock o' the Walk on Holloway's Holly Park estate, a sprawling mess of council flats, inhabited by some of the most depraved, lawless scum in that unhappy area. He had everything going for him. He had been spawned by an alcoholic, part-time prostitute who was a full-time benefit scrounger. In drink, she was prone to complain that she had been caddishly abandoned by Kieron's father, whom she adored, although a little probing cross-examination on these occasions revealed that she had not the foggiest idea of his identity. Kieron's formative years were spent foraging for himself, receiving almost a complete absence of formal education and becoming a sly, vicious, dishonest and arrogant criminal. I hope I haven't left anything out. As he inevitably was brought more and more to the attention of Holloway's police officers, it was clear that he was heaven-sent to Islington's Social Services, who passed their soppy recommendations on to first, the Juvenile Bureau, and later, the Youth and Community Service, who gleefully embraced them.

Young Kieron received caution after caution, even for quite serious offences, until nemesis in the form of his first appearance at the Juvenile Court, reared its ugly head. This caused Kieron only slight trepidation, because he quickly discovered that he could commit offence after offence and then have them dealt with, all on one occasion; or, at least, those offences that his slimy solicitor would permit him to plead guilty to. Even then, that did not present a problem. One conditional discharge followed another, probation orders followed paltry fines and, sometimes, Kieron didn't bother to turn up at court at all. It didn't matter. If he couldn't be bothered to invent some fallacious excuse for his non-attendance when he did turn up for court, his solicitor would provide one for him. Whatever it was would be immediately accepted by the vacant-faced bench of Muppets, sitting at the Juvenile Court. And so it went on, with Kieron smirking as he strolled out of court, past the seething police officers, having received the most inappropriate of sentences for his latest shocking catalogue of car thefts, assaults and burglaries.

One day, Kieron was arrested for a particularly unpleasant burglary, involving a pensioner's saving's of £73. Kieron accepted his arrest with equanimity and without a struggle; he knew nothing would happen to him. As the custody sergeant at Holloway police station took down Kieron's details, he suddenly stopped what he was doing, looked up, smiled and offered his congratulations. It was Kieron's seventeenth birthday. This meant that, Kieron's circumstances had altered: he would now be obliged to attend the Magistrates' Court. However, little changed. His solicitor stepped nobly into the breach at the Magistrates' Court and demanded trial by jury at Snaresbrook Crown Court – on bail, naturally. Now, Kieron had heard of this hallowed Crown Court from his peers: it was a place where one went to, to get acquitted. So he carried on exactly as before, committing crimes, sometimes getting caught for them, sometimes not, often suffering the humiliation of being kept in the cells at Holloway overnight, but the following morning, his faithful brief would apply for bail and, with no objection from the Crown Prosecution Service, all the cases would be committed, on bail to Snaresbrook.

The first crack in Kieron's world appeared when he discovered that he was not going to contest the charges: his slippery brief had instructed a fairly ethical barrister who had spent an evening perusing the committal papers and coming to the inescapable conclusion that his client was as guilty as fucking sin. The next crack in the façade was when he discovered that the people who attended this court did not address him by his Christian name nor beg him to disclose his problems to them. And, lastly, something he would never know, was that the grim-faced judge, to whom he had pleaded guilty to an enormous string of offences, possessed an elderly mother who had herself recently been the victim of a highly unpleasant burglary. In her case rather more than £73 had been stolen, but the shock and distress were very much the same as those experienced by Kieron's victim. Having heard Kieron's shocking antecedents, given with considerable relish by the detective sergeant in charge of the case, and the speech in mitigation given by Kieron's barrister whose expressions of remorse as instructed by his client sounded highly unconvincing, since he, too, had come to the conclusion that Kieron was a thorough-going little shit, the judge barked, 'Stand up!'

'No would you mind standing up, please, Kieron?' thought the young tearaway. Just wait till I get my conditional discharge. As I swan out of the box, he'll get the loudest 'Fuck off, you wanker!' he's ever heard in his life.

'You have been given chance after chance,' the judge grimly intoned, 'and you have abused those chances. Everybody – Social Services, the police and the local authorities have done their best to curtail your activities and make a decent citizen of you without success. You have now pleaded guilty to some of the most unpleasant and anti-social offences I have seen during my time at the bar.'

Yeah, yeah, thought Kieron, as he yawned loudly, making no attempt to disguise his contempt for this boring old fart.

'Any sentence, other than a custodial one in your case, would be a positively evil thing,' the judge snapped. 'On each of these offences, the concurrent sentence is one of eighteen months' detention in a Young Offenders' Institution. Take him down.'

And the best retort Kieron could think of was a very surprised, 'Oh!'

Kieron lasted almost two hours into his incarceration, before he incurred the ire of a very large convicted rapist. Rapidly tiring of Kieron's smart remarks, he marched Kieron into the showers and proceeded to instruct him in an unpleasant ritual, which is known as 'mummies and daddies'. In fact, this was the first semblance of family life that Kieron had known in a long time, and one that made him long for the savage beatings doled out by his alcoholic mother. The rapist's arbitrary action was repeated, on average, twice a week for the rest of Kieron's sentence. Upon his release, the bruised and, I fear, by now syphilitic Kieron discovered that which every police officer at Holloway already knew – that the time spent in the Young Offenders' Institute had not been the reformative exercise that the authorities had wished. So when he was stopped by a couple of aids and was found to be in possession of an offensive weapon, he trembled at the thought of a further custodial sentence and hysterically promised that, if granted bail, he would become a first-rate grass. The magistrates did grant bail, with the proviso that he observed a curfew on the Holly Park Estate between 7 p.m. and 7 a.m. Kieron promptly reneged on the deal and offered not one shred of information. A month later, the aids spotted him walking through the Holly Park Estate at 9 p.m. 'Ah, nah!' gasped Kieron – this is Islingtonian for, 'Oh, no!' – and he fled but, too late. After a short chase, one of the aids pinned him to a wall, with one ham-like hand. 'Right, you little bastard,' he panted. 'You're nicked for breach of bail and, this time, you'll be remanded in custody.'

'Breach of bail?' Kieron echoed. 'I ain't in breach of anything – the CPS dropped the charge against me, last week!'

They had, too. They had yet to let the civilian Crime Support Unit at Holloway know, and even if they had, it would have probably taken a month before the civvies informed the officer in the case. So why had Kieron run? Simply because he anticipated getting a slap from the aids for neglecting to stick up any of his peers. Eager not to disappoint him, there, by the shed containing the over-spilling refuse bins, a little summary justice was meted out.

Any wonder why I loathed dealing with juveniles? Read on, for more of the same . . .

Although, as I've said, Juvies swelled the rear of the diary, they were nevertheless a pain. My fellow aid, Len Faul (whose

emigration to Canada was a considerable loss to the Metropolitan Police) and I arrested a couple of kids whom we had
spotted technically committing a burglary, by reaching
through a grill into a fruiterer's shop (thereby fulfilling
Section 9 Theft Act 1968 by 'entering part of a building') and
stealing fruits of a citrus nature. An arrest for burglary was
considered a very fine arrest indeed and we received the
fulsome congratulations of Detective Inspector Charley
Arnold – that is, until the full circumstances were made
known, when the consolidated mirth of the entire CID office
was turned on us and we were christened 'Sats' and 'Suma' –
Oh dear! It took ages to live that one down.

I was always of the opinion that with magistrates, it was a
foregone conclusion that they would take the side of the juvenile. This was proved beyond reasonable doubt when I was
one half of the night duty CID car, patrolling the Barking
area. At about 2 a.m., I spotted a shadowy figure moving
behind a cigarette machine in Ripple Road. I gently braked
the Hillman Hunter to a halt and stepped out of the car. As I
did so, a young man moved away from the cigarette machine
and walked swiftly away. I started to cross the road towards
him and, as I did so, I called out, 'Hold up, mate – I'm a police
officer – can I have a word?' The young man glanced briefly
in my direction and quickened his pace. By now, I had
reached his side of the road. 'Oi!' I called. 'Police – just a
moment!' He looked over his shoulder at me and continued
on his way. I increased my stride, caught up with him, showed
him my warrant card and said sharply, 'Stand still – I'm a
police officer and I want to know –' That was as far as I got.
He suddenly fumbled at his waist, under his jacket and the
next thing I knew, he was holding aloft a thick leather belt
that was covered in metal studs.

'Fuck off!' he said calmly.

Instinctively, I started forward and, with that, he turned and ran. I chased him for several hundred yards until he ran into a side turning and into the garden of a terraced house. The fence separating the houses was too high for him to scale so he stopped and once more raised the belt. As he swung it at my head, I blocked its descent with my left and punched him hard on the chin with my right. Before I dragged him to his feet, I relieved him of that belt. It weighed about a pound. If he'd hit me with that, it would have taken the side of my face off.

Why had he behaved like that? I never did find out. He knew that I was a police officer, so maybe that was the answer – he'd been up to no good round the cigarette machine. But no – I took him back there and there was no sign of the machine being tampered with. A search of his person revealed that he had no implements for such a venture and a search of the area between me first seeing him and his arrest didn't reveal any tools. He didn't have any money on him for cigarettes, so what was he doing out at 2 o'clock in the morning? Search me. But imagine how thrilled I was when, having initially told me that he was seventeen, at the police station he now confessed that his seventeenth birthday was still several months away.

He pleaded guilty – oh, I'm sorry – I mean he admitted the offence – at the Juvenile Court and was tenderly asked by the drippy magistrate why he'd tried to relieve me of half my face. 'Dunno, do I?' he replied. Every question from the bench was aimed at bending over backwards for this pernicious little turd, and the chairman of the Bench was getting on my nerves.

'Were you in uniform, officer?' he suddenly asked me.

I sighed. 'No Sir,' I replied, 'but then again, CID officers so seldom are,' I added sarcastically but the remark went right over his head.

Having received all the helpful information about him –
"E's a good boy at 'ome, yer Worship,' was the inevitable
response from the boy's long-haired, work-shy father – the
magistrate said sternly, 'Are you aware that the home secretary has directed magistrates to take a very firm line indeed
with this sort of offence?' This was quite correct; some disor-
der had broken out between gangs where offensive weapons
had been used, and the home secretary who had been ineffective for so long that the prime minister had thought that he'd
died and was considering a replacement, was stirred into
action with a few fierce phrases.

'Nah,' replied the disinterested youth and the beak looked
quite shocked to learn that the defendant was not such an avid
reader of *The Times* and the *Telegraph* as he.

'Oh!' he replied. 'Well, I'll have to make an example of you
in any event – fined £5!' If he heard the click of my jaw as it
fell upon the top of the witness box, he gave no indication of
it.

"Scuse me,' said the truculent youth, and I thought, stone
me – the cheeky little bugger's going to ask for time to pay,
but there I was wrong. 'Can I 'ave me belt back?' he asked
and, as I openly gaped, the magistrate turned to me.

'What are your views on that application, Officer?' he
asked.

Trying to keep my grinding teeth under control, I
informed him that now that he had been convicted and sentenced for possessing an offensive weapon, the court was quite
within its rights to order confiscation of the said weapon. A
confiscation order was duly made – but only after a twenty-
minute adjournment.

On another occasion, two young, masked desperados had
burst into a pet shop in Holloway, one Saturday afternoon.
They had demanded cash from the till but the assistant was

unable to comply because, in addition to her terror, the till was a new electronic type to which she was still unaccustomed. They tried to force the till without success and, with the shouting from them and the screaming from the assistant and the customers, they decided to make their escape. Certainly, there was no excuse for their next actions. Shouting, 'Share that among yer!' one of the youths discharged the contents of a canister of CS gas into the air and ran off. The scene was one of terror and confusion: the pets reacted violently to the gas, the customers were choking and gasping and, in the worst case, the gas had got behind the contact lenses of a young girl customer and she was in absolute agony.

'Perhaps one of your famous informants can shed some light on this?' simpered one of the detective inspectors at Holloway police station. I ignored the little creep who, I knew, was a closet rubber-heeler. 'We need this one cleared up, Dick,' said Detective Chief Inspector Fergie Corcoran. 'Any chance you can help?'

'I'll have a go, Guv'nor,' I replied, and pausing only to favour the DI with a sneer, I left the office and made my way over to the Crime Squad.

Sammy the Snout had been lax in honouring his contractual obligations of late, so I whipped him into action with the promise of a big drink, courtesy of the Yard's Informants Fund if he was forthcoming with the names of the miscreants, and a clip round the ear if he was not. Nervously chuckling at my little jest, Sam vowed that his nose would be pressed firmly against the grindstone and, blow me, a few days later, he came up with the goods.

A check in the local collator's records revealed the addresses and antecedents of this charmless pair. Oh, what joy when I discovered that both of them were still shy of their seventeenth birthdays by a few weeks but one of them had a conviction for robbery which was so serious that he had received an immediate custodial sentence. However, this conviction had been quashed on a mere technicality; his culpability was never in any doubt.

I needed to move fast – I wanted to retrieve the CS gas canister as evidence, so I obtained search warrants under the Firearms Act, gas respirators from the Firearms Department, and early one morning both addresses were raided by me and the 'N' Division Crime Squad. The young thugs were brought in and expertly interviewed by the young men and women of the Crime Squad, in the presence of their parents, and both made full confessions. What decent people their parents were; straight and honest as the day is long. God knows what sent this pair of shits off the rails.

They appeared at Highbury and Islington Juvenile Court and both admitted assault with intent to rob, possession of a prohibited weapon and assault occasioning actual bodily harm. The chairwoman (or chair) of the Bench was without doubt the worst magistrate I ever met and, thank goodness, I never met her again. It was clear that she loathed the police and was prepared to accept as gospel anything that was said by the stream of delinquency who paraded before her. In this particular case, she was somewhat stymied because both had admitted the charge.

I outlined the facts of the case in full, studied detail. I described the terror, the stink and hysteria of the pets when the gas was released, the studied brutality of it all when these young thugs were cheated of the contents of the till. I held nothing back; after all, they both had barristers to whine their excuses for them. As I rammed home each point, the chairperson looked intently at me, her face a mask of loathing and contempt. She then switched her gaze to the two young thugs in the dock and her expression would turn to one of pleading.

Say it's not true, her look seemed to say. Scream it at the top of your lungs if you like – say anything you like about this fascist bastard – I'll believe you. But they didn't, and her malevolent gaze would return to me. I can still see it now: seldom have I seen such venom in anyone's face. Eventually, the young tearaways' remorse had been expressed to the court and the silly chair lapped it all up, nodding eagerly at utterances, which were so implausible as to defy comprehension. A report from the Social Services was handed to the Bench and this, amazingly, contained details of the overturned robbery conviction. Because the boy had officially been cleared, it was certainly something that I couldn't have mentioned, and the defence team would have gone to the block before they did, but having read the report, this astonishing creature looked up, smiled benevolently and said, 'This terrible miscarriage of justice which occurred, which sent you into custody for an offence which you hadn't committed; I only hope that you have forgiven everybody concerned and that you bear them no malice.'

'Er – yeah. I mean, no,' replied this totally bemused young scoundrel.

'I expect it's why you committed this offence,' she added, soothingly, 'because you were so full of rage at being framed,' giving me a piercing hate-filled look.

And now it was sentencing time. She turned to the magistrate on her left. I hadn't really noticed him before because I was intent on watching the chair's face with its expressions alternating between adoration and contempt. Like the chair, I don't know who he was and I never saw him again, but he was rather a great man. Short and slim, he was the quintessential grey man. And now, the chair turned to him and quietly suggested what might be a suitable punishment. Whatever it was (and I've a pretty good idea) his head jerked up immediately and I heard him say, quite forcefully, 'You must be joking!' A quiet but obviously fierce argument broke out between the three magistrates and, eventually, the chair decided that there would be an adjournment. As they rose and turned to vacate the court, the second magistrate, obviously feeling that the chair was in need of a little legal guidance, turned to the clerk and said quietly, 'You'd better come too!'

Twenty minutes later they returned, the second and third magistrates' looking quietly resolute, the clerk expressionless, the chair, her face flooded with emotion. Her words, when they came, were choked with passion and she actually apologized as she sentenced them to a well-merited spell in quod. As they were led away and the Bench was about to rise, the second magistrate leaned forward and spoke urgently and softly to the chair. Bright red with embarrassment and with the words dragged out of her, she commended me and my team for bringing these toe-rags to justice. Never have I received a more vindictive commendation, so I enjoyed it all the more. The Bench rose and I solemnly inclined my head. As I did so, the second magistrate half-turned, grinned at me, and winked.

This commendation was reported by the court inspector, and wound up on the desk of that splendid deputy assistant commissioner, Mike Richards OBE, who called me to his office and personally added his own commendation. It was the second time he'd done this, so it was getting to be quite a regular and pleasurable occurrence.

Sammy the Snout was delighted with the generous bursary from the Informant's Fund. 'Am I your best snout, or what, Mr Kirby?' he kept repeating.

'Sam,' I finally replied solemnly, 'there's no one like you!'

Because I moved around so much during my career, I didn't always manage to keep tabs on the activities of my parishioners. The young man who had actually wielded the

CS gas canister, I never heard another word about. Did he renounce his wicked ways and become an industrious citizen? Maybe, but I doubt it. There was too much malevolence in the way the little bastard discharged the CS gas, when there was no need for it. His accomplice, I know, went on to better things and got captured on a Flying Squad plot and received an enormous lump of porridge, but I remember the case with great fondness, because it marked the end of my involvement with juveniles.

Caught – By the Skin of Their Teeth

Some informants could be met on the quiet, often, for the sake of their convenience, close to their homes where I could pay them their reward, murmur a few encouraging words of thanks and that would be that. But sometimes an informant would be so frightened, particularly when the people they'd grassed were pulling out all the stops to discover who had shopped them, that they would demand that the payment of the reward be as far away from their home, the criminals' homes and the scene of the crime, as possible. Billy was one such informant and he was a brave man. He was brave because he was stammering with fright when he gave me the information about the robbers (and when I found out a bit more about them, his fright was quite understandable) but he gave it all the same. And when it came to payment – and it was a big one, the biggest I ever paid out – it was on a bench, in the middle of a deserted park in a town which I had only been to once before to fix the meet. Billy had never been there before and, as far as I could ascertain, neither had the robbers. At the appointed time, Billy approached from one direction, me from another and I had spotters on the perimeter to check that he hadn't been followed in. Our transaction concluded, Billy went one way, I went another and we never met again. Were these precautions strictly necessary?

Well, put it this way: Billy thought so – and if Billy thought so, so did I.

He told me quite a lot about the robbers. And I would have loved to have told the robbers what I knew about them, just to let them know how much I knew. But if I had, it wouldn't have taken too long before they put two and two together and came up with Billy; so I had to bite my tongue. Tragic, really. I just had to be grateful that Billy had stuck up their names. That plus the evidence I'd already gathered made me feel that when I pulled this charmless duo in, there would be a lot more evidence forthcoming. Hopefully . . .

It had been a textbook armed robbery. As the security van with the wages for the factory pulled up and the driver got out, the balaclava-ed robbers leapt from their hiding place. Sticking a pistol against the driver's head, the gunman warned the other guard that, unless cash was thrown out, his companion 'would have his head blown off'. The second guard was in no doubt that the gunman meant what he said. And that, chums, was how this unpleasant pair very quickly netted themselves £23,545.84p.

Running to a Ford Escort XR3 – it had been stolen, two days previously – the two robbers roared off. The driver of the security van was thoroughly shaken up from his encounter with them. It did not deter him from jumping back into his van and whilst the other guard gave out the 'Attack' call on the radio, he set off in pursuit of the robbers.

The Ford screeched to a halt by an alleyway and, as the robbers minus their balaclavas got out, so the driver of the security van crashed his vehicle into the side of their car. As they moved in to tackle the robbers, so the gunman levelled his pistol at them before he and his companion vanished into the alleyway. It would have been madness to have followed them and the guards, who had already acted in a very spirited manner, did not. But they had got a very good look at the pair divested of their disguises, and what was more, given the commotion of the crash, so had several passers-by. But of the robbers there was no sign.

By coincidence, Tony Freeman and I had been patrolling nearby in a Flying Squad car and, hearing the call from the Yard on the radio, we went straight to the scene of the crash. Paul Millen, that superlative Scenes of Crime officer, had similarly heard the call on his radio and he also turned up.

Tony made himself busy, taking details of the witnesses and noting what they'd seen while Paul and I sealed off both ends of the alleyway and searched it. We found a number of discarded items there and the Yard photographer, who had been called out, arrived and photographed them *in situ*. Of the items found, four in particular were of special interest. The first was a jacket: in the pocket of which was a Yale-type front-door key. Next was a pair of leather gloves. A pair of tabs protruded from the ends – there was an identical three-digit number written on them. And, lastly, what was to become the most significant clue of all: the key, left behind in the ignition of the stolen getaway car. There were small indentations on the plastic fob surrounding the key's handle. Paul peered at them. 'You know what?' he said, finally. 'I reckon those are teeth marks.'

During the next week, detailed written statements were obtained from all the witnesses, house-to-house enquiries were carried out and the description of the robbers was circulated. Anybody know anything? No. Anybody who normally didn't have a pot to piss in, suddenly flush with cash? No, again. Informants were prodded into action. What did they know? What had they heard? What was going on? Nothing, nothing and nothing – in that order.

At the end of that week, we staged a reconstruction of the

robbery on that excellent (and now sadly defunct) television programme, *Police 5*. I played the part of the gunman, which was my normal function in these reconstructions – my performance caused the worried Squad Commander to mention that 'Kirby's getting a bit too convincing in these roles'. Perhaps he thought there was a possibility of me going rogue.

The prominence of the leather gloves on the programme paid off. The following day, we received 40 telephone calls, all giving the same information. Those gloves were British Army issue; they were given to troops about to be deployed to Northern Ireland and the three numbers on the tabs were the last three digits of the owner's eight digit army number.

Straightaway, I got on to Army Intelligence and requested details of all army personnel whose army numbers ended in those three digits. I made the mistake of speaking to some pimply faced REMF – this appalling acronym stands for 'Rear-echelon Motherfucker' and it is used to denote those in the army who have never encountered an angry enemy, spending all their military service safely behind a desk. It would be a mammoth task, the pimple stated firmly, and therefore my request was refused. Undismayed by this non-executive decision, I leap-frogged right over this bumptious little squirt and went to a high-ranking officer who couldn't have been more helpful. It took a bit of time, but I was eventually presented with a print-out of the details of all the soldiers whose army numbers ended with my three numbers – all 468 of them.

Over the next two months, the list took up all my spare time. Not that there was much of that, what with investigating other robberies and arresting those responsible, as well as helping out the other Squad officers with their investigations. But whenever I could, I checked and rechecked that list. Some I could dismiss through age. Others might have held promise, so I checked them out. What about . . . this one? No. At the time of the robbery, he was on a training course in Belize. Right – cross him off the list and on to the next one.

The technical boys from C11 had compiled photo-fits from the description given by the witnesses and these I circulated in the police publication, *Confidential Information*, which went to every police station in the Metropolitan Police area. I received not one single response.

Just when I was beginning to hate the thought of picking up that bloody army list again, up popped Billy the Snout. We arranged a meet at a location miles away from the robbery. Billy was a useful-looking chap who looked as though he could punch his weight, but when I met him, he was trembling like a leaf and kept nervously looking over his shoulder, as though he was expecting the blaggers to burst in through the pub door, at any second.

I'm sure the robbers have since seen the errors of their ways and are now pillars of society so I shall refer to the gunman as James and the driver as Stewart. In fact, their real names meant nothing to me, so I researched them. Both of these scoundrels had records of petty crime. Both of them lived in the same area as the robbery and where they had escaped through the alleyway. Both were on bail for a vicious attack on some uniformed police officers which had occurred on their home territory. Since the photo-fits were a very good likeness of them, you would have thought that the uniformed police officers with whom they'd had the dust-up would have been able to identify them, wouldn't you? If they could have been bothered to read *Confidential Information,* that is.

Things became even more interesting after Billy told me that James' sister worked in the factory where the wages were being delivered. Most interesting of all was that James had been arrested eight months previously, after he had been suspected of involvement on a raid on a security van. There was insufficient evidence to charge him with that offence, but a check revealed that James was on the run from the army and had been handed over to the Redcaps.

Got him! I thought and requested James' army number. My jaw dropped when I discovered that the last three digits of his army number bore no resemblance to the three digits on the Northern Ireland gloves. I urgently requested that his number be checked again. Surely I'd been given the wrong number. I hadn't. Feverishly, I checked my list of 468 soldiers again. James' name *must* be there. It wasn't. How could I have been so wrong, I wondered. I had put so much reliance on that list; all that bloody work, all for nothing . . . and then I put my sensible head on. I wasn't wrong. The list was right. In it, there was a clue to the whole mystery. I went through those 468 names again. Out of all of them, only Private Gary Miller was attached to James' regiment.

I had to interview Miller, and as soon as possible. I discovered that he was serving with his regiment in Germany and I rushed in a report, requesting that I be permitted to go there, to speak to him. To my astonishment, my request was turned down. I liked the Squad commander, Jerry Plowman, but I never understood the reason for his refusal; and one simply didn't say, 'Why not?' to Jerry, who was a bit of a stickler for protocol.

I couldn't wait much longer. If any of the money from the robbery was left, I wanted to recover it. Had they spent it and were they planning another robbery? I didn't know, and I had to scoop them in now, with the evidence I'd got. But before I could do that, I had to check out where they were living. I couldn't rely on the information contained on their collator's cards because the addresses they'd been bailed to, following the dust-up with the uniform branch, might well be different. So I had to enlist the aid of the Crown Prosecution Service – and *that* came hard, I can tell you – to discover the addresses. James had been bailed to the family address; Stewart had changed his address and was now living with his brother. So what was the new address? The CPS representative had scrawled it down on the court papers and it was practically indecipherable. Christ, I thought, bitterly, one step forward and two steps back. Slowly, painstakingly, I and some other officers studied the childish, scribbled handwriting and had stabs at what we *thought* it might be; then we compared it with the electoral rolls. Eventually, one of the guessed-at addresses was found to contain a family with the same surname as Stewart. Thank God he hadn't chosen to live with his married sister; I should think that if he had, I'd still be looking for him.

Before making the arrests, I carried out a task that I always did when I had a little leeway on time. I read through all the statements again. Then I checked all the exhibits. This I did with Paul Millen.

Paul held up the car key. 'What we need,' he said, 'is to get impressions of their teeth.'

'Oh, good,' I replied, caustically. 'What'll we do – give 'em an apple each?'

Paul looked over the top of his glasses at me. 'Actually,' he said, mildly, 'I did have a forensic dentist in mind!'

Then there was the front-door key. From the descriptions given by the witnesses, James was wearing the jacket which had been discarded in the alleyway. Since I was going to arrest James, I intended to take this key along with me and if it was found to operate the lock of James' front door, this would be a decisive piece of evidence. However, in both cases, I insisted on using a safety net.

Being wise to the way of defence lawyers, I knew that if the bite marks on the key fob fitted the teeth of one of the robbers, and the Yale-type key fitted James' front door, it could well be alleged at the trial that I had forced the likeliest suspect to bite on the key fob, and that having gained access to the James' family home, I had palmed a latch-key belonging to one of the family, and pretended that this was the one found in the jacket. So two days before the arrests, I had both keys photographed.

Unusually for me, I knocked politely on James' front door. There was a sledge-hammer as back-up, should the need arise but, really, I was hoping that the front door would be opened for me. It was. James was arrested; so was his sister. The key was tried in the door – bingo! – it worked.

At the same time, another Squad team was arresting Stewart. At the police station, both men agreed to provide hair, blood, saliva – and teeth impressions. They were interviewed, charged and remanded in custody. Meanwhile, James' heavily pregnant sister was interviewed. In order to charge her, it would have been necessary for her to have said, 'I set the robbery up with my brother and his mate'. Since she said nothing of the kind and there was only suspicion, as opposed to evidence against her, she was released without charge.

But otherwise, things were starting to look up, for once. Both sets of teeth impressions were compared with the bite marks on the key fob; the marks were conclusively revealed to have come from Stewart. The entire front door was removed from James' address. With the lock taken out, now I took both the lock and the key to the manufacturers in Northampton who examined both and stated that the key fitted the lock, the lock was in perfect working order and that the odds of a key not cut for the purpose actually fitting the lock, were 15,000 to one.

I was on annual leave when I was informed that Private

Miller had been granted home leave. Cancelling my own leave, I went to see him, taking with me the Northern Ireland gloves. Miller stated that he had lost three or four pairs of these gloves and that the gloves that I was showing him, *might* be his. He also stated that he had known James, who had visited him in his barracks on several occasions, and who had decamped, prior to the regiment's posting to Northern Ireland. It was by no means the damning piece of evidence that I'd hoped for but it was nevertheless an important part of circumstantial evidence. Meanwhile, the two guards had picked out Stewart on an identification parade, and a passer-by had identified James, who refused any further participation with identity parades. Well, not bad at all. But the best bit of evidence was yet to come.

The name of James kept going through Paul Millen's head. That he had heard it before, he was certain: but where? Eventually, he got hold of his carbonated book of worksheets, upon which he noted every detail of every robbery he had investigated since coming to the Flying Squad – and there were a lot. And then he found it. Nearly two years previously, he had carried out the forensic examination for the robbery of which James had been suspected, but not charged. He remembered he had taken possession of a jacket which James had been wearing, which was very similar to the one found in the alley. Paul had submitted the jacket to the Forensic Science Laboratory for comparison with fibres taken from the seat of the getaway car – was it the same jacket? At the laboratory, a small sample had been cut from the back of the jacket and, with James languishing in an army clink, the jacket was restored, against receipt, to James' mother. Paul rushed the jacket back to the laboratory – had they retained the sample? They had: microscopic examination revealed that the cut sample fitted the jacket perfectly.

What else? Everything photographable had been photographed and maps of the area had been prepared. I went up in a light aircraft to photograph the area; the prints showed the proximity of James' house to the alleyway, to the scene of the robbery.

I had always thought it a strong possibility that James, at least, would plead guilty to the robbery. So, apparently did his solicitors who had to withdraw from the case. They were a highly respectable company and when James decided that, contrary to what he may or may not have said to them before, not only was he going to plead 'Not guilty' but that he was going to produce notice of an alibi, sixteen months after the robbery had occurred and one week before his trial at the Old Bailey, they had no option but to withdraw, and a fresh company was instructed.

The character who provided the alibi had a shocking criminal record; in fact, he had been convicted with James' father. It seemed unlikely that any sensible jury could listen to his evidence without bursting into incredulous laughter. But these were the days when juries could be hand-picked. James and Stewart each exercised their option to challenge three prospective jurors so that they could get at least a 50–50 chance of having things their own way. The witnesses for the prosecution gave their evidence in an exemplary fashion; even with such a jury, it seemed inevitable that their verdict would be that of guilty. But when the jury failed to agree upon a verdict, a retrial was fixed for four months hence. Disappointed though I was, it was an acceptable result.

When a case is ordered to be retried, many police officers throw up their hands and say, 'Well, let's hope for the best' — or worse still, 'That's it, then'. I didn't. I'd seen what had happened in the first trial and I resolved to strengthen the evidence as much as possible. Stewart had called his own forensic dentist to rebut the evidence of our own expert and he had been allowed to be present in court whilst our expert gave his evidence. When he came to the irrevocable conclusion that our witness's evidence was spot-on and there was no doubt that Stewart had indeed made those tooth impressions, he was hastily dismissed by the defence: he was lucky to avoid an infuriated Stewart punching him.

There's a saying in legal circles – 'There's no property in a witness'. Well, I thought, if the defence don't want their expert forensic dentist witness, I do. I told the prosecuting counsel this, in a pre-retrial conference, and he had never heard the like before. 'Good Heavens!' he kept repeating. And in the end, 'Well, why not?' Why not, indeed? I had a quiet word with the former defence star witness and persuaded him to come over on to the side of the angels.

What else? Private Miller had been a conditional witness in the first trial, which meant that the defence were content to allow his statement to be read in court, without him appearing in person. It also meant they were content for him not to blurt out anything in cross-examination which might compromise their client's case by saying the wrong thing. Well, I wanted him to say the right thing. So I went and saw him again and this time he told the whole truth. The Northern Ireland gloves *had* been his, he stated; and the three digits on the tabs had been written by him. At my initial interview with him, he had been confused and worried about Queen's Regulations.

So the retrial looked far more promising: to start off with, that is. The first jury that was sworn in had to be discharged for legal reasons. A second jury was sworn and the retrial got underway. The witnesses were called once again and the defence demanded that I was excluded from the court. So it wasn't until much later that when I went into court, I casually glanced at the jury and then took a longer, harder look. There was a jury member whose face stirred a chord in my memory. I made a few enquiries and what I had suspected was confirmed: the juror was a convicted criminal. This was brought to the attention of the judge, who stopped the trial, dismissed the jury and swore in a third one.

When the prosecution witnesses discovered that they would have to come and give evidence for a fourth time, they were understandably furious; worse, one of them (and a most important witness) refused point-blank to turn up. I told the prosecuting barrister who shrugged his shoulders. 'We'll get a witness summons and force him to appear – arrest him, if necessary,' he replied dismissively. I shook my head. I'd never done this in the past and I wasn't going to start now. That would *really* put a witness's back up and if anything was guaranteed to make him 'lose his memory' it would be being dragged along to the Old Bailey. Instead, I went round to his house, suffered a torrent of abuse from him and, when he ran out of steam, sat down with him and talked. I talked to him for a long time. Finally, he started talking with me. He turned up again at the Bailey; and, again, he was a star witness.

The defence went all out for an acquittal. Private Miller took a lot of flack but stuck to his guns. The police in general – and me, in particular – took a tremendous amount of flack. I was cross-examined about James' sister and this was both to brand me as a villain and also to win the sympathy vote from the jury. I agreed that the sister had been released without charge.

'At the time of her arrest, my client's sister was pregnant, was she not?' asked the defence barrister. I agreed that this was so.

'And during her interview, she was frightened, wasn't she?' the barrister insisted. I replied that I had not personally interviewed the girl, but I accepted that this could well have been the case.

'Pregnant – and frightened,' defence counsel stated. 'And she might well have been frightened, Sergeant Kirby, because here was a girl who had never been in trouble with the police before. Isn't that right?'

'Wrong,' I replied flatly. 'She has a conviction for assault occasioning actual bodily harm.'

The defence counsel paused. 'It was a very minor assault, wasn't it?'

'Depends what you call minor,' I replied. 'The circumstances of the case were that she attacked a girl in a pub because, it seems, the victim had the effrontery to be the daughter of a serving police officer. She displayed her displeasure by pulling out handfuls of the girl's hair by the roots.'

This was definitely what the defence counsel didn't want the jury to hear. 'I suggest that the defendant's sister had unwisely had too much to drink,' he stammered, trying to draw back rather a lot of lost ground.

'Yes, I shouldn't be surprised,' I agreed. 'Some sort of celebration was underway; in fact, by coincidence it was held on the same night as the robbery occurred.'

'Yes, yes!' the barrister almost shouted. 'No further questions!'

Towards the end of the prosecution's case, a remark was made by the defence which implied that a serving soldier, from the same regiment that James had served so ingloriously, had committed the robbery. It was a disgraceful remark, intended to throw even more doubt in the jurors' minds. I had to work quickly. With only a name to go on, within six hours, I had identified the soldier, discovered that he had since been discharged from the army, traced and interviewed him and obtained a statement in which he was able to say that, at the time of the robbery, he was not even in the United Kingdom. This was confirmed after I had obtained statements from Colchester Barracks and the Army Records Office at Exeter. These statements were served on the judge, prosecution and defence, just before the close of the prosecution's case and the defence were grudgingly obliged to admit that, no, this soldier could not possibly have carried out the robbery.

I was at home, enjoying the remainder of my interrupted annual leave when Tony Freeman telephoned me from the Bailey. 'We got a verdict,' he said abruptly. My throat was dry. 'Go on,' I said. 'Six months,' Tony said, 'for assaulting the police officers.'

Christ, I thought, wearily, and this time I was so certain they'd go down. 'Oh, yes,' Tony added, after that long pause. 'And eight years for the robbery!'

It had taken the jury just two hours to come to a unanimous verdict. Eight years. It wasn't enough, I thought – but, then, it never is.

Paul Millen and I were commended by the commissioner. Both of us had been recommended for 'detective ability' but only I received that citation; Paul's was for 'determination and ability'. I thought it a shame at the time and I still do. It was Paul who spotted the marks on the key fob which Stewart had nervously gnawed upon while he was waiting for the robbery to go off; I don't suppose I'd have even noticed them. And as for his work with the jacket, well . . .

As far as I was concerned, Paul who had convicted them, literally, by 'the skin of their teeth', could have taken his job description of 'Scenes of Crime officer' and chucked it out of the window. He was as much a detective as anybody on the Flying Squad.

Tales From a Riverside Inn

It was the close of . . . one of those days. The night before, I had tossed and turned in bed, my thoughts racing. From the day that I planned my first operation until I retired, it was always the same. Was the information good? Had I enough troops? A thousand and one ifs, ands and buts buzzed around inside my head; it was a relief when the alarm clock went off at 4.30.

Then, I had to brief the other Flying Squad officers, and drive across London to Hammersmith to raid premises which contained a pretty trio of villains and the contents of a high-class burglary from a quality store in the West End, which they were planning to disperse through a top-class receiver.

My car was the first of three Flying Squad cars to draw up close to the premises, and as I got out, I patted my jacket to ensure that the search warrant was safely there. Suddenly, I heard my name whispered from the shadows: it was the informant, who breathlessly told me that the gang, thinking quite rightly that 'something was up', had shifted the stolen property to another address overnight, from where they were just about to dispose of the gear. He gave me the new address, his teeth chattering, either from the cold or, more likely, fear. He had good reason: the team of screwsmen had a nasty reputation for violence when they were thwarted.

And thwart them I was going to, but my mind was working overtime. If the gang had shifted the gear, was it to this address, or had they merely given the address, secure in the knowledge that if it was raided, there could only be one person who was the informer? Was the property still at this original address? Was the informant in with the others and trying to double-cross me? Or was the property still at the address a few yards away and the informant's bottle had gone? So if I went to the new address and the property wasn't there, the informant could say it must have already been shifted? Right, Richard, I thought, cut out the paranoia and think sensibly. Had the informant been a good'un in the past? Yes. Should I trust my instincts? Yes.

As I got back into the Squad car, called the other cars up on the car-to-car set and told them there'd been a change of plan and to follow me, I had one other sobering thought. Had I got a search warrant for this new address? No. Could I conceivably get one in time? No, again. If we crashed in to this new address – and that was exactly what I had in mind – and there was nothing there, it would provide the perfect excuse for that swine of a deputy assistant commissioner who hated my guts, not merely to kick me off the Squad but also kick me straight back to uniform. But as the Squad car sped across West London, I remembered the words of that great Flying Squad officer, Ian Forbes: 'The CID has no place for cowards or look-before-you-leap types. They must be resolute and determined men who are ready to act upon information, no matter where it comes from.'

That did stiffen my resolve and as we crashed in through the door of the warehouse, I sighed with relief as I saw not only a couple of very surprised screwsmen but also a huge amount of stolen clothing with West End labels still attached. The third member of the team was not present, but a search of the office revealed evidence to tie him in with the job, and then the two screwsmen sighed and rolled their eyes, as their names were called out by a lorry driver and his assistant who strolled in, saying they'd come to collect the gear. Comically realizing the *gaffe* they'd committed, they then compounded matters by trying to escape, but the highly amused Squad officers restrained them without too much trouble, so they came in, as well. Then the hard slog began: the property had to be photographed *in situ* and then removed, and the owners contacted to identify it formally. The prisoners were taken to the local police station, and then their home addresses searched. When criminals pull a nice job off, few of them can resist creaming off a little of the stolen property and taking it home with them, and this bunch was no different. Then there were interviews, telephone calls, reports detailing damage to property, viz, one front door, snatched meals, the informant to meet again regarding the possible whereabouts of the gang leader and yet more telephone calls.

With everybody working flat out, by the end of the day the prisoners were locked up. The lorry driver and his mate were considering whether their best course of action was to become prime prosecution witnesses against the receiver who had sent them, or to end up in the dock, charged with conspiracy. Momentous decisions like that are best ruminated over, during a night in the flowery. One of the screwsmen had suggested in a particularly oily fashion that, given the right incentives – dropping him completely out of the case – he might be able to finger the gang leader . . . only might, mind. Since I already knew the identity of the gang leader, I let him know that the best way that he could help himself would be to 'do the royals' when they were all standing in the dock together and these words left him a little crestfallen. But best of all was the feeling of relief which swept over me. From distinctly shaky beginnings, just about everything had gone well. The Squad commander was delighted and said so, to my little chum the deputy assistant commissioner, who exited left, muttering.

I looked at my watch – 6.30. I stood up and stretched myself. My friend and driver, Tony Freeman, strolled into the Squad office. 'Come on, Tony,' I said. 'Home.' The big Squad Rover nosed out of the Yard's underground car park and headed east, but as we reached the Victoria Embankment, we discovered it was blocked solid with a mixture of traffic and roadworks. Tony swung the car south, across the River Thames, only to find that Southwark Street was similarly blocked.

There is a pub in south London which has a terrace which overlooks the Thames; it is a haven of peace for the parched traveller. Our good intentions disrupted, it was to this cool waterhole that we headed.

The heat of the day had started to subside. Tony and I carried our drinks out on to the terrace and chose a table that was both shady and secluded. As the brown waters of the Thames slapped against the wooden posts a dozen feet or so below us, we chatted about the events of the day: just when things were about to go horribly, catastrophically wrong, some quick thinking and a large amount of luck had snatched us from the jaws of defeat and had crowned the day with success. 'We could do with a few more days like this,' Tony chuckled. I nodded. 'Some things go boss-eyed for any number of reasons,' I admitted. Tony agreed and, to illustrate the point, recounted the story of 'Knuckles' Docherty and the case of mistaken identity.

Detective Sergeant Dennis 'Knuckles' Docherty was a large, raw-boned thug of a police officer. His liking for gratuitous violence made him much feared amongst the criminal fraternity in Knuckles' small corner of the East End. His favourite interview gambit was to ask the suspect, 'Are you 'aving it, or not?' If the prisoner unwisely answered, 'No', Knuckles' rejoinder was, 'Well, tell me when you've 'ad enough!' and with that, he would proceed to knock the stuffing out of his opponent until the answers which Knuckles wanted to hear were forthcoming. None of the lowlifes who were Knuckles' staple diet ever complained about his conduct: the thought of the retribution that would follow was too terrifying even to contemplate.

On this particular evening, Knuckles had returned to the police station, somewhat the worse for wear after a session in the local pub. As he entered the vestibule, so he saw a rather downcast man sitting on the seat. Knuckles glared at him. 'Wot you want?' he demanded ungraciously. The man looked up. 'Oh, I'm here about the little girl that got indecently assaulted,' he muttered. '*What?*' roared Knuckles. '*One of those dirty bastards, are yer!*' and without further ado, he pulled the man to his feet with one large hand and proceeded to bash the living shit out of him with the other.

The commotion brought the station officer rushing outside and, pulling Knuckles off of his unfortunate victim, explained that the man was in fact the father of the indecently assaulted child, who had been waiting until the divisional surgeon had completed her examination of his daughter.

Knuckles had the grace to mutter an apology to the battered visitor, but he would have none of it. Wiping the blood away from his nose, he replied, 'No problem, mate! If that's what you're going to do to the dirty bastard who frightened my daughter, I don't mind in the least!'

And Knuckles, who would have lasted all of three seconds in today's caring, sharing police service, wandered away into the night; and Heaven help anyone whom he encountered who even resembled a child molester.

*

Tony and I laughed so much over the story that some of the pub's clientele had started looking in our direction, so I softened the moment by taking the opportunity of getting another round of drinks. When I returned, I treated Tony to another tale of disappointment: this time, to the detriment of the bad guys.

As a detective constable on night-duty with a couple of aids to keep me company, we had become involved with the Flying Squad after information had been received that a warehouse was going to be broken into. We plotted up around the premises and the order to attack was given. Two of the burglars, who had been busy loading the stolen goods into the back of a waiting lorry, turned and fled into the warehouse. The third member of the gang, who had singularly failed to discharge his duties as a look-out, was flattened by the aids.

The rest of us ran into the warehouse, which was in complete darkness. Of course, none of us had a torch, so someone groped around for the light switch. All of a sudden, there came a high-pitched howl from above our heads which was getting louder and nearer. As the light switch was found and light flooded the interior of the warehouse, so one of the burglars who had sought to evade capture by hiding in the roof space and had lost his footing, landed with a terrific thump at our feet. The comedy of errors was now officially underway.

As the burglar lay groaning on the floor, his leg twisted at an unnatural angle, so Detective Sergeant Fred Cutts of the Flying Squad, a curious combination of pianist and wrestler, knelt by him murmuring what purported to be supportive words, although somebody unkindly observed that it was more likely that Fred was telling him what would happen to his other leg, if he didn't come across with the whereabouts of his associate.

With an excess of zeal, rather than common sense, a police

dog was released in an effort to find the reclusive burglar: the giant German Shepherd's eyes (which appeared to be surrounded by scar tissue), gleamed. Almost two stone over its recommended bodyweight, it promptly let out a howl of delight and launched itself forward, burying its teeth in Fred Cutts' forearm. Fred howled in turn and he punched the animal, until the handler, muttering apologies to Fred and imprecations to the dog, pulled it away.

Up to the roof space we climbed, Fred rubbing his tender forearm, and we looked around. Where on earth could he be? All that was up here was the water tank and he couldn't be . . .

Suddenly, Fred's eyes narrowed as he spotted what appeared to be a small, pink dorsal fin, belonging to a tiny shark, protruding from the waterline. Reaching forward, Fred gently grasped this small isosceles triangle between thumb and forefinger and squeezed. Within seconds, the owner of the nose erupted from the water tank and, emitting loud sobbing noises, he was permitted to get some air into his lungs, before being escorted to the nick.

The three screwsmen looked a sorry spectacle in the charge room. The lookout was still traumatized from being squashed and was looking nervously at the aids who were openly arguing about whose diary he should appear in the back of – and if you think that's bad English, I'm sure you get my drift. The first of the two climbers was looking forward to receiving swift medical care and the last member of the trio just stood there, still dripping as the surrounding puddle grew bigger and bigger. 'D'you know what?' he said, sadly. 'I only got out of stir last week; and that was for screwing, as well.'

There was a moment's silence.

'Ever thought of doing cheque frauds, instead?' I said helpfully.

*

259

Tony and I laughed as we sipped our drinks. It was appreciably cooler now. Tony looked across the river. 'Traffic's getting easier,' he observed but, before we could leave, he felt impelled to recount one final story.

The night-duty at Forest Gate police station had brought in a well-known local car thief for a spot of TDA – unauthorized taking of a motor vehicle, to the uninitiated – and the evidence to support a charge was rather flimsy. He had been spotted at 3 o'clock in the morning, walking quickly away from an abandoned vehicle, which had just been stolen. Nobody had actually seen him *in* the car. The young car thief knew this and sneered at attempts to induce him to confess that this had indeed been the case. The night-duty CID was therefore summonsed. The detective constable who was 'K' Division's sole representative for investigating criminal matters between the hours of 10 o'clock in the evening and whenever he finished, arrived, and first questioned the arresting officers. Was it possible, he urgently probed, that they had made a mistake and *had* seen the thief – the *well-known* car thief, he stressed – actually in the car? The arresting officers were rightly shocked at the imputation and rejected the very idea. So next, the DC decided to interview the prisoner in the CID office, as was the norm in those days. Not only did the prisoner refuse to acknowledge his complicity in the matter of the TDA, but being fully aware of the paucity of evidence in this case, decided to push his luck rather. 'Them wollies what pulled me in, ain't got no evidence, mate,' he sneered. 'I fink you'd better let me go, sharpish, before I fuckin' sue yer!'

Nowadays, I expect CID officers are far more tolerant of lippy young men, but that was not the case in those long-gone days, particularly not in the case of this particular DC who had a justifiable reputation for wildness.

Without a word, he picked up the CID typewriter and threw it at the window. There was an ear-splitting crash as it disappeared through the shattered window, followed a couple of seconds later by a more muffled thud as the typewriter exploded into several hundred component parts, one floor below, on the pavement in the Romford Road.

As the prisoner looked on, goggle-eyed, the DC casually remarked, 'You can fuckin' have that one with me!' and, apart from charging him with the TDA, also charged him with malicious damage to property belonging to the Metropolitan Police, to wit, one typewriter.

Justice moves in funny ways. The magistrates convicted the car thief of the TDA; the malicious damage charge was thrown out, the Bench commenting that although the charge had been properly brought, there appeared to be 'an element of doubt'.

Tony and I finished our drinks and set off for home. As we drove north, across Blackfriars Bridge where, within a few months, the hanging body of Roberto Calvi would be discovered and conjure up more imaginative conspiracy theories than any of those made against the Flying Squad at the Old Bailey, I thoughtfully reflected that no matter how successful one day might be in London's Metropolitan Police, cock-ups were always waiting, just around the corner.

Just the Ticket!

'Did you make a note of that, Officer?' was one of the questions most asked by defence counsel in court, knowing, of course, that you hadn't. The matter referred to was usually either so trivial that it didn't require recording or that it hadn't happened at all – except in the fertile mind of the defence barrister, his weasel solicitor or, less likely, the gormless miscreant whom they were representing. The matter was best dealt with by Gerry Gallagher, that genial giant from Ulster, during one of our Flying Squad trials. 'If, indeed it were said,' he replied to that particular question, 'I would have considered it so trivial that I would not have recorded it.'

'But surely,' the defence barrister persisted, 'you have a duty to accurately record everything said by a defendant?'

'If I considered it relevant, the answer is "yes",' Gerry replied, 'but if I had recorded everything that passed between your client and myself, I'd still be writing now!'

'Quite right,' the judge interjected, effectively stopping that time-wasting sort of commentary, used only to confuse further a jury who had already been confused to a state of bamboozlement. Others were not so lucky – you won't be surprised to learn, that I'm referring to yours truly.

Norman Bolton was a tall, good-looking and very genial detective sergeant (2nd class) at Romford police station when I was an aid. I believe he was one of the youngest officers ever to be promoted to that rank. (Why he never sought further promotion was beyond me, because he was supremely capable.) Whenever an irksome job needed doing, he would swoop upon me, as unerringly as a hawk on its prey. Looking at me with steady, unflinching eyes, he would clap me on the shoulder and say, 'Dick – I know I can rely on you to do this – you're my best aid.' I should have instantly realized that some dreadful, time-consuming lumber was going to be dumped on me, but nevertheless I drank in Norman's blandishments with a bashful grin on my vacant face; Norman had a charming way of getting his subordinates to do his bidding, which is more than could be said for many of his contemporaries. So when Norman asked me to accompany him to Romford town hall to assist in an investigation of theft, I was delighted.

The car park at the town hall charged half-a-crown (12 pence) for parking and this sum was collected by a pair of middle-aged employees at the gate, who issued the car drivers with a ticket. Someone at the town hall had busied himself and had discovered that all the money was not being accounted for and suspicion fell on these two attendants. Not a fraud on a grand scale, you understand, perhaps one half-crown being pocketed out of every couple of pounds lodged. Two very apprehensive car-park attendants were taken to the police station and very quickly admitted their full culpability in this minor scam and both made detailed, written confessions, outlining their part in the offence. The reason for their actions, they said, was to supplement the pittance that they were paid by the town hall. They were a couple of nice old boys and I had a long chat with one of them afterwards. Jack Evans was, by then in his mid-fifties and he was short, slim with smartly Brylcreemed brown hair, with hardly a bit of grey in it. Greyness was reserved for his eyes, which had seen a great deal of death and danger, for during the Second World

War, Jack had been a member of No. 2 Commando. He described to me the terrible losses that his, and other units had suffered on the Dalmatian island of Brac. His colourful commanding officer, Lieutenant-Colonel 'Mad Jack' Churchill, DSO & Bar, MC, who had been known to lead his troops into battle, either by playing the bagpipes or wielding a claymore, had been wounded and captured by the Germans. His namesake, who now sat in front of me, had also been wounded and, I managed to prise out of him, mentioned in dispatches.

My pal, Joe Wambaugh, once wrote that compassion is an essential part of a good police officer's make-up and this is a sentiment with which I thoroughly concur. I'm not talking about sloppy sentimentality, either – and, in this case, I thought that we owed compassion to a couple of middle-aged men who had served their country well and whose blameless life had been affected by filching the odd half-crown to supplement their miserly wages. I had a quiet word with Norman and we returned the 100 yards to the town hall, to plead their case. That they would lose their jobs was inevitable; and, with the lack of suitable references, they would be hard pressed to find another, but was it really necessary to prosecute them? Yes, it was, replied a stern and unflinching town hall, snug in the respectability of their fiddled luncheon expenses and car allowances. It would act as a deterrent to others, they added, and as Norman and I pleaded and argued on their behalf, the more resolute the pompous town hall became. So back to the nick we trudged, charged the pair of them and bailed them to the next appearance of the Magistrates' Court. 'I'll do the paperwork,' Norman said, so I gratefully excused myself, sought out Len Faul, Dick Miles or some other suitable companion, and went out on to the streets to bring a little alarm and despondency to the real criminals of the parish.

A couple of weeks later, as I walked through the office I

caught sight of Norman Bolton and, out of interest, I asked, 'What happened to those two old boys at court, Sarge?'

'One of them pleaded guilty,' he replied, 'and I gave him a leg-up and he was fined a tenner. The other one – what's 'isname? – Evans – wanted a solicitor, so the case has been put over for a couple of weeks. Don't know why,' he added. 'I told him not to bother – I'd have given him a leg-up, as well.' And of course, Norman would have done: scrupulously fair, he would have detailed the mitigating factors of the case as much as he would have stressed the parsimony of the town hall.

A few more weeks went by. 'Sign this statement, will you?' Norman asked, setting down the neatly typed form 991 in front of me. I ran my eye over it and saw that it referred to the arrest and interview of the car-park attendant. I checked the statement against the notes contained in my pocket book and signed the pages. 'I thought this was going to be a quick plea, Sarge?' I asked. Norman nodded. 'So did I,' he replied, 'but the poor old bugger's been conned into going for trial. Any dates to avoid?'

A year passed and then Norman and I were warned to attend the North-East London Quarter Sessions. The first intimation that something was wrong was when I saw Jack Evans going into court. I smiled and nodded to him and I was about to call out a greeting when he sedulously avoided eye-contact and went into court without uttering a word. Strange, I thought, especially when I remembered how well we'd got on together.

There was nothing for me to do whilst the trial got under-way, so I hung about, read and re-read my *Daily Mail* and waited until such time as I was called into court. As the court rose at lunchtime, Norman emerged from the courtroom. I started to walk towards him, half expecting him to tell me that the defence had thrown in the towel and that we'd have lunch together, but Norman, white-faced, gave me a barely imperceptible shake of his head and walked straight on. So that was the second intimation that something was amiss.

After a solitary lunch, the court resumed and I was called into the witness box. As I took the oath, I noticed a wave of hostility radiating from the jury, and whoever it was who said that bad things come in threes wasn't far wrong. Just how bad, I was about to find out. My evidence in chief was very quickly dealt with, because my evidence was identical to Norman's and as the prosecution barrister sat down, so the defence counsel got lugubriously to his feet. 'Did you make a record of all the conversation that occurred between you and my client?' he asked.

'Not everything, no,' I replied. 'Only what was relevant.'

'Because I notice you made no reference to my client's heart condition,' he continued. 'Perhaps you did not think that particularly relevant, h-m-m?'

I was rather confused. 'I wasn't aware that your client suffered from a heart condition, sir,' I replied.

The barrister raised his eyebrows. 'Really?' he asked in mock surprise. 'I would have thought that you might have been given a clue by the fact that he had pills for his heart condition in his pocket when he was arrested.'

'I wasn't aware of that,' I replied, nor had I been. If I'd thought the old chap had had something wrong with his heart, I'd have sent for the divisional surgeon straight away.

'Weren't you?' enquired the counsel. 'Perhaps you'd look at this?' and handed over a copy of Evans' charge sheet. 'Look at the prisoner's property section – the seventh item down. Do you see "One packet of tablets" listed?'

I inspected the charge sheet. 'Yes,' I replied, 'but I didn't know that they were tablets for a heart condition.'

'Nor, I suspect, did you really care,' the barrister smoothly intoned, and, before I could repudiate this slur, he quickly inserted a question (which is a favourite defence barrister's trick) 'because now, I want to come to my client's interrogation.' This is another little trick, using an emotive word, such as 'interrogation', intended to convey to the jury a picture of a damp dungeon, a trembling prisoner and someone, very much like me, setting up the thumbscrews.

'There came a time, did there not, when you told my client that you wanted a statement from him,' the barrister said.

'Well, no,' I replied. 'I asked him if he wanted to make a written statement.'

'You wanted a statement,' the barrister snapped, as though I had never qualified the question, 'and I suggest that my client replied –' and here, he pretended to consult his papers – '"Yes sir, I'd like to state that I had nothing to do with stealing the money from the town hall."'

'He did not,' I replied but hardly were the words out of my mouth before the barrister snapped, 'and it was then that a blinding pain radiated across my client's chest, causing him to gasp out to you, 'Please sir, it's my heart – please give me one of my pills!'

I was dumbstruck. 'That's nonsense!' I retorted, but the barrister ploughed on, as though I'd never spoken. 'It was these tablets that you held in front of his eyes,' he stated, holding up a small box of tablets. 'Yes, members of the jury!' he added dramatically. 'Those same tablets which were described on the charge sheet, and I further suggest that you taunted him by waving these tablets under his nose, saying, "You want one of these? Well, you won't get one until I hear what I want you to say! We've got a case on our books, you're in the frame for it and you're going down for it!" And the defendant, this sick man –' and here, he flung his arm in the direction of the prisoner in the dock – 'feeling he could take

Just the Ticket!

no more, whispered, "Write down what you like, sir – I'll sign it, only for God's sake, please give me one of my pills."'

I was so furious that half of me wanted to vault over the top of the witness box, punch this flabby piece of garbage in the face and shout, 'You lying slag!' Since the other sensible half of me urged prudence, I could still hardly get the words out to deny these disgraceful allegations: something the barrister wanted because it would appear to the jury that he'd caught me out and I was too mortified to reply.

It was obvious to me that the jury wanted to acquit Evans there and then, but the case ran its course and, in a completely unnecessary plea to the jury, the defence barrister's *tour de force* contained the words, 'The Nazis couldn't break Jack Evans' spirit. No, members of the jury, it took another 25 years and someone called Kirby to do that!' and as Evans surreptitiously wiped his eye in the dock, the jury barely bothered to step out of the jury box before acquitting him.

'Sorry, Dick,' Norman afterwards said, 'I knew what was coming but I couldn't warn you when you still hadn't been called to give evidence,' and of course, he was quite right.

I had conflicting emotions about the outcome of the case. In one way, I was glad that Evans had got off, because we hadn't wanted to charge him in the first place. Certainly, he'd done wrong, but was it such a terrible act? I didn't think so. And, apart from that, he'd done bloody brave deeds during the war, actions which, if they'd been demanded of me, would have caused me to faint on the spot. So while I was glad he'd kept his good character, I felt furious about the way in which I'd been savaged in court.

There's a stone, set in the Naval cemetery on the island of Vis, which commemorates the men of the Allied forces who fought and died on the islands of Dalmatia. In part, it reads:

Just the Ticket!

> Here dead lie, because we did not choose
> to live and shame the land from which we sprung.
> Life to be sure is nothing much to lose
> but young men think it is, and we were young.

In my bitterness that day, I thought that Jack Evans had somewhat tarnished that inscription. Over thirty years have passed by since then; so was I being just a bit uncharitable with my resentful views about Evans on that day, so long ago? Now that I'm in my sixties, I'm ashamed to say, I was.

Glossary

bender	(1) A suspended sentence (2) A politically unacceptable name for a homosexual
Binney Medal	A medal awarded annually to civilians who perform acts of bravery in support of law and order. It was instituted after Captain Robert Binney RN lost his life in 1945, attempting to intercept a car driven by criminals who had carried out a smash and grab.
brass	A prostitute.
brief	(1) A search warrant (2) A legal representative
carpet	Three months' imprisonment
divisional surgeon	A general practitioner, called by police to examine prisoners, victims and police officers.
do (or doing) the Royals	To turn the Queen's evidence. When a defendant gives evidence for the prosecution against co-defendants, in order to curry favour during sentencing.
flowery	*Rhyming slang*. Flowery dell = cell
half-a-stretch	Six months' imprisonment

Glossary

imprest	A sum of money, held by the head of a department in the Metropolitan Police, for use by that department's officers whilst carrying out enquiries, and to be strictly accounted for.
lay down	A remand in custody
leg-up	Mitigation given by a police officer, in respect of a prisoner in court, usually when the prisoner is not legally represented. If the prisoner does have legal representation, the barrister in question will often take umbrage, tartly remarking that the officer is doing his (i.e. the defence barrister's) job. The correct rejoinder to this, is, 'Yes, and a fucking sight cheaper, too.'
Maltese Syndicate	A gang of Maltese who ran and controlled groups of prostitutes in the Soho area of London, from the 1940s onwards.
middling	Acting as a go-between in the disposal of stolen property.
muppet	Impolite name for a lay magistrate (or Justice of the Peace).
Obeah woman	Ladies from Jamaica, said to possess supernatural powers which they could be persuaded to exercise, in return for a sum of money.
Pimply	A derogatory term used to describe the youthful impetuosity of a jumped-up junior member of a governmental department.
previous	Previous convictions

272

rass	Afro-Caribbean expression, meaning 'Up your arse' – actually considered quite acceptable in some circles.
screwing one's loaf	Exercising perspicacity
screwsman	A burglar
spilling one's guts	Confessing
stretch	Twelve months' imprisonment
tom	(1) *Rhyming slang*. Tom foolery = jewellery (2) A prostitute
whizzers	Pickpockets
wiping one's mouth and walking away	Remaining silent in a dignified manner
wollie	An impolite term for a uniformed police officer
wrap up	(1) To tie up a person especially during a robbery. (2) A terse demand for silence

Dick Kirby joined the Metropolitan Police in 1967 and spent over half his service in the Flying Squad and the Serious Crime Squad before the dark cloud of appeasement and political correctness was cast over the capital in 1993, when he was medically discharged.

He is the author of *Rough Justice – Memoirs of a Flying Squad Detective* (Merlin Unwin Books, 2001) and he contributes to police periodicals on a regular basis.

From his home in Suffolk, Dick Kirby now lives life at a more leisurely pace with his family, writing, corresponding with friends all over the world, reading, listening to music and tending his garden which, like its owner, is small but beautiful.

Lightning Source UK Ltd.
Milton Keynes UK
30 December 2009

148010UK00001B/16/P